Wisconsin Herb
Cookbook

Design at left by William Morris (1834-1896)

Cover photos:
Wisconsin Pastoral: Brent Nicastro
Food Inset: Joe Paskus
Food Styling: Suzanne Breckenridge

Wisconsin Herb
Cookbook

Suzanne Breckenridge & Marjorie Snyder

Prairie Oak Press
Madison, Wisconsin

First edition, first printing

Prairie Oak Press
821 Prospect Place
Madison, Wisconsin 53703

Designed and produced by Flying Fish Graphics, Blue Mounds, Wisconsin
Printed in the United States of America by BookCrafters, Chelsea, Michigan

Library of Congress Cataloging-in-Publication Data

Breckenridge, Suzanne.
    Wisconsin herb cookbook / Suzanne Breckenridge and Marjorie Snyder.
    p.   cm.
    Includes index.
    ISBN 1-879483-32-7 (paperback : alk. paper)
    1. Cookery (Herbs). 2. Herbs. 3. Herb gardening—Wisconsin.
I. Snyder, Marjorie. II. Title.
TX819.H4B697   1996
641.6'57—dc20   96-23118
                                                              CIP

Contents

Foreword

In the more than 20 years of living in Wisconsin, we have come to realize the importance of a definitive book on growing and cooking with herbs. One that would give tips for growing in our extreme Zone 4 climate—and hope that all is not lost in the tundra. A book that would be positive about what to expect from our growing season and rejoice in the knowledge we actually do have good earth.

A book that would help both the novice and experienced gardener come to terms with our environment and wisely use what is available.

A book that would provide recipes for all tastes and all levels of cooking abilities—recipes to challenge and recipes to start you on your way to confident cooking.

A book with the hope that home cooking and home gardening are the future.

A book that would help teach how to use herbs effectively in everyday cooking.

Most of all, we hope that with this book all your questions get answered and your senses heightened.

Marjorie A. Snyder
Suzanne Breckenridge

May, 1996

Acknowledgments

Producing a book like this is like building a house. You may have some of the furnishings, raw materials and building site, but designing the floor plan, choosing colors and hiring a competent construction crew is the key. We've been fortunate. From the top of the house down to the basement we've been surrounded with supportive and professional staff.

Thanks to Jerry Minnich who went out of his way to trust us and let us pick our own herb cooking style; who left us to our own devices even though we were often unsure; who treated us as equal professionals; and who took us to great restaurants for dinner meetings!

Thanks to Caroline Beckett and Frank X. Sandner, the book designers who were always helpful, courteous, accepting of our suggestions and made it all look so easy.

Special thanks to Suzanne's daughter, Sarah, who put our recipes in print, organized some of our thoughts, corrected our spelling and taught two moms that computers aren't scary. Thanks to our other children Ethan Breckenridge and Ryan and Dana Snyder who have cheerfully tasted and retasted countless recipes, worn out shoes walking between our houses with sample dishes, and offered praise and criticism in pleasant moderation!

Thanks to our students throughout the many years of cooking classes and wherever we took our road show for giving us honest feedback.

Thanks to Anne McNitt who first introduced us to cooking with herbs and let her class be our stage.

To our good friend and great cook, Donna Taylor, who sorted out our recipes into a logical sequence and gave advice on what the cooking public wants to know.

To our many friends and relatives who shared meals, mostly experimental, over the years and gave us praise and polite criticism.

Thanks to Suzanne's mother, Lurana Hultquist, who willingly tried and tasted everything first; and to Marge's Tante Friedel who encouraged her with the knowledge that cooking is in her blood.

Last, but certainly not least, to our husbands, Chuck Snyder and Bruce Breckenridge, for driving to grocery stores in the middle of the night, for feeding children when we forgot, for washing dishes in bathroom sinks when the pipes froze, and giving us love and encouragement when things got downright depressing.

Introduction

"Where did you and Suzanne meet?" This is the question our students always are curious to know. I guess they think we're going to say "at LaVarenne in France or the Culinary Institute in New York." Then we tell them, and they seem somewhat disillusioned—maybe I'm reading into it. Actually, I thought our chance meeting was rather unique—we met on the beach. Why, that's the way romance novels begin! I'm afraid our husbands didn't think much about it when be both came home and said we had met a new neighbor who also had a daughter the same age as ours. This was a big deal. Wheels started turning and visions of new playmates spun through our heads since we both lived in a neighborhood where there weren't many kids.

I don't particularly like sun, and I like sand and water even less, at least being out in it, so when I discovered that another Mom was willing to take my daughter to swimming lessons in exchange for playtime and baby-sitting, I jumped at the chance. Suzanne is a sun-worshipper and I am not; in that respect we are exact opposites and over the years of being friends and partners, this is probably the only thing we don't agree on. Not bad.

In the process of our daughter-exchanges, we did what most mothers do when watching their kids play. We talked and eventually our talk got around to what we both did. At that time we were both full-time Moms on part-time schedules. . . isn't that the case for everyone? Suzanne was teaching at our local Junior-Technical College in the Art Department. Her specialty was ceramics. I was teaching at the same place but in the Business Department.

It was summer and Suzanne and I both had interests in gardening. She had a beautiful flower garden, growing things that aren't supposed to grow, but somehow did. I tried to play Earth Mother and grow organic vegetables and chickens for future free-range dinners; thankfully, city ordinances prohibited the latter. We also discovered in our talks that we lived around the block from one another—a fact that proved very handy in later years.

As the first summer continued, Suzanne and I would talk about recipes, not uncommon even today. We were really interested in trying all kinds of foods since neither of us had much background in ethnic cuisine, or herbs for that matter.

One day a brochure of non-credit classes was stuck in our mail and we noticed that a local woman was offering a class on Herbs. Just Herbs. So when fall arrived and our daughters started kindergarten we signed up for the class. I hadn't taken a class since college and I don't think Suzanne had either. The class was taught by a delightful and very knowledgeable woman named Anne McNitt. She was from Chicago or Milwaukee, or like everyone else we had met in Madison, from somewhere else. The class was in the evening and it had about six or seven equally herbally-challenged people! It met in a smelly chemistry lab of a high school. Try and counteract the scent of sulfuric acid with herbs! Anne was filled with information. In fact, I still have her handouts (done on a mimeograph machine no less) and my notes, which I actually consulted while writing this book. It was her enthusiasm that sparked something in both Suzanne and me. She lived and breathed herbs and she made it seem like that's just the way life should be. It didn't take long for us to get just as interested.

Anne asked if any of us would be interested in bringing in some herbal treats. Suzanne and I volunteered to make a few of our favorites and work on a few together. It was at this moment we knew we shared more than a common interest; we shared a common taste. As we talked we found out we both had a wonderful gift. We can talk about a flavor and we both know what the other is tasting. Not many people in the food business can say that. We prepared several things. One was a lovely dill-flavored salmon mousse with scales made from slivered almonds tinted pale orange-pink! The class enjoyed it and they asked that we teach them how it was made.

We decided to take their advice and teach exactly what they wanted. Herb Cooking. That spring we worked on a schedule. Suzanne with her graphic arts background designed beautiful brochures; I wrote them up and we sent them out to our former classmates who passed them along to friends and pretty soon we had a full enrollment. We met at my house since the kitchen was bigger than Suzanne's. Suzanne, in all these years still miraculously turns out wedding banquet feasts out of her kitchen the size of a dining room table! The classes were successful. We continued for many years offering classes on Cooking with Herbs. They were both fun and exhausting.

We called ourselves The Herb Forum. Word of mouth kept our classes filled; eventually some of our students got us interested in sharing our knowledge publicly. They asked that we write for a local newspaper, *Isthmus*, and a local magazine, *Wisconsin Trails*. We worked as the Food Editors for *Wisconsin Trails* for ten years and still wrote regularly for *Isthmus*. During that time Suzanne increased her family.

Her son was born. We began experimenting with herbal products. We started selling Herbal Sauces, Pestos, Mustards and Vinegars at the then newly opened Dane County Farmers Market. We like to think of ourselves as front-runners in the condiment craze. We bought gigantic stainless steel stockpots and began cranking out vinegars. During those summers we never experienced sinus problems; cauldrons of vinegar and mustard pretty much cleared our heads! We were quite successful at this condiment venture, but eventually it became too much and the Farmers Market rules for homemade products changed. We had to decide to expand into a full-time job or venture in another direction. We chose the latter. We started catering, another adventure that almost broke our backs.

We also tried to get the public to learn what we had found so fascinating—herbs. We and six others started the Madison Herb Society, an organization that today boasts over 200 members. We helped design Madison's first public herb garden at Olbrich Park, gave many public lectures there, and sponsored local chefs who did programs for us.

Finally, it was time for us to put some of our recipes to the test, so we wrote our first book, *The Wisconsin Country Gourmet*, a beautiful full-color cookbook published by Wisconsin Trails. We are still very proud of that work. Recipes in it were based on our earlier magazine articles and we still find them good enough that we use them ourselves. Now there's an endorsement!

We continued to teach classes. But after a rather untimely accident in one of our classes that involved my cat we decided to move on.

Well, that was 15 years ago. Since then we opened and closed a catering business, and joined two other women for another cooking school adventure. I had another daughter, and have taken our Herb Cooking Show on the road—in the style of Laverne and Shirley. That brings us to today. After all the classes and all the articles we've written, we finally decided to put together a unique version of Cooking with Herbs *a la* Suzanne and Marge. We hope you enjoy it.

Marjorie A. Snyder
Madison, Wisconsin
May, 1996

History, Growing Ideas & Uses of Herbs

History

Herbs have a sneaky way of becoming an obsession when given half a chance. Once you start learning about them and begin using them you'll find out what a fascinating part they've played in antiquity, and still play in our personal lives. They're a delight to the touch, smell, and taste, and are the subject of countless stories from history, mythology, literature, medicine and witchcraft. They become part of your life. But for those of you not yet bitten by the herb bug, where do you begin? How do you go about using herbs? Where do you start? Can you start out small? What if your family doesn't like them? Whew. There are a lot of questions to answer.

Fortunately, as herbalists who have done our share of trial and error, we thought we'd better start at the real beginning before swamping you with details about herbs, cooking, and gardening. First things first. Just exactly what is an herb? After much thinking and consulting botanicals and herbals, we only became more confused ourselves. Then we decided to do the scholarly thing and consult a real source: the dictionary. We discovered that our trusted Webster's dictionary didn't offer as much help as we thought. The definition we found was. . . "an herb is a seed plant of which the stem does not become woody or persist (as a shrub or tree) but remains more or less soft and succulent and dies to the ground (or entirely) after flowering. . . ." This definition covers a great deal, includes more plants than we can name, and excludes some plants we know are herbs. Using Webster's definition, even tomatoes and snap-dragons are classified as herbs, but rosemary is not! So we continued our search and came across a few local herbalists who found their answer years ago. Simply, we discovered, they narrow the field down considerably with an easy "litmus" test. An herb or spice to them is a plant that falls into one of five categories. It should either be decorative, fragrant, medicinal, culinary, or used in dyeing. This seemed a logical approach, and being cooks, we decided to concentrate only on the culinary plants.

Most herbs are native to the Mediterranean and can tolerate poor soil, light watering, and very little fertilizer. The part of the herb used for cooking is mainly the green leaves, and in some cases the seeds or flowers. Spices are a little different. By definition, they resemble herbs, but instead of growing in mild climates, they prefer tropical areas. They're almost always brown or yellow in color and the roots, pods, seeds and bark are their prized features.

Herbs were not used in cooking at first; rather, they were used in religion and medicine. There is no real documented date when most herbs were discovered. Legend tells us that people learned about herbs by observing animals and how they reacted to various plants. If eating a particular plant resulted in a certain behavioral or physical change, such as lethargy, then it was thought the plants had caused it. This, of course, is also how poisonous plants were discovered!

Centuries later, specific plants that produced known effects were confined to a Physic Garden. They were grown in monasteries and studied by both the clergy and doctors. One of the theories that explained the medicinal properties of herbs was the Doctrine of Signatures. In essence it was thought that the appearance of a plant, its color, scent, and shape indicated the disease for which a cure was provided. For instance, red flowering burdock was used to purify the blood. This is not now a widely accepted theory, but it is the origin of many herbal names. The study of herbs continued, but still mostly by the medical profession. Somewhere along the way witchcraft emerged. Herbs were used to cast spells—a few berries from Deadly Nightshade would cause mild delirium. Herbs were given in varying degrees for specific spells, so witchcraft was now linked to medicine and herbs.

Eventually herbs started to become familiar in everyone's home. Women became keepers of the herbs. Wives and mothers were in charge of the household and this included the health of the family. They often had to administer simple herbal remedies. Then the real breakthrough occurred. More and more people began living in cities. Their food was not as fresh, and they needed some way to preserve it. People began to use the same plants they used for medicine to preserve meats and vegetables—in reality to disguise the sometimes rancid foods. Herbs now were being used for cooking. Fortunately things have evolved even further and herbs are now used to enhance the best flavors of food rather than masking the worst.

Growing Ideas

To help you explore the world of herbs and see how flavors improve, we've chosen a basic culinary sample of 12 easy-to-grow and widely used herbs. Following their in-depth descriptions, we've briefly outlined another group of 24 herbs that we couldn't do without. They're not as common in every garden, but eventually you'll probably want to include some of them, too. They all grow successfully in Wisconsin's Zone 4 climate.

After deciding to plant an herb garden and before plowing up the back forty, there are other things to consider. How many plants do you want? Which plants do you want? How many are needed for a family? What kind of space do you have? And how much time and money do you want to spend on this adventure?

Ideally, you should have your backyard soil or your chosen garden site tested. And don't forget the orientation of your site—is it sunny, partially sunny or all in the shade? It's better to have this decided and analyzed now than to undo all your good intentions later.

Design

One of the most exciting things about growing herbs is the actual design of the garden. An herb garden is a place of enchantment—no matter what size. And here is your chance to be truly creative—even more than in a flower garden. Throughout history herb gardens were designed around a theme. Of course you can intersperse them in border gardens, in vegetable gardens, in perennial gardens or annual beds, but making them a focal point in your over-all garden scheme is more fun.

There are hundreds of books that will give you precise guidelines. (We've included several designs at the end of this chapter.) Some use age-old designs like the knot garden—an old Elizabethan idea of intermingling plants to form a maze. Those, like the ones in castle courtyards, were intricate and large enough to actually walk through. Today many of these still exist in England, Italy, and France. Many public gardens in this country have reproduced them, but in much smaller scale. You can do this yourself in your own backyard in miniature form.

There are other traditional herb garden designs you could use as inspiration. Some of these possibilities are: a Lemon garden, Silver garden, Blue, White or Pink-flowering herb garden, Shakespeare garden, Biblical garden, Italian garden, and the list goes on. Besides a specific theme garden, you can choose a garden that fits a specific landscape feature—water element, small driveway garden, hillside garden, the old Colonial backdoor kitchen garden, even an all-container garden. You're limited only by your imagination. Once you've decided on a theme and a design, the plants to be included must be given some thought, along with the site orientation—sun, shade or partial shade. The following page offers some ideas:

3

Ground Cover Herbs:

> Sweet Woodruff, Mints, Creeping Thyme, Creeping Oregano, Winter Savory

Rock Garden Herbs:

> Rosemary, Thyme, Dwarf Sages, Savory, Corsican Mint

Bee Garden Herbs:

> Hyssop, Marjoram, Mint, Lemon Balm, Savories, Thyme

Container Herbs:

> Chives, Common Thyme, Corsican Mint, Scented Geraniums, Lemon Verbena, Ginger, Marjoram, Pineapple Sage, Rosemary, Nasturtiums, Calendula, Salad Burnet

Hanging Basket Herbs:

> Creeping Thyme, Creeping Rosemary, Nasturtiums, Mint, Scented Geraniums, Creeping Savory

Tea Plant Herbs:

> Chamomile, Lemon Balm, Sage, Mint, Rosemary, Lemon Verbena, Bee Balm, Pineapple Sage, Thyme

Partial Shade Herbs:

> Chives, Basil, French Tarragon, Lovage, Sweet Woodruff, Mint, Chervil, Parsley, Lemon Balm

You need patience the first year of your herb garden. It's a learning experience! You'll quickly discover what plants do well and which you'll want to remove. You'll also discover which plants need more or less sun, and more or less water. This is true even for container and hanging basket herb gardens.

Planting

It's been said that sowing seeds directly into the soil will result in the strongest and hardiest plant specimens. In our Zone 4 climate, that's probably an accurate statement. But if you choose to buy plants rather than starting them from seeds, select large, bright green, bushy, bug-free plants for a good start and a burst of show in a short time. Know the plant dimensions before you begin to plant. What is the adult height and width of your plant? Does it spread slowly or grow more upright? Does it reseed itself or must you plant new ones each year? Plan this out on paper and label your plants as they are placed in the garden. Don't rely on your memory to pick out your tiny plants from a weed once they start growing!

Most of the perennial plants can be put into the ground in Wisconsin as soon as the soil is warm enough to be worked. In new beds, dig 10"-12" deep and remove as much clay and stone as possible. If the soil has too much clay or is too full of rocks, you may need to remove all of it and start over with good top soil and a light mix of manure. No matter what our soil is like, we always add a little lime to sweeten the herbs and a little peat moss to loosen the soil. Each year after that we work compost around the beds and supplement with more lime. We keep our herbs mulched with either cocoa hulls or leaves and grass clippings and work them in the following spring. This cuts down on weeds and means less watering.

Because herb gardens are generally more formal in design than other gardens, it's nice to frame them either with bricks (which is traditional), railroad ties, wattle fences (an old Colonial-designed fence that's woven out of willow branches), decorative wooden fences, or hedge plants like boxwood, germander or santolina. Paths should also be carefully planned. Use bricks, flagstone, cedar bark, or finely crushed stone. Choose a texture to balance your design.

Once your herb garden is planted, maintaining it is very easy. Herbs are virtually maintenance-free, pest resistant, and with their sweet fragrance, a pure pleasure to weed. It only takes a few minutes each day to care for your garden, unless you have acres! In the beginning you'll probably spend more time weeding since vigorous weeds can overcrowd young plants, but by the middle of the summer your plants will have established themselves and after that it's only fun.

Using Herbs

Using your garden is the next step. Fresh is best. Pick the fragrant leaves and flowers and use them in your recipes From experience, we suggest you take it slow. Don't use too many herbs at one meal or in one dish; they can be overpowering. Like the chocolate chip cookies made with curry power produced when I once told my class to experiment with spices and their favorite recipe! In the recipe section of this book we've included sample menus to get you on your way to successfully combining and using herbs. Almost all of them contain herbs, but not so many as to be overwhelming.

As the season grows on, so will your herbs and you will be faced with another dilemma—a rather nice one. What are you going to do with all these herbs? Preserve them. The two most common methods are freezing and drying. Dried herbs are fine to use in recipes, in some cases even better than fresh. Dried herbs are more concentrated than fresh ones, so in recipes you'll use less of them. The ratio is three to one; that is 1 tsp. dried is equal to 1 tbl. fresh.

Freezing Herbs

Some herbs freeze better than others, but in any case, thawed frozen herbs become soggy (aromatic, but soggy). They don't look as appealing in salads or as garnishes, and are best used in soups, stews or other cooked dishes. Basil, tarragon, dill, Italian parsley, and chives are most commonly frozen. Rinse the fresh leaves, shake them dry and for everything but chives, strip the leaves from the stem and place on a cookie sheet. Freeze for a few hours. When completely frozen, remove from sheets and place in plastic boxes with lids. Label and freeze. For chives, simply mince the stalks and place in a small freezer container. Some people make purees of their herbs and freeze them into ice cubes. Just be sure you label the containers!

Drying Herbs

To dry herbs you have four choices: Hang Drying, Quick Drying, Decorative Drying and Tray Drying. One is sure to fit your needs. For any method, pick the fresh herbs in the late morning, after the dew has dried off and shortly before the afternoon heat sets in. Wash them under cool running water and dry with paper or cloth towels.

Hang Drying: Gather the herbs into small bunches and tie with string or rubber bands. Hang them upside down in a well-ventilated room, attic or kitchen. If the room is dusty, place the bunch in a paper bag that's been perforated with holes and tie the bag around the stems. It's not particularly attractive, so place it in a dark or infrequently used room. Basil should be dried like this because exposure to light causes the leaves to turn black.

Quick Drying: Spread the herb leaves, whole or stripped from the stalks, on a cheesecloth or parchment paper-covered rack in the oven at its lowest setting. Leave the door ajar and stir occasionally until they are crisp. You'll be surprised that this will only take a few minutes.

Decorative Drying: You need a deep cardboard box with a lid. Pour in 2" of a drying medium, like borax powder, extra fine sand, silica gel or equal parts of cornmeal and borax. Lay the flowers (stems removed) or leaves in the medium and pour more on top to completely cover. The flowers and leaves will dry in five to seven days. Use these only for decoration.

Tray Drying: This method requires a few building supplies. Use a wooden frame, such as an old window, or make one any size you want. Cover it with very fine screening and staple securely to the frame. You can make several; they're very good for drying flowers for decoration. Place the leaves on top and let dry in the summer air or in a well-ventilated warm room. Stir the leaves daily. They'll dry in about seven to ten days.

The newest method for drying and preserving your herbs is with a microwave or dehydrator. They're just as effective as the natural methods. Because appliances vary so much in power, we suggest you follow your manufacturer's directions for exact times and methods.

Storing Herbs

When your herbs are completely dry, strip them from their stalks if this hasn't been done already, and place in containers with tight-fitting lids (mason jars, old jelly jars, tin containers, and ceramic jars all work well.) Label and store in a dark place away from direct sunlight. Many people store herbs on a shelf above a stove, but this causes the herbs to dry out too quickly and lose their aroma. Freshly dried herbs will keep their fragrance for a year or longer. Smell for flavor. If the herbs smell musty or have no scent, it's time to toss them on your compost pile! We find most herbs dry well, with the exception of parsley, cilantro, and chervil. Their dried flavor is similar to shredded green construction paper!

On the following pages you'll find specific information about growing each culinary herb. It's best to start from seeds or plants and we've included the growing conditions, varieties and uses for herbs in your kitchen. For more detailed information, see *The Wisconsin Garden Guide* by Jerry Minnich.

A Basic Kitchen Garden

	Type	Light	Height	Start From	Uses
BASIL *Ocimum basilicum*	A	FS	1 1/2'	seed	Pasta, tomatoes, soups, zucchini, salads
CHIVES *Allium schoenoprasum*	P	S	2'	plants	Breads, soup, fish, omelets, salads
CILANTRO *Coriandrum sativum*	A	FS	1'	seed	Salsas, tomatoes, Asian, Thai, Mexican foods
DILL *Anethum graveolens*	A	FS	3-4'	seed	Pickles, fish, salads, cheese dips, soups
MARJORAM *Origanum marjorana*	A	FS	12-18"	plant	Pasta sauces, eggs, salads
MINT *Mentha species*	P	S	1"-3'	plant	Tea, fruit dishes, salads, desserts
OREGANO *Origanum vulgare*	P	FS	4"-1'	plant	Salads, pasta sauces, pizza, meats
PARSLEY *Petroselinum crispum*	A	S	8-18"	plants	Everything
ROSEMARY *Rosmarinus officinalis*	TP	S	6"-3'	plant	Dressings, potatoes, lamb, fish, bread
SAGE *Salvia officinalis*	P/A	FS	2-3'	plant	Dressings, bread, pork
TARRAGON *Artemisia dracunculus*	P	S	2-3'	plant	Poultry, vinegars, salads, chicken
THYME *Thymus vulgaris*	P	FS	2"-12"	plant	Beef, chicken, soup, salads

A= Annual   P= Perennial   TP= Tender Perennial   FS= Full Sun   S= Sun, but can tolerate some shade

8

12 Easy-to-Grow Kitchen Herbs

Basil (*Ocimum basilicum*)

Type: Annual

Light Conditions: Full sun to partial shade

Moisture & Soil: Prefers moderately rich soil; don't overwater

Varieties: Over 20 types: we suggest purple or opal, lemon, cinnamon, Thai, ruffled, sweet or Italian, bush, holy and camphor

Propagation: Seeds, plants

Growth Habit: 18"-24", grows upright and bushes out about 10" per plant. Easy and quick to grow from seed. Sow directly into the ground after all danger of frost is gone. It's the first herb to succumb to frost. Leaves are bright green, except the opal, and should be pinched back as soon as it flowers.

Suggestions: We suggest one package of seed for average kitchen use, plus one of each plant variety for experimenting. The bush variety makes a wonderful border plant.

Historical, Mythological & Medicinal Lore: In Greek, basil means king. It represents love, honor and devotion. During the Middle Ages newlyweds had sprigs of basil scattered around their doors and windows to insure marital fidelity. It was one of the Elizabethan strewing herbs—herbs that are scattered on the floor to create a pleasant smell when crushed underfoot. In India the plant is used in aromatherapy and brings enlightenment and harmony, plus it is used as a disinfectant against malaria.

Not all associations are pleasant. The name basil was derived from "basilisk," a serpent-like creature that could kill with a look, and for many years was linked with poisonous beasts. In Salem, Massachusetts, a pot of basil was strong evidence of the presence of a witch.

Culinary Uses: A pot of basil is said to keep flies away. The scent of the leaves is "perfumey," a combination of clove and pepper with a hint of licorice. It's often used in Italian cooking and is closely associated with tomato-based dishes. It goes well with eggplant, zucchini, mushrooms, eggs, meat and poultry dishes. It's most well known for pesto, a sauce made from basil leaves, oil, cheese and nuts. Pesto is used on pasta, over tomato salad, in salad dressing, soups, and for purists as a dip for crusty bread.

Chives (*Allium schoenoprasum*)

Type: Perennial

Light Conditions: Sun to partial sun

Moisture & Soil: Rich garden soil, average watering

Varieties: Garlic or Chinese

Propagation: Division, plants, seeds

Growth Habitat: Grows to about 2'. Should be clipped regularly throughout the season to about 6"-8" or it falls over and looks ragged. Grows well in pots, even indoors. Can be sown directly into the soil. Every three to four years it should be dug up and divided to promote healthy plants.

Suggestions: Chives make a good border plant, if clipped regularly. In early spring delicate purple blossoms form and can be used in salads, or dried for arrangements. When added to vinegar it tints it a lovely lavender color, unfortunately if not removed soon enough the flavor is very strong and unpleasant smelling.

Historical, Mythological & Medicinal Lore: It is an old European custom to hang bunches of chives in doorways to ward off evil spirits. In Chinese medical history chives' volatile oil is said to have a tonic effect and helps control high blood pressure.

Culinary Uses: Use chives fresh at the end of cooking or for garnishes. Heating chives causes them to disintegrate. Its mild onion flavor is favored in egg dishes, salads, soups, marinades and cheese. Difficult to dry successfully, most often it's commercially freeze-dried. It's one of the herbs in the French Fines Herbes. Whole chive stems are often used as decorative ribbons around bunches of cooked carrots, asparagus and green beans.

Cilantro (*Coriandrum sativum*) also called Chinese Parsley or Coriander

Type: Annual

Light Conditions: Full sun

Moisture & Soil: Prefers dry soil. When it's very hot it tends to bolt, like spring lettuce.

Varieties: None

Propagation: Seeds

Growth Habitat: Grows to about 12"-18". The leaves look like a ferny parsley plant.

Suggestions: Grow from seeds and sow throughout the growing season since in northern climates plants tend to go to seed quickly. It's the only plant we know that's both an herb and a spice. The leaves are the herb, but when it goes to seed, the seeds are considered to be a spice. Cilantro has an unusual taste and it's one of those herbs that you either will love, or as Suzanne says, learn to love!

Historical, Mythological & Medicinal Lore: Coriander's name is from the Greek word for "bug" because of its pungent odor. It is used in many cultures. Chinese herbalists used it in a drink as an aphrodisiac, linking it to immortality. Seeds were found in the Egyptian tombs and sprouted after thousands of years. In India the plant is said to cool hot stomachs, banish gas and aid digestion. Early Romans crushed the seeds and inhaled the aroma to relieve dizziness; they called it "dizzycorn." And it's one of the bitter herbs mentioned in the Bible for Passover

Culinary Uses: A favorite herb of ours. Use it only in fresh form—dried has no flavor. It's found in many ethnic cuisines: Thai, Mexican, Indian, Moroccan, Spanish, and African. In Thai cooking, the roots with their nut-like flavor are used as well.

Coriander seeds are ground and used extensively in baking in northern European countries. It has a slight orange taste. We use it in poaching pears and in desserts with apples, gingerbreads, cooked fruits, cookies and cakes. It's also part of the spice combination known as curry powder.

The leaves are indispensable in cooking. We use them in salsas, salads, tortilla dishes, pasta sauces, and with fish and chicken.

11

Dill (*Anethum graveolens*)

Type: Annual

Light Conditions: Full sun

Moisture & Soil: Poor but well drained soil. Water moderately.

Varieties: A variety sometimes called dwarf or Dukat is a new hybrid that reportedly grows only to 12" and has mostly feathery leaves

Propagation: Seeds

Growth Habitat: Regular dill grows to about 3'-4' with flower head and seeds

Suggestions: We grow Dukat dill from seed in the spring and early fall.

Historical, Mythological, & Medicinal Lore: Dill is the Norse word meaning "to lull" and often has a soporific effect on babies. In Colonial times the dill seed was given to church parishioners to nibble in hopes of suppressing hunger pangs that developed during long sermons.

Culinary Uses: The feathery leaves or weed with its unmistakable flavor is used as often as parsley. It's particularly good in egg and potato dishes, with cucumber, shellfish, smoked fish, poultry, cheese, carrots, peas, green beans, cabbage, cooked root vegetables, rice, mixed with cottage cheese, over lamb, veal or chicken while roasting, and added to gravies.

The seed has more intense flavor and is mainly used in breads, chutneys and pickles.

Marjoram (*Marjoram hortensis* or *Origanum marjorana*)

Type: Annual

Light Conditions: Full sun

Moisture & Soil: Prefers a slightly alkaline soil, needs good drainage, moderate watering

Varieties: Pot marjoram

12

Propagation: Plants, seeds

Growth Habit: A slender upright plant 12"-18" tall, it flowers in early summer with white and pink flowers that grow in a knot-like cluster. It needs constant pinching to promote bushiness. Slow to germinate from seeds. Easy to grow from plants or cuttings.

Suggestions: Since leaves are so small, we plant several for average consumption. Some we grow in containers. This sweet smelling herb doesn't get the recognition it deserves. We use it in many foods.

Historical, Mythological & Medicinal Lore: A symbol of happiness often woven into a bride's headpiece. Because of its sweet aroma, Venus was said to have created marjoram. It was used during Elizabethan times as a strewing herb.

American Indians used it in many ways. It was drunk as a tea, used as a gargle for sore throats, and the leaves were chewed to make the breath sweeter.

Culinary Uses: The flavor is sweet and perfume-like. Often used in vinaigrettes, salads, egg dishes, soups, with fish, sausage, onions, potatoes, tomatoes, pizza, mushrooms, and chicken.

Mint *(Mentha species)*

Type: Perennial

Light Conditions: Partial shade to shade

Moisture & Soil: Rich, moist soil, water more frequently than other herbs

Varieties: Many types. We suggest: apple, orange, pennyroyal, Corsican (tender perennial), chocolate, lemon, grapefruit, spearmint, peppermint, pineapple, Kentucky Colonel, Korean (anise flavored).

Propagation: Cuttings, division, plants, seeds

Growth Habit: A very invasive plant that spreads by underground runners. It grows from 1" (Corsican) to 3'. Use plants, cuttings, or acquire by division. Has lavender blossoms in late summer that attract bees. Plant in areas that you don't want anything else to grow; in containers sunk in the ground, or surround the plant with metal strips.

Suggestions: We grow peppermint, spearmint, orange and Corsican (in pots). One plant is more than enough for a family.

Historical, Mythological, & Medicinal Lore: Mint is the symbol of hospitality and wisdom. In India it was used to scent a room by hanging bunches in doorways. In Medieval times it was used as a strewing herb. Hebrews sprinkled it on the floor of synagogues to freshen the air, and Greeks and Romans polished banquet tables with mint leaves to promote healthy appetites.

Today mint plays a large role in medicine as the active ingredient in most menthol flavors. It was once used to treat hiccups and its soothing effect eases nausea and vomiting. Ancient medicine men used the leaves to combat dog bites, prevent indigestion, cure mouth ailments and heal skin diseases. It is said if you rub the leaves on your face, neck, and arms it repels mosquitoes. Planted close to the house it will discourage mice from entering.

Ancient Greeks believed that when Pluto, god of the underworld, fell in love with Mentha, his wife Persephone flew into a jealous range and turned Mentha into this herb and left her to grow in the forest forever.

Culinary Uses: Fresh leaves are best, but it dries beautifully. You can candy the leaves for use in cake decoration. Corsican mint has the most intense mint flavor and was originally the main ingredient in Creme de Menthe. It's used extensively in Middle Eastern cooking and said to tame the heat of foods in Thai cuisine.

It's rich in vitamins and minerals and is particularly good in desserts, fruit salads, sauces, lamb dishes, and as a refreshing tea, hot or iced. It goes well with peas, carrots, green beans, spinach, cabbage, new potatoes, chicken, applesauce, poached pears, chocolate, fruit cocktails, and jellies.

Oregano (*Origanum vulgare*)

Type: Perennial

Light Conditions: Full sun

Moisture & Soil: Needs well drained good soil. Allow for spreading. Water evenly.

Varieties: Many types. We suggest golden creeping, Greek, Mexican, Dittany of Crete, Cuban, and Puerto Rican; sometimes called wild marjoram.

Propagation: Plants, cuttings, division, seeds

Growth Habit: Sprawling plant and some varieties are suitable for hanging pots. Grows from 4" to about 1'. It flowers in mid to late summer with pink and purple blossoms. Should be replaced every three to four years as it becomes woody and bitter tasting.

Suggestions: We grow several varieties, some for groundcovers like golden, and others for culinary use like Greek or Mexican.

15

Historical, Mythological & Medicinal Lore: According to legend, a Greek servant of a cruel king was carrying a large bottle of a favored perfume and accidentally dropped it. The servant was so terrified he fainted. The gods saw the unconscious boy and saved him from the king by turning him into a fragrant herb— oregano. Then they hid him deep in the forest to protect him from the king's rage.

In Latin, oregano means "joy of the mountains." Livestock that grazed oregano meadows were said to have tasty meat. Early herbalists combined the leaves with honey and applied it to scrapes, bruises, insect bites and aching muscles. American pioneers used it as snuff and rolled the leaves into cigarettes.

Culinary Uses: It's called the pizza plant. It has a sharp taste, a little like thyme. Found extensively in Italian cooking, Mexican and Spanish recipes. Use fresh or dried with beef, pork, lamb, salad dressings, marinades, with beans, lentils, eggplant, summer squash, stews, pasta sauces, and cheese spreads. It dries well.

Parsley (Petroselinum crispum)

Type: Biennial, treated in this climate as an annual. Second year growth tends to be bitter tasting.

Light Conditions: Partial sun

Moisture & Soil: Grows in moderately rich soil, water evenly

Varieties: Italian, curly, and Hamburg (grown for the root)

Propagation: Plants, seeds

Growth Habit: Grows 8"-18" depending on variety. Very, very slow to germinate from seed. Soaking seeds in water overnight helps. Plants are preferred. Curly parsley is more compact and used as an edging plant. Italian gets quite tall and full. Once it flowers, the flavor becomes bitter tasting. Doesn't make a good potted plant because of the long tap root.

Suggestions: We plant three to four Italian parsley plants for our kitchen use—it has more flavor than the curly variety. Parsley is so good for you it should be a staple in any kitchen. It contains incredibly high amounts of vitamins A & C and large quantities of iron, calcium, iodine, and more beta carotene than a large carrot. It's the most universal herb.

Historical, Mythological, & Medicinal Lore: Early Greeks fed it to chariot horses to make them run faster and wove it into wreaths for athletes to ensure speed and victory. The early Romans used it as a breath cleanser, especially after orgies to mask alcoholic odors. The custom of placing parsley on dinner plates probably has its basis in that old tale.

Culinary Uses: A universal herb that can be used with any food or in combination with any herb, except desserts. Italian parsley has the favored taste, curly parsley is often used as garnish. It keeps fresh in the refrigerator if stored in a glass of water. Combined with garlic and lemon zest it's called gremolata, an Italian garnish added to stews and risottos. It's the main ingredient in Bouquet Garni and Fines Herbes. Only use it fresh—it loses its flavor when dried.

Rosemary (*Rosmarinus officinalis*)

Type: Tender Perennial in our climate

Light Conditions: Full sun

Moisture & Soil: Grows in light, dry and slightly alkaline soil. Add lime for sweetness. Indoors in winter it must be watered two to three times weekly.

Varieties: Many varieties. Some we use are creeping or trailing, pink, golden, white, and Tuscan blue

Propagation: Cuttings, layering, plants, seeds

Growth Habit: Grows to 3' or more. Can be easily trained as a topiary or bonsai plant. Some varieties (the trailing and creeping ones) are used in hanging baskets. Slow growing and best started with plants or cutting. Keep your rosemary in good-sized clay pots and sink in the ground during the summer. Must be brought inside in winter. Keep in a cool, very sunny room and water very frequently.

Suggestions: We suggest two plants per household or more. One that's upright and trained like a small tree, the other in a hanging basket.

Historical, Mythological & Medicinal Lore: The name rosemary is Latin for "dew of the sea" because it grows along the craggy cliffs of the Mediterranean. It is also called the herb of remembrance as in Shakespeare's Hamlet: "There's Rosemary, that's for Remembrance. . . ." Greek scholars tucked rosemary sprigs in their hair when studying to help them remember what they learned. Some stories say that rosemary was used to try to awaken Sleeping Beauty.

In Elizabethan days, rosemary sprigs were tied with colored ribbons, then the tips dipped in gold and given to wedding guests to symbolize love and faithfulness. Brides would give sprigs of rosemary to their grooms on the wedding morning to ensure love, wisdom, and loyalty.

In the Middle Ages it was also used as strewing herb. The strong, pungent, resinous oil of rosemary is used in perfumes, toiletries, insect repellents, furniture polish, disinfectants, moth repellents, mouthwashes, headache medicine, sleeping powders, and as a hair rinse for blondes.

Culinary Uses: It has a pine-camphor-citrus aroma that's used fresh or dried. Dried rosemary is like hard pine needles and should be crushed with a mortar and pestle before adding to food. Avoid ground rosemary, it has almost no flavor. Rosemary makes a refreshing tea when mixed with sage and mint.

Great in rich dishes like pork or lamb, and blends well with potatoes, egg dishes, rice, apples, oranges, poultry stuffing, venison, eggplant, squash, grilled fish, mushrooms, lentils, vinegars, and marinades.

Sage (*Salvia officinalis*)

Type: Perennial/Annual

Light Conditions: Full sun

Moisture & Soil: Likes well-drained alkaline soil; don't overwater

Varieties: Hundreds of varieties, perennial and annual. We use dwarf sage, purple, tricolor, honeydew melon, pineapple sage, common sage

Propagation: Cutting, layering, plants, seeds

Growth Habit: Grows 2' to 3' and very bushy. Best started with plants. Common or garden sage has beautiful violet, blue, and magenta flowers. Renew plants every five to six years. Prune old growth in the spring after flowering. Makes a good background or hedge plant because of its lovely gray-green foliage.

Suggestions: One common or garden sage plant is enough for general kitchen use. The others are more for decoration. We use pineapple sage as a container plant.

Historical, Mythological & Medicinal Lore: Salvia in Latin means "I am well" and was called the longevity herb. In Medieval times sage was thought to impart wisdom and improve the memory. It was first used as a tonic or cure-all tea in the spring after a long winter. Superstition says when all is well, sage will flourish.

Today, some North American Indians use bundles of a certain type of sage for "smudge sticks."

They dry it and light it to produce smoke. It is then waved around rooms, houses, and cars to disperse and remove any gloomy spirits.

As a cosmetic, it's a popular hair rinse for brunettes, and also whitens teeth!

Culinary Uses: Sage dries well, but has sharp sticks—often referred to as rubbed sage. Chopping in a mortar and pestle will help.

Sage is said to counteract the fatty tastes of certain foods like pork, veal, goose, pheasant, duck, and sausage. It's used to flavor cheese (English Sage Derby), fish chowders, winter squash, and, of course, in poultry stuffing. In Italian cooking it's often used in desserts with apples and pears. Avoid ground sage, it has very little flavor.

Tarragon (*Artemisia dracunculus*)

Type: Perennial

Light Conditions: Full sun, tolerates a little shade

Moisture & Soil: Soil should be light and loamy; needs good drainage

Varieties: French and Russian

Propagation: Cuttings and plants

Growth Habit: Grows 2' to 3' tall and spreads 15"-18". Shelter it from cold winds. French tarragon does not flower or set seeds.

Suggestions: Only buy French tarragon for cooking. Russian tarragon looks similar and grows a little larger with white flowers, but the leaves taste like a blade of grass! French tarragon has the characteristic licorice taste. One plant is enough for kitchen use.

Historical, Mythological, & Medicinal Lore: Tarragon is called the herb of virtue, yet it's considered an aphrodisiac. Tonics were given to restore romantic feelings in married couples, and brides chewed fresh leaves before their weddings to freshen breath and ensure a blissful marriage.

19

The French call tarragon "esdragon" or little dragon. Its dragon-like root system can strangle the plant if it is not divided every few years. And it was thought to have powers to heal bites of snakes, serpents and other venomous creatures.

Marie Antoinette established the herb's exotic reputation. The queen loved the licorice flavor of tarragon and assigned one lady-in-waiting the sole duty of picking perfect fresh leaves each day for her salad. She insisted the girl wear new white leather gloves each day and crush the leaves only slightly so no juice would stain them. The task was performed with such precision and attention that the phrase "handle with kid gloves" evolved.

Culinary Uses: Probably the least well known herb to beginning cooks. Most popular in French cuisine in dishes like Bernaise sauce or in Fines Herbes. It's prized in vinegars, great with fish, peas, spinach, asparagus, chicken, shellfish, cauliflower, eggs, cheese, tomatoes, mushrooms, sauces, butters, and fresh in salads.

It dries very well, but can turn brown if left too long.

Thyme (Thymus vulgaris)

Type: Perennial

Light Conditions: Full sun

Moisture & Soil: Soil should not be acidic, but can be stony or contain a little sand. Water regularly

Varieties: Hundreds of types, some we suggest are Doone Valley, English, silver, woolly, caraway, coconut, creeping, English, golden lemon—upright and creeping, Mother of Thyme, nutmeg, and oregano. It has beautiful flowers, ranging in color from white to red, that bees love. Good in landscapes because of its texture and growth habits.

Propagation: Cuttings, layering, plants, seeds

Growth Habit: Grows from 2"-12". Can be grown from seeds, but purchasing plants is preferred and allows for more variety. Great in rock gardens, in between flagstones or in wall gardens. The upright varieties are good in containers, and the creeping varieties make fine hanging basket plants. Can be brought indoors in the winter. Shelter from strong winds when outdoors.

Suggestions: We have many varieties in our gardens. Great as container plants. We particularly like the Lemon varieties and Oregano-flavored thyme.

Historical, Mythological & Medicinal Lore: In Greek history it was the symbol of strength and bravery. Soldiers were given an infusion made from it to renew their strength. Sprigs of it were added to their uniforms and often it was sewn into scarves. Shakespeare referred to it in *A Midsummer Night's Dream*: "I know a bank where the wild thyme grows. . . ."

It was one of the strewing herbs in castles and the early colonists used it as a moth repellent.

The noted herbalist, Nicholas Culpepper, used it as a remedy for shortness of breath, and today it's a principal ingredient in cough medicines and some antiseptic salves.

Culinary Uses: Use fresh or dried. It dries very well and keeps its flavor longer than most herbs. A universal herb with a strong pungent flavor. Used in meat sauces, soups, with onions, tomatoes, peas, eggs, poultry stuffing, lamb, beef, pork, rice, carrots, onions, and biscuits. One of the main herbs in Bouquet Garni and in some Fines Herbes. Avoid ground thyme. It has very little flavor.

Secondary Kitchen Herbs

The following 24 herbs we use frequently in our cooking, but they are not as often found in Wisconsin gardens. Some are indispensible, some are less familiar, others you may not have heard of. All will add flavor and fun to your cooking. All can be grown in Wisconsin, though some take more pampering than others.

Anise Hyssop (*Agastache foeniculum*)

Type: Perennial

Propagation: Plants

Growing Conditions: Full sun, grows to 3', prefers well-drained soil

Facts: Sometimes called "anise mint." The seed and the purple flower are used in cooking. Imparts a sweet licorice taste of anise seed. Used to sweeten food sometimes without the addition of sugar. Makes a delightful tea. Add leaves to fruit salads.

Borage (*Borago officinalis*)

Type: Annual

Propagation: Seeds, reseeds freely

Growing Conditions: Full sun, grows 1'-3', prefers dry, poor light soil

Facts: Soft furry-like leaves taste like cucumber and are added to salads and vegetable dishes. The beautiful pink-blue starry blossoms are used in summer drinks, ice cubes, ice rings and dried for decoration.

Calendula (*Calendula officinalis*)

Type: Annual

Propagation: Seeds, plants

Growing Conditions: Full sun, grows to 1', prefers light sandy, moderately rich soil

Facts: Can be grown in pots. Also known as "pot marigold." Prized for its lovely yellow-orange flowers which are used as a saffron substitute, only for the color. Add to green salads, rice dishes, creamy soups, cheese spreads, sandwich spreads and dips. Petals are slightly peppery and when mixed with garlic and dill makes a good herb seasoning for tossing on steamed vegetables.

Caraway (*Carum carvi*)

Type: Biennial, treated as an annual in Wisconsin

Propagation: Seeds, sow in late summer for next spring, reseeds freely

Growing Conditions: Full sun, grows 12"-18", prefers average soil, good drainage

Facts: Spicy seeds are traditionally added to rye breads, cabbage dishes, coleslaw, seed cakes, soups, stews, and sauerkraut. Carrot-like leaves are used as garnish. The edible root tastes something like parsnips.

Chamomile (Matricaria recutita)

Type: Annual

Propagation: Seeds, reseeds freely, average soil

Growing Conditions: Full sun, grows 2"-12"

Facts: Also called German chamomile. The flowers are used for tea to aid in digestion and to soothe stomach aches. Roman and English chamomile are a perennial ground cover. Sometimes chamomile is added to fruit salads and desserts. Can be grown in a container.

Chervil (Anthriscus cereifolium)

Type: Annual

Propagation: Seeds, reseeds freely

Growing Conditions: Semi-shade, grows to 9"-10", prefers moist, rich light soil

Facts: Chervil resembles parsley in appearance, but is more ferny. It is best used fresh, and doesn't dry well. Add to cooked foods at the last minute. Has a mild anise-like taste. Great added to steamed spring vegetables like peas, potatoes, asparagus and carrots. Goes well with chicken, fish, egg dishes, vichyssoise and sometimes added to Fines Herbes, Bouquet Garni and Bernaise Sauce.

Cumin (Cuminum cyminum)

Type: Annual

Propagation: Seeds

Growing Conditions: Full sun, lots of warm days, grows about 10", average soil with good drainage

Facts: Member of the parsley family. Has a very strong pungent odor and used in Middle Eastern, Mexican, Indian and North African cuisine. Seeds are most flavorful and should be crushed in a mortar and pestle before adding to chili, tomato sauces, beans, beef dishes, breads, cauliflower, carrot dishes, couscous, sausages, and some cheeses.

24

Fennel (*Foeniculum vulgare*)

Type: Perennial/annual

Propagation: Seeds

Growing Conditions: Full sun, grows 1-1 1/2', prefers rich moist soil

Facts: There are two varieties, Florence and common. Florence is harvested as a vegetable and common for seeds. Prized by the Italians for its globe-like edible bulb. Possesses a sweet anise-celery flavor. Baked in cream sauces, braised, eaten raw in salads, pasta sauces, marinated, and makes a delicious creamy soup. To use the bulb for cooking, harvest before plant flowers.

Garlic (*Allium sativum*)

Type: Perennial

Propagation: Bulbs

Growing Conditions: Full sun, grows to 12"-24", prefers rich, moist garden soil

Facts: Needs a long growing season to harvest large bulbs. It may be necessary to leave in the ground until the following season. Varieties include elephant and Rocambole. Plant cloves of garlic bulb. Can eat leaves, like chives. When tops fall over and die down it can be harvested. Uses are extensive and defined by personal taste. Eat raw in salads, vinaigrettes, marinades, or made into sauces and mayonnaises (aioli).

Ginger (*Zingiber officinale*)

Type: Tender Perennial

Propagation: Bulbs

Growing Conditions: Full sun, grows 1'-3', prefers moist, well drained soil

Facts: A tropical plant that can be grown in containers and brought in during the winter. After one year dig up roots from young sprouts. Has bamboo-like stems and leaves. Mist occasionally when brought indoors. Like garlic, ginger has infinite uses. Available candied or crystallized for cakes, tarts, confections, cookies, jellies; also found in ground form and used fresh in marinades, salsas, curry dishes, Thai, Mexican, Caribbean, and Asian foods.

Lavender (*Lavandula species*)

Type: Perennial

Propagation: Plants, seeds

Growing Conditions: Full sun, grows to 18"-24",

25

average soil and good drainage

Facts: Called the king of fragrant herbs. Many varieties, not all hardy in Wisconsin. The seed, flowers and leaves are edible. Used in desserts like cakes, cookies, salads, and one of the herbs in Herbes de Provence.

Leeks (*Allium ampeloprasum*)

Type: Biennial

Propagation: Seed or transplants

Growing Conditions: Full to filtered sun, grows 18"-20", needs moist soil

26

Facts: Leeks are treated as an annual and should be planted in trenches 4"- 6" deep. Pile the soil around the stems as they grow to produce long white edible stalks. Mulch well. Some gardeners overwinter leeks for spring harvesting.

Leeks should be washed well before using; the inner leaves usually hide dirt and stones because of mounding. Leeks have a more delicate flavor than onions. Called the king of the soup onions—vichyssoise is the most famous soup with leeks. Leeks are often included in soup stocks. An excellent vegetable-herb used a great deal in Italian cooking, in salads, or cooked in quiches and braised dishes.

Lemon Balm (*Melissa officinalis*)

Type: Perennial

Propagation: Seed, root division, cutting, layering, plants

Growing Conditions: Sun to partial sun, grows 2'-3' and about 24" wide, prefers moist rich soil. Self sows.

Facts: From the mint family, hardy and spreads. Can become invasive. Lemon Balm has a mild citrus scent, more in its fragrance than flavor. Makes wonderful tea—hot or iced. Reminds you of lemon peel with a minty sweet accent. Used in fruit salads, jellies, tarts, tea breads, rice, and with chicken and fish.

Lemon Verbena (*Aloysia triphylla*)

Type: Tender perennial

Propagation: Root cuttings, plants

Growing Conditions: Full sun, grows from 2'-8', prefers well drained soil; perfect in containers

Facts: More of a tropical plant. Has white flowers in late summer. The flavor has an intense citrus taste making it a favorite in cooking or in teas and punch. Add to berries for sweetness without much sugar. Dries well. Use in rice, muffins, tea cakes, salad, jellies and sorbets.

Lovage (*Levisticum officinale*)

Type: Perennial

Propagation: Plants, seeds

Growing Conditions: Sun to partial shade, grows 6"-10", average garden soil

Facts: Looks like a giant celery stalk, has an even more pronounced flavor. Sometimes called the Bloody Mary plant because the stalks are hollow and make a good straw for the famous drink. Leaves can be dried, but lose their fragrance quickly. To preserve it for winter use, it can be pureed with a little water and frozen in ice cube trays. Very good in soups, stocks, stews, poultry dishes, and in Bouquet Garnis. Use sparingly.

Nasturtium (*Tropaeolum majus*)

Type: Annual

Propagation: Seeds, plants

Growing Conditions: Sun, grows to 6", average garden soil

Facts: The brilliant orange, yellow, and red flowers are prized for adding to salads and decorating

desserts. The flowers are edible and so are the peppery-tasting leaves. The buds are pickled and make a mock-caper.

Perilla (*Perilla frutescens*)

Type: Annual

Propagation: Seeds, plants

Growing Conditions: Full sun, grows to about 3', average garden soil

Facts: Reseeds itself with abandon. Often mistaken in our climate for a perennial opal basil. There are two varieties—one with green jagged leaves, the other with dark opal jagged leaves. The flavor is similar to cinnamon-basil. A popular Japanese herb, called "shisho." It's a common ingredient in gourmet or Mesclun salad mixes. Beautiful foliage—can be grown in large containers.

Pineapple Sage (*Salvia elegans*)

Type: Annual

Propagation: Cuttings, plants

Growing Conditions: Full sun, grows to about 3', prefers loamy soil

Facts: Part of the large salvia family. Has beautiful

red blossoms. The leaves with their beautiful pronounced pineapple flavor are used in salads, fruit dishes, teas.

Salad Burnet (Sanguisorba minor)

Type: Perennial

Propagation: Seed, plant, cuttings

Growing Conditions: Full sun to partial shade, grows to about 12", average to moist garden soil, with good drainage

Facts: Beautiful lacy-looking plant that is often overlooked in the garden. Remove flowers as they develop to promote vigorous growth. Has a delicate cucumber flavor making it great for people who have trouble digesting cucumbers. Used in salads, vinegars, tea sandwiches, vinaigrettes, soups, sauces, and added to cream cheese.

Savory (Winter: Satureja montana or Summer: Satureja hortensis)

Type: Winter is a perennial; Summer is an annual

Propagation: Seeds, cutting or plants

Growing Conditions: Sun to partial shade. Winter grows to 12", Summer grows to 2'. Prefers light,

well drained soil.

Facts: The flavor of summer savory hints of basil-lavender. The winter is more pungent, like thyme-marjoram. It's popular in German cooking, particularly with beans and sausage dishes. Also good in soups, with lentils, pork, veal, and sauces. Winter savory makes a nice evergreen-type plant in your landscape. Summer savory is often planted in hanging baskets. Both have a slight peppery taste.

Scented Geraniums (Pelargonium species)

Type: Annual

Propagation: Cutting, plants

Growing Conditions: Full sun, grows to about 1 1/2'-2' tall, prefers average garden soil

Facts: Makes a great container plant. Hundreds of varieties with aromatic foliage. The flowers are secondary to the leaves. Typical scents are rose, with many varieties—lemon, apple, chocolate mint, ginger, cinnamon, nutmeg, orange, peppermint, strawberry, coconut, etc. The leaves are used in jams and jellies, pound cakes, muffins, cookies, cakes, tea, sugars, and tarts.

Shallots (*Allium ascalonicum*)

Type: Annual/perennial

Propagation: Bulbs

Growing Conditions: Full sun, grows to about 1', prefers well drained rich soil

Facts: Another member of the onion family. Planted by separating bulbs. Grows like spring onions. Planted in fall for harvesting the next year, like garlic—it will then be larger than if planted in the spring. Has a mild, delicate onion flavor prized by cooks. Use in any recipe calling for a little onion taste. Great roasted with other vegetables—it caramelizes and becomes sweet.

Sorrel (*Rumex species*)

Type: Perennial

Propagation: Full sun, grows to about 1-3', prefers rich, moist soil

Growing Conditions: Seeds, self sows, root division, plant

Facts: Easy to grow. Prized for its lemon-spinach flavor. Leaves are best used in early spring and late fall. Cut down the seed-flower heads to promote new growth for the fall. Used in French cooking. Heat of the summer turns the leaves bitter. Add leaves to salads, coleslaw, and instead of lettuce in sandwiches. Makes great cream soups, especially with potato. Add to stuffings for trout and other fish.

Sweet Woodruff (*Galium odoratum*)

Type: Perennial

Propagation: Shade, grows to about 4"-6", prefers acid, moist soil

Growing Conditions: Seed, root division, plants

Facts: A beautiful ground cover that grows well in partial or all shade areas. Has deep green leaves and white flowers in the early spring. Unusual herb in that it has very little flavor when fresh, but when dried has a faint vanilla scent. Used in may wines, punch, vinegars and cobblers.

There are many other culinary herbs that can be added to your garden. As you become more acquainted with cuisines from around the world, you may decide to include them in your repertoire. Some may take some tender loving, and some may just be relegated to attractive house plants. No matter what, we're sure whichever plants you decide to include in your garden, you will be pleased.

29

Herb Garden Designs

With the following four garden designs we tried to provide a variety of ideas and materials to work with. Our *Formal Garden* is divided into four sections with an intersecting path. The path could be made from brick (our first choice), crushed rock, gravel, etc. The four squares need not all be herbs. If you like, plant the two rear squares with flowering perennials or vegetables.

The *Pizza Garden* was designed as fun for the whole family, especially children. It helps them learn the relationship between growing and using produce and herbs in a familiar food—pizza!

Our *Kitchen Garden* was designed so you can step out your door and snip fresh herbs for any dish you are preparing. It can be adapted to any size, and expanded as your interests grow. Remember there are no rules, so feel free to add annual or perennial flowers.

Our *Salad Garden* will keep your salad bowl, plus your neighbors', full all summer and well into autumn. This is an easy design to reduce or expand. Remember: this is *your* garden, so be creative and enjoy!

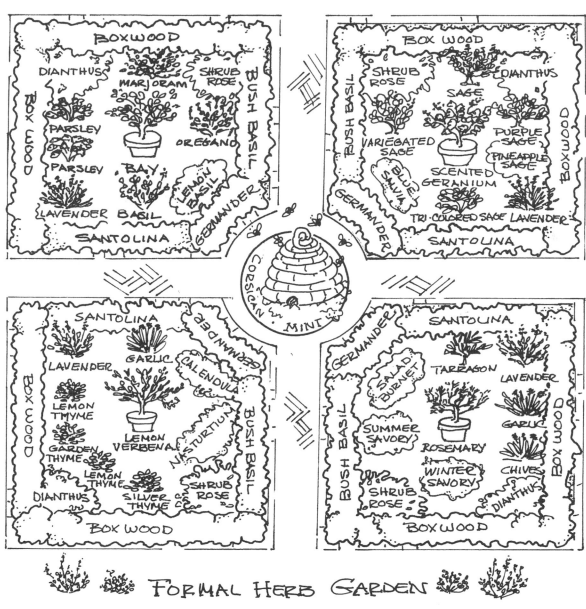

FORMAL HERB GARDEN

Plant List: basil: bush, garden, & lemon; bay, boxwood, calendula, chives, dianthus, garlic, germander, lavender, lemon verbena, marjoram, Corsican mint, nasturtium, oregano, rose-shrub, rosemary, sage: garden, pineapple, purple, tri-colored & variegated; salad burnet, santolina, savory: winter & summer; scented geranium, tarragon, thyme: garden, lemon & silver.

32

KIDS PIZZA GARDEN

Herb & Vegetable Plant List: basil: bush & sweet; Japanese eggplant, garlic, marjoram, onions, oregano, parsley, peppers: banana, green, Hungarian & jalapeno; scallions, tomatoes: plum, red & yellow pear.

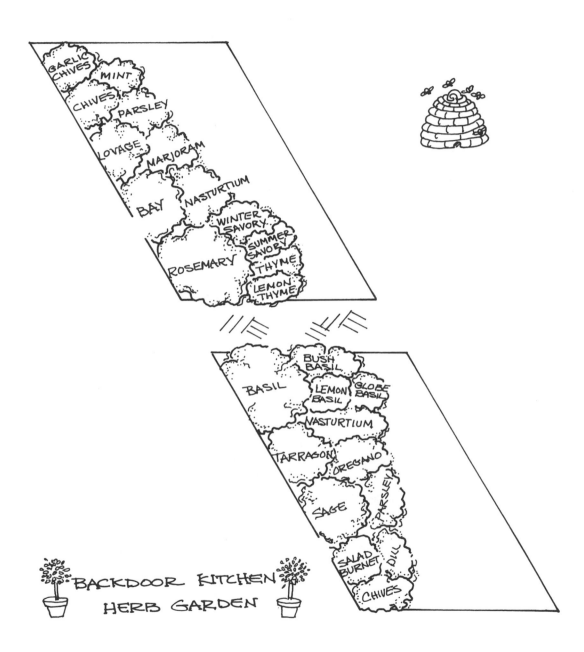

GARLIC CHIVES
MINT
CHIVES
PARSLEY
LOVAGE
MARJORAM
BAY
NASTURTIUM
WINTER SAVORY
SUMMER SAVORY
ROSEMARY
THYME
LEMON THYME

BUSH BASIL
BASIL
LEMON BASIL
GLOBE BASIL
NASTURTIUM
TARRAGON
OREGANO
PARSLEY
SAGE
SALAD BURNET
DILL
CHIVES

BACKDOOR KITCHEN HERB GARDEN

33

Plant List: basil: bush, globe & lemon; bay, chives: garden & garlic; dill, lovage, marjoram, mint, nasturtium, oregano, parsley, sage, salad burnet, savory: winter & summer, thyme: garden & lemon.

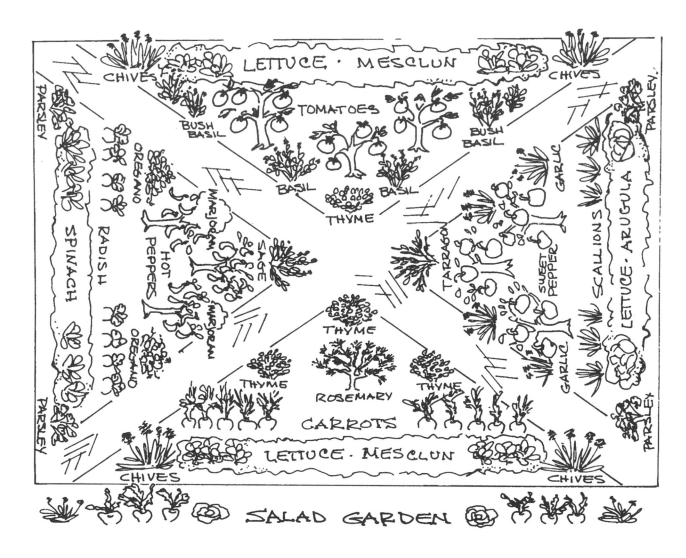

LETTUCE · MESCLUN

CHIVES

PARSLEY

TOMATOES

BUSH BASIL

CHIVES

BUSH BASIL

PARSLEY

SPINACH

RADISH

OREGANO

MARJORAM

HOT PEPPERS

MARJORAM

OREGANO

BASIL

SAGE

BASIL

THYME

TARRAGON

GARLIC

SWEET PEPPER

GARLIC

SCALLIONS

LETTUCE · ARUGULA

PARSLEY

THYME

THYME

ROSEMARY

THYME

PARSLEY

CARROTS

LETTUCE · MESCLUN

CHIVES

CHIVES

SALAD GARDEN

34

Herb & Vegetable Plant List: basil: bush & sweet; carrots, garlic, lettuce: arugula & mesclun; marjoram, oregano, parsley, peppers: banana, green & jalapeno; radish, rosemary, sage, spinach, thyme, tomatoes.

Appetizers & First Courses

An appetizer or first course acts as a dramatic entrance to a meal. It should tease the diner and set the mood for what's to come. Appetizers can be served informally around the kitchen stove, at the dining room table with the candles lit, or in a separate room for a more elegant feel.

The flavors should sparkle and the presentation should be thorough—cheese spreads served out of yogurt containers may be environmentally friendly, but miss the mark on style! Suzanne and I both feel that visual appeal is as important as wonderfully prepared food. Always provide plates, napkins and small utensils, even if your dish is considered "finger food."

When choosing your appetizers, consider them in relation to the whole meal. Pleasing contrasts are the rule. If your entree is rich and heavy, your first course should be light and simple. If your main course is simple, like pasta, or light fish or chicken dishes, then this is your chance to begin with an elaborate appetizer—something you've always wanted to try but never got around to doing—a paté, for instance.

Suzanne and I often go to restaurants and order only appetizers. We find that small samples of several things are just enough, they give us a fairly accurate indication of what a restaurant is really like, and besides we like to try all kinds of foods.

In the following pages of appetizers and first courses, we've included a wide range of flavorful dishes. Some are very simple and use only a few ingredients, some are more elaborate and may need last minute attention, others can be made ahead and frozen until just before serving. Remember, unless your appetizers are the entire meal, keep the portions small. You don't want your guests filling up before the main course is served!

For ease in preparation, mix dry ingredients and seafood ingredients in separate bowls and set aside until ready to fry.

Caribbean Seafood Fritters
serves 10

1/2 lb. shrimp, peeled, deveined and chopped in large pieces
1/2 lb. scallops, chopped in large pieces
1/2 c. EACH finely minced celery and onion
1 tbl. fresh lovage (optional)
2 tbl. lime juice
2-4 tbl. jalapenos, finely chopped (to desired hotness)
2 tbl. tomato paste
1/2 tsp. cayenne
2 c. flour
1 tsp. dried oregano
1/2 tsp. ground cloves
1 1/2 tsp. salt
1 tsp. baking powder
1/2-1 c. water
oil for frying (pour in skillet to a depth of 1")
1 recipe Cucumber Relish

Mix seafood, celery, onion, lovage (if used), lime juice, jalapenos, tomato paste, spices, and herbs. Let sit 10-15 minutes for flavor to blend. In a small bowl combine salt, flour, and baking powder. Stir into seafood mixture. Slowly add water as necessary to make a fairly thick batter, like muffin batter.

Fry by tablespoons (in batches) in hot oil. Drain on paper towels and serve with Cucumber Relish.

Cucumber Relish

1 tsp. salt
2 cucumbers, peeled, seeded and chopped into small dice.
2 bunches fresh cilantro, chopped
2 tbl. green chiles (mild) canned or fresh
2 limes, juiced
2 tbl. minced onion
2 tbl. fresh chives
salt and freshly ground pepper

Salt the cucumbers and place in a colander for 30 minutes. Rinse and drain and pat very dry. Add remaining ingredients and season. Chill 30 minutes.

Shrimp

We prefer shrimp with shells on. Since almost all shrimp come to the Midwest frozen, we believe shrimp with their shells on are superior in flavor and texture to those which have been shelled and precooked.

Depending upon the use, size is important. For grilling, use large or extra large shrimp; for salads, soups, and sauced entrees, use large to medium shrimp.

Shrimp is labeled by the number of shrimp per pound.

Jumbo: 5-15
Extra Large: 16-20
Large: 21-30
Medium: 31-40

37

When we picnic at American Players Theatre in Spring Green, we enjoy a glass of wine with friends, and serve this tart while waiting for the meat to grill.

Rosemary, Caramelized Onion & Goat Cheese Tart
serves 10

Pastry
 1 1/4 c. flour
 1 stick unsalted butter, cut in pieces (should be very cold)
 1 tsp. salt
 1 egg yolk
 3 tbl. ice water

In a food processor or bowl with a pastry blender, combine flour, butter, salt and egg yolk until it resembles coarse meal. Add the ice water, 1 tbl. at a time, using on-off motion with the food processor. Do not allow pastry to form into a ball.

Place on counter and knead with the heel of your hand. Form into a flat ball and chill. Roll out to fit a 10" flan pan. Prick with fork and freeze. Bake at 425° for 5-10 minutes until lightly golden brown.

Filling
 2 large onions, cut in half and sliced thinly
 2 tbl. butter
 2 tbl. oil

1 tsp. sugar
1/2 tsp. salt
freshly ground pepper
1/8 tsp. cayenne
7 oz. goat cheese
4 oz. (1/2 c.) sour cream
2 eggs
2 tbl. fresh rosemary, chopped
1 sweet red pepper, roasted, seeded and chopped

In a skillet sauté onions, butter, and oil, tossing until very soft. Turn heat to low and add sugar, cover and continue to cook an additional 10-15 minutes. Add salt and ground black pepper and cayenne. In an electric mixer or food processor thoroughly blend goat cheese, sour cream, eggs, and 1 tbl. rosemary. By hand, mix in red pepper and pour into prepared tart shell. Place onions and remaining rosemary on cheese mixture evenly. Grind fresh black pepper on top. Bake at 350° for 40-50 minutes.

Tart Pans

We always use a removable flan pan—usually 10". Check to make sure the pan is made of heavy metal and won't bend while twisting in opposite directions with your hands. The black coated pans are not a good choice, since they seem to rust.

39

Avocados

Remember to purchase the fruit one to two days in advance, which gives it time to ripen. The skin should be uniform in color, without cracks, bruises, or punctures. Make sure the skin yields to light pressure. To remove the skin, try Suzanne's method:

Cut the avocado in quarters, just cutting through the skin. Peel.

Or use Marge's method:

Cut avocado in half lengthwise and with a small paring knife twist to separate from pit. Scrape out avocado with knife or spoon. To keep the fruit from turning brown, sprinkle with fresh lemon or lime juice.

Be creative with this crowd-pleasing appetizer. Roll in sliced smoked turkey or smoked salmon for a unique flavor.

Tortilla Pinwheels with Green Chiles
serves 8-10

1 8-oz. package cream cheese, at room temperature
1 small (3.5 oz.) package goat cheese (or substitute additional cream cheese)
1/2 small jar (4 oz.) horseradish mustard (if watery, drain well)
4-5 large flour tortillas (11") (We recommend El Rey, from Milwaukee, Wisconsin)
1 c. fresh cilantro, stems removed
1 c. sliced black olives
1 1/2 c. red onions thinly sliced
1 small can mild green chiles, drained
1 7-oz. jar roasted red peppers, drained and sliced thin
1- 2 avocados, peeled and sliced (sprinkle with lemon juice)
2- 3 hot fresh chiles: jalapenos, serranos, Hungarian banana, etc.

In a food processor or with a hand mixer, combine cheeses and horseradish. Blend well. Taste and adjust seasonings. Set aside.

To Assemble: Lay tortillas on work surface and spread each tortilla with the cream cheese mixture almost to the edge. Sprinkle on each tortilla an equal portion of remaining ingredients, and roll up very tightly. Wrap each in plastic wrap. Chill. Can be made up to 1 day in advance. Just before serving cut into 3/4" slices.

Besides the toppings listed here, let your imagination go wild—try other marinated vegetables or smoked fish.

Crostini
serves 6

1 loaf French bread, preferably baguettes, cut into 1/2" slices
1/4 c. butter, melted
1/4 c. olive oil
2-3 large garlic cloves, finely minced

Combine butter and oil with garlic, brush mixture on bread slices. Toast in a 350° oven or under a broiler until just lightly brown.

Toppings:
Gorgonzola Cheese Spread

6 oz. goat cheese
8 oz. cream cheese
4 oz. Gorgonzola cheese
cream (if needed)

Combine all cheeses (at room temperature) in a food processor until smooth and creamy. Add a little cream to thin if mixture is too thick. Chill covered up to 3 weeks. Spread on Crostini slices and top with Marinated Roasted Peppers, Fresh Tomato & Basil, or Shrimp topping.

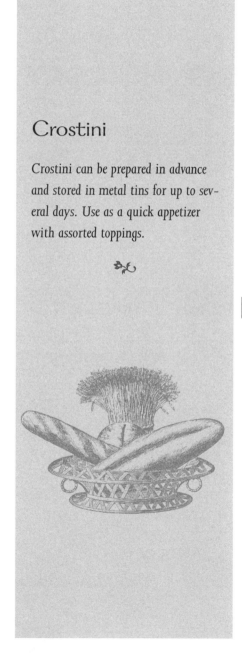

Crostini

Crostini can be prepared in advance and stored in metal tins for up to several days. Use as a quick appetizer with assorted toppings.

41

This simple cheese is best made 1-2 days ahead of serving. It allows the herbs to blend and mellow. Fines herbes is a French term referring to finely minced herbs, usually tarragon, chives, parsley, and chervil.

Fines Herbes Cheese

1-8 oz. package cream cheese, softened
3 tbl. blue cheese
1 tbl. fresh parsley, finely minced
1 1/2 tbl. fresh tarragon, finely minced
1 small garlic clove, minced
2 tbl. cream or half-and-half (if necessary)

Soften cream cheese and blue cheese. Add herbs and garlic. Mix well. Thin with cream, if necessary. Cover with plastic and chill several hours to develop flavors. Serve with French bread, pumpernickel bread or apple slices.

Herbed Goat Cheese

1 small package (4-6 oz.) softened goat cheese
1 8-oz. package cream cheese, room temperature
1 tbl. mixed fresh herbs or 1 tsp. dried (basil, marjoram, thyme, parsley, chives)
milk (if needed)

Combine all in a food processor or in a bowl. Add milk to make a spreading consistency. Spread on Crostini slices and top with Marinated Roasted Peppers, Fresh Tomato and Basil, or Shrimp topping.

Sun-Dried Tomato & Green Olive Tapenade

1/2 c. boiling water
1 1/2-2 c. sun-dried tomatoes
1/3 c. olive oil
1/3 c. pitted hot green olives
2-3 garlic cloves, coarsely chopped
1 tbl. capers
1 tbl. lemon juice
1 1/2 tsp. dried basil
freshly ground pepper
salt
2 tbl. fresh Italian parsley, chopped
1 recipe Herbed Goat Cheese Spread

Pour boiling water over tomatoes and let soak for at least 10 minutes or until soft. When pliable, drain and set aside. In a food processor combine tomatoes and soaking liquid, olive oil, olives and garlic. Process until a semi-smooth texture. Add capers and remaining ingredients and whirl gently, pulsing once or twice to combine. Taste and season. Keeps refrigerated and covered for several weeks. To serve, spread Crostini with Herbed Cheese and a small amount of topping.

Shrimp Topping

2 large tomatoes, red, yellow or combination, *seeded, drained and chopped*
1 red pepper, *seeded and chopped*
1/2 c. red onion, *chopped*
1/2 tsp. dried oregano
1/4 c. + 1 tbl. fresh cilantro, *chopped*
1 jalapeno, *seeded and chopped*
dash sherry vinegar
olive oil
freshly grated black pepper
1/2 lb. cooked shrimp, *cut in large pieces*

Combine the tomatoes, pepper, onion, herbs, jalapeno, and a dash of vinegar in a bowl. Add a small amount of oil, just to bind. Taste and adjust seasonings. Gently mix in shrimp. Set aside 1 hour at room temperature, adding remaining cilantro. Place a small amount of the mixture on Crostini.

Quick Appetizer 1

To a 4 or 6 oz. package of room temperature goat cheese, add 3-4 finely chopped sun-dried tomatoes (packed in oil). Mix by hand. Season with black pepper.

43

Quick Appetizer 2

Make small balls of the Herbed Goat Cheese and roll in toasted sesame seeds, finely minced fresh herbs, or toasted crushed nuts and spear with toothpicks.

44

Fresh Tomato & Basil Topping

4 fresh Italian tomatoes, seeded, drained well, and chopped coarsely
2 tbl. olive oil
salt and freshly ground pepper
2 tbl. fresh basil, chopped
1 tbl. small red onion, minced
1 tbl. balsamic vinegar
1-2 tbl. Asiago cheese, crumbled

Combine tomatoes, oil, salt, pepper, half the basil, red onion, and vinegar. Gently mix and taste. Season. Just before serving, spoon mixture on toast and sprinkle with remaining basil and cheese.

Here's what to do with all of those red bell peppers at the end of the season when they're finally reasonably priced! We usually double or triple this recipe.

Marinated Roasted Pepper Appetizer
makes 2 cups

3 large red bell peppers*
3 large green peppers (or use all red peppers)*
1/2 c. oil
1/4 c. red wine vinegar
2 tbl. sherry vinegar
2-3 garlic cloves, minced
1 tbl. fresh basil, minced
salt and freshly ground pepper

Roast peppers in broiler*. Cut into 1/2" strips. Combine with other ingredients and chill. Bring to room temperature to serve. Serve on toasted Italian bread (Crostini) or on top of herbed cheese and crackers.

* Can also use a 12 oz. jar of roasted red peppers (not pimentos). Add 1 tbl. honey if flavors are too acidic.

Roasting Peppers

Roasting any variety of peppers eliminates the bitter skin and gives the flesh a mellow sweet flavor. There are several ways to roast peppers. The oldest method is to skewer a pepper with a long-handled fork and hold it directly over a gas flame. An easier method is to use your broiler (gas or electric). Place the peppers on a foil-lined baking sheet as close to the heat source as possible. As the pepper blackens (blisters), turn often until it is uniformly charred. With either method, place the peppers in a plastic bag after roasting and let sit at room temperature until they are cool enough to handle—usually about 30 minutes. Peel off the softened skin and clean the pepper of any seeds or membrane. You're now ready to use the peppers in any dish. Covered with olive oil and stored in the refrigerator, they will last several weeks.

This dainty appetizer can be made ahead, refrigerated, and reheated—be sure to keep it covered with foil to prevent it from drying out. It's such a popular appetizer, we usually double the recipe.

Wild Rice Blinis with Caviar
serves 4

1 1/2 c. wild rice, slightly overcooked
1 egg
4 tbl. flour
2/3 c. milk
1/2 tsp. salt
1/2 tsp. baking powder
1 tbl. sugar
1 tbl. minced scallions
5 tbl. butter, melted

Place wild rice, egg, flour, milk, salt, baking powder, sugar, scallions, and 2 tbl. melted butter in a blender or food processor. Blend until well-combined and a semi-coarse consistency. Melt 1 tbl. butter in a large Teflon-coated skillet on medium heat. For each pancake, add 1 1/2-2 tbl. batter. Pancakes should be 1 1/2-2" in diameter. Fry 2 minutes per side or until golden and done. Add butter as needed.

Serve immediately with one of the following toppings (see toppings below). Blinis can be made ahead, covered and refrigerated. To reheat, cover with aluminum foil and heat in a 325° oven until warm.

Blinis

We're taking liberties here by calling these tiny pancakes blinis. Actually a blini is of Russian origin—a yeast-raised buckwheat pancake with a slightly sour taste. With wild rice the texture is coarser, but the flavors are similar.

46

Toppings:

1 1/2 c. sour cream, regular or low fat.
1 jar EACH black and red caviar

1 1/2 c. sour cream, regular or low fat.
1/2 tbl. prepared horseradish
1 tbl. minced fresh dill (extra sprigs for garnish)
6 oz. lox, cut in match sticks

1 1/2 c. Herbed Goat Cheese Spread (see Index)
2 c. Marinated Roasted Peppers (see Index)

1 1/2 c. sour cream, regular or low fat
1 1/2 -2 tbl. minced fresh herbs (tarragon, dill, marjoram, basil)
1/2 lb. cooked shrimp, cut in half lengthwise

1 c. sour cream, regular or low fat
2 tbl. fresh cilantro, minced
1 ripe avocado, diced
1/2 lb. cooked shrimp, cut in half lengthwise

Quick Appetizer 3

Mince finely chopped dill, parsley and chives into softened cream cheese. Add a little olive oil and season with salt and lots of freshly ground black pepper. Use to stuff raw mushrooms or hallowed out cherry tomatoes for a quick hors d'oeuvre.

47

Phyllo Triangles

Flat sheets of phyllo dough are available in 2 sizes, 1 lb. (14" x 18") or 8 oz. (9" x 13"). Either will work for appetizer triangles. Cut the smaller sheets into 4 strips and the larger sheets into 6. Once the filling is added and the triangles are folded, place on baking sheets in a single layer and freeze. When completely frozen, remove to plastic boxes with sides and store between sheets of wax paper. Then, any time you want to make a quick appetizer, pull out a few, place on an ungreased baking sheet, and bake until golden.

Marge and I make these triangles in large quantities and freeze them. They're one of our most popular appetizers. Besides the filling below, use curried chicken, shrimp with tarragon, roasted peppers, and our Herbed Goat Cheese.

Italian Sausage Phyllo Triangles
serves 15

1 lb. hot Italian sausage
1/4 c. Dijon mustard (herbed with basil or other Italian seasonings)
1/2 c. heavy cream
2 tsp. dried basil (reduce amount if mustard contains herbs)
1/4 tsp. freshly grated nutmeg
1/2 c. chopped red bell pepper
phyllo sheets (about 10)
melted butter (about 1 stick)

Remove casing from link-style sausage. Crumble and place in a skillet and brown. Remove and drain on paper towels. Return to pan and add mustard, cream, basil and nutmeg. Cook and reduce until thick and creamy. Add red peppers, taste and adjust seasonings. Chill.

To Assemble:

Using a pastry brush, butter one sheet of phyllo, place another sheet on top and butter lightly. With longest side facing you, cut into 6 long strips, about 2 1/2" wide. Place a small amount of the chilled mixture on bottom and roll up flag-style. Place on baking sheets and bake at 350° for 15-20 minutes. They can be frozen before cooking.

Another method of folding is to use one sheet of phyllo, short side facing you. Butter and fold sheet over towards you. Cut into 4 or 5 strips. Place a small portion of the sausage mixture on the bottom and roll up like a flag.

This recipe makes an attractive and tasty gift at holiday time. Place in a hinged French canning jar and tie with raffia strands. Be sure to include a note saying to store in the refrigerator.

Herbed Feta
serves 4

1 tbl. dried rosemary or
    1 1/2 tsp. fresh, minced
1 garlic clove, minced
1 tbl. lemon juice
2 tbl. olive oil
1/2 lb. feta cheese cut into
    1/2" cubes
Greek olives

In a mortar, grind rosemary. In a small bowl combine garlic, lemon juice, rosemary and beat in oil slowly. Place feta in bowl and gently toss. Cover and chill. Keeps several weeks in refrigerator. Serve with olives.

49

50

Marge loves making patés, particularly during the holidays. Often she'll make several small ones from one basic recipe and vary the textured ingredients, such as apricots instead of pears, golden raisins instead of currants, and different spice and herb combinations.

Pear & Ham Paté
serves 10-12

2 lbs. pork steak (should have some fat)
1/2 c. currants
1/4 c. port
1 lb. ground turkey or chicken
1/2 c. shelled natural pistachios
1 1/2 tsp. freshly ground nutmeg
1 1/2 tsp. ground allspice
1/3 c. dried apricots, cut into large pieces
1/2 lb. smoked ham or pork chops, cut into large chunks
6 large cloves garlic, minced
2 eggs
1/2-1 tsp. paté seasoning (See Index)
2 pears, peeled and cut into small dice
salt and freshly ground pepper
1 lb. bacon

Grind pork in food processor in batches. Mixture should be very smooth, but not too fluid. Remove to a large bowl. Soak currants in port for 30 minutes. Combine with all ingredients, except bacon, and mix well with hands. Fry 1 tbl. of the mixture for a taste test. Adjust seasonings at this point.

In the bottom of a loaf pan or paté pan arrange bacon strips in a staggered pattern with every other row draped over the side of the pan. When observed from above, every other strip should extend beyond the side of the pan about 3 inches, on both the right and left sides of the pan. Spoon in paté mixture, rap pan on surface to eliminate any air pockets. Fold bacon strips over paté mixture. Cover with more bacon and top with foil or lid (poke air holes in foil.)

Place paté pan or loaf pan in a bain marie (larger pan filled with hot water half way up sides of pan.) Bake in a 325° oven for 2 hours or until temperature registers 160° internally. Remove and pour off excess fat. Let sit 10-15 minutes and pour more fat off. Cool to room temperature and place foil on top and weight with cans or bricks and refrigerate overnight. (The bricks compress the meat mixture making it easier to slice.)

Serve with herbed Dijon mustard and small sour pickles and French bread. The paté can be stored in the refrigerator for up to 2 1/2 weeks.

Patés vs. Terrines

These two words are often used interchangeably, but historically were different. A paté was the savory mixture, and the terrine was the container used to hold it. Either word is acceptable now. Patés are easy to make and are impressive first courses. Use well-marbled meats—you need some fat to keep the mixture moist during cooking. After the long cooking times (usually 1 1/2-2 hours) pour off the accumulated liquid. Use interesting food in the mixture: diced apricots, pistachios, smoked ham, turkey, pears, apples, currants, dark and golden raisins, sliced blanched leeks, or asparagus, to name a few. When you cut your paté slices, you'll see a mosaic of colors and textures.

Be sure to season your patés generously. Make a sample patty and fry it to check. Remember, patés are served cold, and chilling foods tends to dilute flavors, especially salt.

Cooking Wines & Liqueurs

Don't be tempted to buy grocery store cooking wine when a recipe calls for it. They are so full of chemicals and salt they contain little flavor. Use wines and liqueurs to add unique flavors to simple recipes. Remember that the alcohol is burned off once the liqueur is heated. Buy good quality brands and store them in dark, dry cupboards away from direct sun. Many wines and liqueurs have a long shelf-life, including sherry, brandy, Madeira, Marsala, dry white vermouth (used whenever a recipe calls for white wine), creme de menthe, creme de cassis (black currant), amaretto, etc.

This old-fashioned spreadable paté is made with chicken livers. Relax, though, it's so delicious, rich, and meaty tasting, you'll be a convert!

Sage & Calvados Paté
serves 10-12

2 tbl. butter
1/2 lb. chicken livers
1/4 lb. fresh mushrooms, chopped coarsely
1/4 c. scallions, sliced
2 tbl. chopped chives
1/3 c. Calvados (apple brandy) or sherry
2 cloves garlic, minced
1/4 tsp. dry mustard
1 tbl. fresh sage, minced
1/2 tsp. dried thyme, minced
1/4 c. soft butter
salt and freshly ground pepper

Melt butter in skillet and sauté livers and mushrooms, scallions, and chives for five minutes. Add wine, garlic, mustard, sage, and thyme. Cover and simmer 10 minutes or until livers and mushrooms are very tender. Uncover and continue cooking until liquids are almost evaporated. Whirl in a blender and add butter. Taste and adjust. Store up to two weeks in the refrigerator. Serve with French bread or crackers.

Here's something to do with all of the zucchini that mysteriously appears in the garden.

Zucchini, Leek &
Roasted Red Pepper Quiche
serves 10

1 Paté Brisee (pastry shell; see next page)
1 tbl. Dijon mustard
3 c. grated zucchini, unpeeled
salt
1 leek, chopped
2 tbl. butter
1 1/4 c. heavy cream
1 c. grated Gruyere or aged Swiss cheese
4 eggs, lightly beaten
1 roasted red pepper, julienned
1 tsp. freshly grated nutmeg
1 1/2 tsp. dried marjoram
salt and freshly ground pepper

Prebake pastry in a preheated 400° oven for 10 minutes. Cool. Spread bottom of pastry with Dijon mustard. Set aside.

Reduce heat to 350°. Place zucchini in a colander and sprinkle with a little salt and drain 5 minutes. Rinse well and squeeze very dry.

Sauté leeks in the butter until soft. Remove and set aside. Combine the cream, cheese, and eggs and beat very

Pastry Shells

Pastry shells can be prepared ahead and frozen for up to 6 months. Be sure to seal tightly in plastic or foil. No need to thaw to prebake.

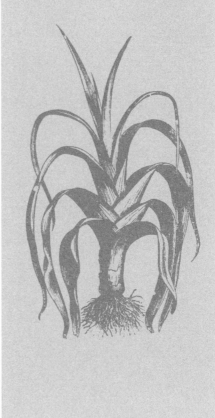

53

Tailgate Picnic Menu

*Zucchini, Leek & Roasted
Red Pepper Quiche*

❦

*Saltimbocca (Pork Rolls)
with Sage Sauce*

❦

White Bean Salad

❦

*Ginger Almond Torte with Fresh
Raspberry Sauce*

❦

*Serve with California Chardonnay,
Valpolicella, or Chianti Classico wine*

well. Add the pepper, herbs, leeks, salt, and freshly ground pepper to taste. Mix. Place the zucchini on bottom of the pastry shell. Spread evenly. Pour cheese-egg mixture over top and sprinkle with additional cheese, if desired. Bake 35 minutes or until top is puffed and golden and a knife inserted in the center comes out clean. Let stand 5 minutes before slicing. Can be made ahead and stored at room temperature.

Paté Brisee

> 1 1/4 c. flour
> 1/4 tsp. salt
> 6 tbl. cold butter, cut into bits
> 2 tbl. shortening (like Crisco solid)
> 2-3 tbl. ice water

In a bowl mix flour and salt with a pastry blender or food processor. Add shortening and butter with quick on-off pulses. Mixture should resemble coarse meal. Add ice water in small amounts. Toss gently. Remove and knead on a lightly floured surface a few seconds. Flatten into a circle, cover with plastic wrap and chill 30 minutes. Roll out to fit a 10" removable-bottom flan pan. Prick bottom with a fork several times and place in freezer for at least 30 minutes. Partially bake in a 400° oven for 10 minutes or until lightly golden.

This is a great appetizer to prepare ahead of time, in fact we like to double this recipe: serve by itself, or with French bread as part of an antipasto platter.

Eggplant Caponata
serves 6

2 medium eggplants, peeled and cut into 1/2" cubes
salt
1/2 c. (+) vegetable oil
2 tbl. good quality olive oil
2 medium onions, finely chopped
4 garlic cloves, finely chopped
4-5 sun-dried tomatoes, dried and finely chopped
1 c. pitted green olives, coarsely chopped
1 tbl. capers
1 tbl. sugar
1/2 c. balsamic or sherry vinegar
1/3 c. fresh minced Italian parsley
salt
freshly ground black pepper

Sprinkle eggplant with salt and drain in a colander for 30 minutes. Rinse with water and press out liquid, pat very dry. Heat vegetable oil in a skillet and fry eggplant; add more oil if needed. Cook till just done, but still slightly firm. Drain on paper towels. Discard vegetable oil.

In same pan add olive oil and sauté onion, garlic, sun-dried tomatoes, olives, and capers for several minutes.

Antipasto

A great Italian invention to tide you over until dinner, or as a delicious picnic or appetizer meal.

Antipasto literally means "before the pasta course." Today it's usually a small assortment of little surprises: marinated vegetables, cheeses, thinly sliced sausages, and crusty bread. It's very easy to make, especially if you keep a well stocked pantry.

Have on hand canned marinated artichokes, olives, hard cheeses, tuna in oil, roasted peppers, and frozen foccacia. Place each in separate small bowls and spice them up with a sprinkling of herbs, such as fresh or dried basil, oregano, rosemary, good olive oil, and freshly ground pepper.

❧

55

Eggplants

When choosing eggplants remember to look for shiny dark purple skins without any soft spots, dents, or brown areas. Peel the skin with a vegetable peeler, slice and salt. The salt removes the bitter taste. Let sit a half hour and rinse. Don't forget this step, or the eggplant will be very salty!

Add eggplant, sugar, and vinegar. Simmer 5 minutes. Add parsley. Taste and adjust flavor with salt and pepper. Chill. Serve cold or at room temperature. (It also freezes beautifully.)

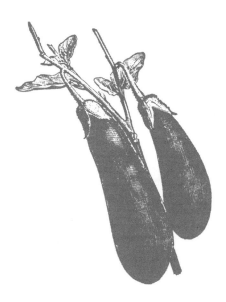

Suzanne's daughter, Sarah, has become a pro at making pizzas for her friends. Never mind the pepperoni and tomato sauce, she experiments with favorite food combinations like spicy chicken and salsa, or portabella mushrooms with brie.

Quick Food Processor Pizza Dough

1 c. water
2 tbl. olive oil
3 1/4 c. flour (can substitute 1/2-3/4 c. whole wheat flour)
2 tbl. sugar
1 tsp. salt (increase if using whole wheat flour)
1 pkg. dry yeast
1 egg

Heat water and oil until it reaches 110° (we find an instant-read thermometer handy for this.) Place 1 1/2 c. flour, sugar, salt, and yeast in food processor. With motor running, add water and oil and whirl 2-3 seconds. Add egg, process again. Sprinkle 1 1/2 c. flour and process until it forms a ball. Knead on a floured surface for 3-4 minutes. Divide into thirds and stretch or roll thin and fit in pizza pans, or cover with plastic and let rest 30 minutes (this eliminates elasticity).

Recipe makes 1-12" x 18" cookie sheet + 1 pizza pan or 3-12" pizza pans.

Pizza Dough Variations

While the dough is in the food processor, add one of the following additions or use your imagination and add some of your favorite herbs, or other savory ingredients.

Pepperoni
3 oz. finely minced pepperoni
1/4 tsp. red pepper flakes
dash cayenne pepper

Basil & Black Pepper
1 tbl. dried basil
2 tsp. coarsely ground black pepper

Rosemary
1 tbl. fresh rosemary

57

Toppings:
Mushrooms, Basil & Pancetta Pizza
(makes enough for 2-10" x 15" baking pans)

1 oz. dried assorted mushrooms and 1 c. boiling water
2 tbl. butter
1 tbl. oil
3 -4 oz. pancetta, cut in 1/4" dice
1 -1 1/2 lb. fresh mushrooms, assorted varieties
juice of 1/2 lemon
1 medium onion, halved and sliced
6 cloves garlic, minced
1 tsp. fennel seeds
2 tbl. sherry
1 tbl. fresh basil, minced
1/2 c. Parmesan cheese
2 c. shredded *Asiago* cheese
salt and coarsely ground black pepper
olive oil

Prebake pizza crust for 5-7 minutes at 400°. Soak mushrooms 30 minutes. Remove and discard tough stems. Slice mushroom caps and reserve. Strain liquid. Reserve and set aside. Melt butter and oil and sauté pancetta 1-2 minutes until done. Remove to a bowl. Sprinkle fresh mushrooms with lemon juice and add to pan with onion, garlic, fennel seeds, sherry, dried mushrooms, and reserved soaking liquid. Cover, reduce heat to low, and cook until mushrooms are soft. Remove mushroom mixture to pancetta bowl with a slotted spoon. Raise heat and reduce liquid till slightly thick. Stir often. Pour over mushrooms and add basil. Taste and adjust with seasonings.

To Assemble:

For one pizza, spread half the mushroom mixture over pizza dough and sprinkle on half the Parmesan and half the Asiago. Season and bake in preheated 400° oven for 10-15 minutes or until brown and cheese is melted.

Caramelized Onion, Gorgonzola & Fresh Rosemary Pizza

(makes enough filling for 2-10" x 15" baking sheets)

59

4 tbl. butter
4 tbl. oil
4 very large onions, halved and thinly sliced
3/4 c. Gorgonzola cheese, crumbled
2 tbl. fresh rosemary, chopped coarsely
salt and freshly ground black pepper to taste

Melt butter and oil in large skillet. Add onions and cook over low heat until light brown and caramelized. Stir often to prevent burning.

To Assemble:

Spread onion mixture over pizza dough. Dot with cheese and sprinkle with rosemary. Season. Bake at 400° for 15 minutes or until dough is slightly brown and cheese melted.

Eggplant, Roasted Red Pepper & Goat Cheese Pizza
(makes enough for 2-10" x 15" baking pans)

1 eggplant, peeled and cut into 1/2" slices
olive oil
salt and pepper
1 recipe Basil Vinaigrette with marjoram
1 tbl. minced fresh garlic
3-4 oz. goat cheese, crumbled
1/2-3/4 c. roasted red peppers cut into 1/4" slices
1 tsp. dried marjoram
1/2 c. grated Parmesan cheese

Prebake pizza crust for 5-7 minutes at 400°. Place eggplant on baking sheet and brush with oil. Season with salt and pepper and broil 3-4 minutes. Turn over, brush with oil and broil another 3-4 minutes until soft. Brush eggplant slices with Vinaigrette.

To Assemble:

Brush pizza crust with a thin layer of oil. Sprinkle on garlic, goat cheese, eggplant, peppers, marjoram and Parmesan. Bake at 400° for 15 minutes or until golden brown.

60

Thai Shrimp & Cilantro Pizza
(makes enough for 2-10" x 15" baking pans)

8 oz. raw shrimp, peeled and deveined

Marinade
1/3 c. bottled Thai Sweet Chili Sauce
2 tbl. oil
1 tbl. vinegar
1 tsp. ginger root, minced
1 garlic clove, minced

Topping
1/2 tsp. sesame oil
1 c. mozzarella cheese
2 carrots, peeled and finely julienned
4-6 scallions, finely julienned
2/3 c. fresh cilantro, chopped
2 tbl. fresh basil, shredded
2 jalapeno peppers, seeded and julienned
1/4 c. Parmesan cheese

Marinate shrimp in chili sauce, oil, vinegar, ginger, and garlic. Toss well and let sit for 30 minutes.

To Assemble:

Cook pizza crust for 5-7 minutes at 400°. Remove and sprinkle with sesame oil and place topping ingredients in the following order: 1/2 c. mozzarella, shrimp (removed from marinade), carrots, scallions, cilantro, basil, peppers, 1/2 c. mozzarella, and Parmesan. Bake at 400° for 10 minutes or until shrimp is done.

Pizza Parties

Hosting a pizza party is fun, and different from years gone by. To begin with, the pizza toppings are unusual. Dough making is the same, but we've included some variations that you'll want to try.

Prepare the dough a few days ahead and keep it refrigerated. The day of your party, roll out the dough to fit your largest baking sheets (10" x 15" works well). Prebake them for about 5-7 minutes at 400°. Cover dough with plastic and stack up until ready to use—this can be done early in the day.

Next, assemble your ingredients on trays for each type of pizza. When guests arrive, get them to join in assembling pizzas. Round out the meal with a salad, wine or a good Wisconsin beer, and a simple fruit dessert.

❦

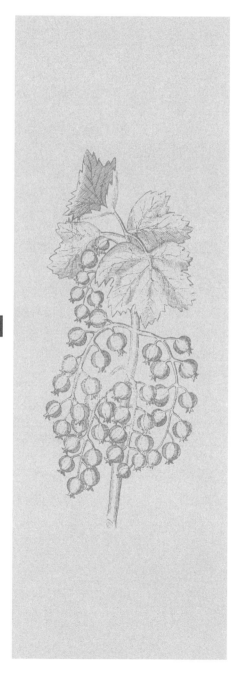

Shrimp Phyllo Purses
serves 15

1 16-oz. pkg. phyllo dough
melted butter

Filling
3 slices bacon, chopped
2 cloves garlic, minced
3 tbl. jalapeno, minced (or to taste)
1/2 c. scallions, chopped
1/2 lb. shrimp. peeled, deveined, and chopped
1 tbl. curry powder (or to taste)
1/2 c. currants
7-8 oz. herbed cheese (or Boursin)*
1/3 c. coarsely chopped salted peanuts
1 tbl. chutney

Sauté bacon 2 minutes, add garlic and jalapenos. Continue cooking and add scallions, shrimp, and curry powder. Cook until shrimp are just done and have turned pink-orange. Remove from heat and mix in currants, cheese, peanuts, and chutney. Taste and adjust flavors. Cool.
To Assemble:
Place one sheet of phyllo dough on a counter. Brush lightly with butter, repeat until there are 3 layers. Cut into 3"-4" squares. Place 1-2 tbl. of the filling in the center of each square. Gather the four corners together and
*Boursin is a brand name herbed cheese.

squeeze halfway down to form a pouch. Place in ungreased mini-muffin tins and bake at 375° for 15-20 minutes or until golden. Serve immediately with lemon, jalapeno, or chili flavored aioli (see Index).

Prosciutto

Prosciutto (Italian ham) is slightly smoky and salty, a cross between Canadian bacon and country-cured ham.

It's served as an antipasto wrapped around fresh melon pieces or blanched asparagus, and lends an assertive taste to cooking. Prosciutto must be sliced very thin, almost transparent. Most Italian specialty food stores carry both domestic and imported prosciutto. Prices and quality vary, ask for a sample to determine your favorite.

63

Giardiniera

Giardiniera is an Italian condiment of mixed pickled vegetables. It's often part of an antipasto platter or a garnish with boiled dinners. In some neighborhood Italian restaurants in Chicago it's used as a pizza topping.

The marinade is made of wine vinegar and herbs. It's rather tart and slightly acidic, but great with crusty bread and robust red wine.

Unlike the usual American pickled vegetables, Giardiniera is not sweet and doesn't contain dill. Many vegetables are used—carrots, celery, pearl onions, small cucumbers, cauliflower, and peppers. In some gourmet shops you'll find it displayed on counters—beautifully layered in large designer canning jars.

Turn this dish into an entree by cutting the slices larger or leaving the rolls whole. It's great at picnics or buffets in the summer.

Chicken Giardiniera
serves 12 as an appetizer or 10 as an entree

4 whole chicken breasts, halved, skinned, boned and pounded to
   1/8"-1/4" thick
24 very thin slices of Genoa salami
1 tbl. EACH butter and olive oil

Filling
2/3 c. Hot Giardiniera, drained
1 egg yolk
4 oz. plain or herbed goat cheese
8 oz. cream cheese, room temperature
1 garlic clove, minced
3 tbl. toasted walnut halves, coarsely chopped
3 tbl. fresh Italian parsley, minced
1 tsp. dried basil
1 tsp. dried marjoram
salt and freshly ground pepper

Place Giardiniera, egg yolk, cheeses, and garlic in a food processor and whirl until just combined. Mixture should have some texture. Remove to a bowl and mix in walnuts, parsley, herbs, salt, and pepper. Taste and adjust. Can be set aside to chill in the refrigerator for up to several days.

To Assemble:

Cover the work surface with wax paper and lay out the pounded chicken breasts in a row—shiny side of breast down. Place 3 slices of Genoa salami on each and spread with 2-3 tbl. of the Giardiniera mixture on top. Roll chicken up like a jelly-roll, and place seam-side down on a plate. Cover with plastic wrap and chill 2 hours or overnight.

Melt butter-oil in a large skillet. Dredge chicken rolls with a little flour. Sauté in pan, turning to brown on each side. Add more oil if necessary. Remove rolls to a baking dish that will hold the chicken snugly together. Cover with foil and bake for 25 minutes or until done in a 350° oven. Cool. Cover each roll with plastic wrap and chill 8-10 hours or overnight. Cut off ends and save for munching! Slice rolls 1/2" thick and arrange on a platter. Serve cold or at room temperature with aioli.

66

Sun-Dried Tomato Aioli

2 garlic cloves, chopped
1/4 c. sun-dried tomatoes
2 tbl. seasoned rice vinegar
1 egg
3/4 c. oil
salt and freshly ground pepper

With motor running, add the garlic to a food processor or blender. Whirl till finely chopped. Add sun-dried tomatoes, vinegar, and egg and whirl until smooth. With motor running, very slowly add the oil until all is used up. Taste and adjust flavors. Store up to 3 weeks in the refrigerator.

One summer Suzanne and I, and two good friends, Tomi Gutterman and Lucy Ito, formed a group called the Jaguar School of Cooking. We gave classes on barbecues, grilling, and picnics. One of the students' favorite dishes was this flavorful appetizer/side dish/vegetarian entree of Lucy's. See if you don't agree.

Marinated Eggplant Rolls
serves 8-10 as an appetizer

3 small eggplants, unpeeled, cut lengthwise into 3/8" slices
salt
olive oil
6 oz. goat cheese, room temperature
4 oz. cream cheese

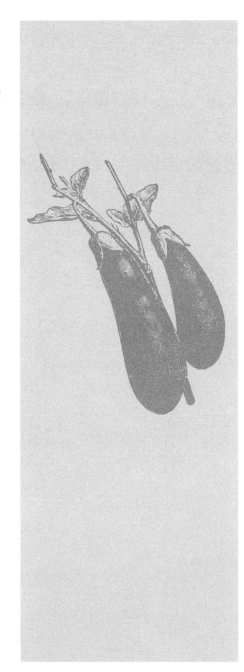

Marinade
2 garlic cloves, chopped
1/4 c. fresh Italian parsley, chopped
1/4 c. fresh basil leaves
1/3 c. red wine vinegar
1 c. olive oil
salt and freshly ground pepper

Place eggplant slices on paper towels, lightly salt, and allow to set for 30 minutes. Preheat oven to 400°. Rinse off salt and pat eggplant slices very dry.

Drizzle olive oil on a baking sheet that has sides. Arrange eggplant slices in a single layer, and drizzle more olive oil over eggplant. Place in oven and bake until soft

Appetizer Cocktail Party

Crostini with Shrimp Topping
Sun-dried Tomato
& Green Olive Tapenade

❧

Rosemary, Caramelized Onion
& Goat Cheese Tart

❧

Italian Sausage Phyllo Triangles

❧

Marinated Eggplant Rolls

❧

Pear & Ham Paté

❧

Rosemary Walnuts

❧

Serve with a California or Italian
Brut Sparkling wine,
Champagne Cocktail, or Kir Royale

68

and lightly browned, about 5 minutes on each side. Combine cheeses, set aside.

When cool enough to handle, spread each eggplant slice with cheese and roll into "cigars." Place rolls in a glass or ceramic shallow pan.

To Make Marinade:

In a food processor with motor running, put in garlic and mince. Add parsley and basil and mince again. Transfer to a bowl and add vinegar. Whisk in olive oil and season with salt and pepper. Taste and adjust.

Pour marinade over eggplant rolls. Cover with plastic wrap and chill for at least 24 hours. Remove from refrigerator and serve at room temperature.

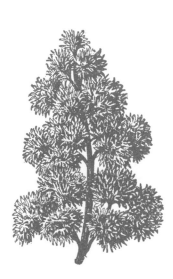

Quesadillas can be prepared ahead. Cook as below and place on a foil-lined baking sheet. Cover with more foil and keep warm on a 350° oven.

Quesadillas with Brie & Pears
serves 10-12

1/2 c. butter
1/2 c. vegetable oil
1 pkg. flour tortillas, medium to large size
8 oz. brie, white rind removed, room temperature
1-2 pears, unpeeled, cored and very thinly sliced
1/2 c. fresh chives, whole stems
Salsa (Cranberry Jalapeno or Melon Salsa) (See Index)

Melt butter and oil, adding about 1 1/2 tsp. to a large hot skillet. Place one tortilla into pan and arrange several pear slices over half. Dot with crumbled brie (about 2 tbl.). Add 2-3 chive stems. Fold tortillas in half and brush with the melted butter-oil mixture. Turn several times until tortillas are golden and cheese begins to melt. Add melted butter-oil mixture only as needed. Remove, cut in wedges and serve with a favorite salsa, such as Cranberry Jalapeno, or Melon Salsa.

Brie

Originally from France, Brie is known as the Queen of Cheeses. Today it's produced throughout the world, even here in Wisconsin. Belmont Brie is a well-known example.

Brie comes in wedges or rounds. It's characterized by a soft white edible crust and a creamy, buttery center. For the best flavor, purchase fresh cut wedges, rather than pre-cut. Once brie is cut, it no longer ripens and begins to diminish in flavor. Remember to serve at room temperature for maximum taste.

69

This is a very versatile snack. Other flavor combinations are possible by adding different herbs to the original recipe, such as 1 tsp. homemade or commercial chili powder, 1 1/2 tsp. Italian seasoning, or 1 1/2 tsp. dill weed. Experiment and add your own favorite herb or mix.

Pita Chips

1 pkg. pita bread
1/2 c. butter, room temperature
3 tbl. fresh parsley, finely minced
1 garlic clove, finely minced
salt and freshly ground pepper

Mix butter with parsley, garlic, salt, and pepper. Cut pita bread into eighths and separate. Spread the inside portion with the butter mixture. Place on a baking sheet and bake in a 375° oven for 15-25 minutes or until crisp. Remove and cool on a rack. Store in airtight containers until ready to use. Serve with soups and chili, or with herbed cheese and dipping sauces.

Serve this attractive hors d'oeuvre with toast points or a good quality water cracker such as Carr's or Bremner's Wafers.

Goat Cheese, Torta with Sun-Dried Tomato Pesto
serves 6-8

5 oz. goat cheese
2 oz. cream cheese, at room temperature
3 oz. feta cheese
1/2 recipe Sun-Dried Tomato Pesto
2-3 sun-dried tomatoes, finely julienned
2 tbl. fresh basil, chopped

In a bowl combine the goat cheese and cream cheese. Add feta, combine lightly, creating a coarse texture. Line a 1 1/2 c. ramekin (or straight sided bowl) with plastic wrap. Place 1/2 cheese mixture in the bottom of the ramekin, press down smoothly. Spread 2-3 tbl. pesto on top of cheese mixture, smooth evenly. Refrigerate overnight or at least 4 hours.

When ready to serve, invert torta on serving platter. Remove plastic wrap. Place some pesto around bottom of torta. Decoratively sprinkle juliennes of sun-dried tomato and basil on top.

Sun-Dried Tomato Pesto

3-4 large cloves garlic
1 c. sun-dried tomatoes (if not pliable, reconstitute in hot water,
    omitting the 2 tbl. hot water)
2 tbl. hot water
4 tbl. Parmesan, grated
1/2 c. olive oil
1/2 c. walnuts or pine nuts
freshly ground pepper

In a blender or food processor, while motor is running, add garlic. Next add tomatoes and water and combine well. Slowly add Parmesan and oil, then walnuts. Season to taste with pepper.

Feta Cheese

Feta is a fresh Greek cheese made of goat or sheep's milk. Unlike chevre, feta is shaped without a rind, packed in a brine or salt, and allowed to ripen.

The texture is soft and crumbly with a tangy, salty flavor. Feta has many uses—crumbled into salads, minced with tomatoes, melted in pasta sauces, marinated, or just enjoyed as an appetizer with cured olives.

71

Salads: Side Dishes & Main Dishes

This was one of the most difficult chapters for us to do. Not because herb salads are hard to make, but because in the course of writing this book, we had developed many more recipes than we needed. Working around the size constraints of the book was more of a challenge than inventing recipes!

We have tried to provide our readers with a selection of simple green salads to accompany dinner, such as our Boston Lettuce & Goat Cheese Salad with Honey Vinaigrette, or the intriguing Fennel & Lychee Nut Salad. Side dish salads are exemplified by the colorful Couscous Salad, or the crispy Middle Eastern Bread Salad. Also included are salads for picnics and buffets. Those are the hearty main dish varieties like Chicken with Black Bean Salad, or the spicy Asian Noodle Salad. We hope you have as much fun preparing these recipes as we did.

Wisconsin Winter Dinner

Butternut Squash Soup

Pork Tenderloin with a Calvados-Lingonberry Sauce

Wild Rice Pilaf with Hazelnuts & Cranberries

74

Spinach, Red Onion & Orange Salad with Poppyseed Vinaigrette

Poached Pear Tart

Serve with a ...nia Merlot wine

A tart-sweet salad that goes especially well with spicy food like our Southwest Chicken or Shrimp in Black Bean Sauce.

Spinach, Red Onion & Orange Salad with Poppyseed Vinaigrette

serves 4

10-12 oz. fresh spinach, trimmed and washed
1 small red onion, halved and thinly sliced
2 oranges, peeled and sliced
1 c. blue cheese, crumbled

Vinaigrette

3 tbl. honey or sugar
1 1/2 tsp. dry mustard
1 tsp. salt
1/3 c. flavored vinegar (raspberry, blueberry, red wine, etc.)
2 tbl. minced scallions
1 tbl. grated onion
3/4 c. oil
1 1/2 tsp. poppy seeds
1/4 c. fresh chives, minced

Arrange spinach, red onion, and oranges on a large platter. Combine vinaigrette ingredients and taste. Add more sugar if needed. Just before serving pour a little on salad and toss lightly. Sprinkle on cheese and serve.

After a weekend of outdoor events or any busy weekend, we serve this nutritious dish on Sunday nights with hot homemade bran muffins.

Winter Fruit Salad
serves 4

2-3 Granny Smith apples, cored, unpeeled and diced in
   1/2" chunks
1 orange, peeled and chopped in large pieces
1 c. seedless grapes
1 banana, sliced (optional)
2-3 pears, unpeeled, cored and diced in 1/2" chunks
1 c. Swiss cheese, cut in 1/2" chunks
1 c. sharp aged cheddar cheese, cut in 1/2" chunks
1/2 c. toasted whole almonds
1/2 c. toasted whole pecans
2 tbl. minced fresh mint
3 tbl. honey

Combine all ingredients and let sit 30 minutes before serving.

Toasting Nuts

If you toast nuts (pecans, almonds, walnuts, pinenuts) before adding them to recipes the flavors are heightened. It's such a simple step, but often overlooked. Even if a recipe doesn't call for this process, we generally do it—particularly for salads, garnishes, or in tarts. The procedure is simple. Place the quantity of nuts called for in a recipe on a baking sheet and put into a preheated 400° oven. Toast for 4-5 minutes. Remove and toss gently and continue toasting for another 2-3 minutes. Be sure to check often, since nuts burn quickly. The general rule is, if you can smell them toasting, it's probably too late!

Tomatoes

Besides growing the old reliable tomatoes like Better Boy, Early Girl, and Big Boy, venture out and add a few heirlooms to your garden.

Try sunny yellow Chello Cherry, rosy-pink Japanese Odorike, golden-orange Mandarin Cross, bi-colored Old Flame, or the sweet French varieties. Look in gourmet seed catalogs (see Index). They'll not only add color to your garden, but a plate of these sliced tomatoes will look like a rainbow.

When your garden is filled with sweet tomatoes, this simple dish will show them off.

Tomato & Sweet Onion Salad
serves 6-8

4 large tomatoes
1 large sweet onion, very thinly sliced
2 tbl. fresh basil, chopped, or 1 tsp. dried + 1 tbl. fresh parsley
1/4 c. good olive oil
2 tbl. red wine vinegar
salt and freshly ground pepper

Cut tomatoes in 1/4" slices. Arrange in a single layer on a serving platter. Separate onions into rings and scatter over tomatoes. Sprinkle with salt, pepper and basil. Combine oil and vinegar and drizzle over salad. Cover with plastic wrap and chill 2-4 hours. Return to room temperature to serve.

This is another creative salad. The fruit can also be kiwi, mango, banana, or raspberries. For variety, use more than one flavor mint.

Summer Fruit Salad with Yogurt-Mint Dressing
serves 4-6

1 8-oz. carton plain or vanilla yogurt
2 tbl. honey
1 tsp. grated orange rind
1/2 tsp. grated fresh ginger
3 tbl. minced fresh mint
6-8 c. assorted sliced and cut up fruit (strawberries, melons, pineapple, grapes, cherries or blueberries)
lettuce leaves (optional)

Combine the yogurt, honey, orange rind, ginger, and mint. Mix well. Chill several hours. Just before serving, line individual plates with lettuce. Place about 1 cup of assorted fruits on top of lettuce. Spoon a generous dollop of the yogurt mixture on top of the fruit on each plate and serve with a mint sprig.

Salad Fruit

When cutting up fruit, make sure you leave strawberries for the very end, since they are very fragile and tend to break down sooner than melons and pineapples. We also keep cut pineapples away from other fruits until the last minute—the acid in pineapple causes other fruits to deteriorate more quickly.

77

Radicchio

The current popularity of radicchio (pronounced RA-DEEK-E-O) is evident in restaurants across the country. Although a common sight in Italian grocery stores, this chicory is relatively new to most Americans. It can be grown locally, but does take some pampering. Its distinctive ruby-red color adds a bright spot to salads, but if not properly shaded during the growing process, will turn a green or deep copper color.

Radicchio has a slightly bitter taste that goes well with other assertive greens, like escarole or endive, and benefits from strong-flavored vinaigrettes.

We must admit this is a strange combination of ingredients, but they work brilliantly together!

Boston Lettuce & Goat Cheese Salad with Honey Vinaigrette
serves 6-8

1 head Boston lettuce
1 small head radicchio
1 small bulb fennel, thinly sliced and chopped (about 1/3 c.)
1/2 c. goat cheese, crumbled
1/2 pt. strawberries, whole or sliced
1/2 c. toasted whole pecans*
freshly ground pepper

Arrange torn lettuce and radicchio on individual plates or a large platter and sprinkle with fennel, goat cheese, and strawberries. Drizzle dressing over and toss gently. Add pecans, more strawberries, if needed, and a grinding of pepper.

Honey Vinaigrette
1/2 c. olive oil
3 tbl. fruit flavored or tarragon vinegar
2 tsp. balsamic vinegar
1 1/2 tsp. dried marjoram
2 1/2 tbl. honey (or to taste)
3/4 tsp. salt

Place all ingredients in a jar and shake well. Add a dash of salt.   *Toast whole pecans in a 400° oven for 8-10 minutes.

Marge's husband, Chuck, serves this salad when he makes Cajun food—a specialty of his. He finds the "element of danger" involved in making a Cajun Roux a real challenge.

Artichoke Salad with Sun-dried Tomatoes
serves 6-8

Vinaigrette
6 tbl. olive oil
3 tbl. balsamic vinegar
2 tbl. red wine vinegar
1 tbl. fresh basil, chopped
1 tsp. Dijon mustard
salt and freshly ground pepper

Salad Mixings
1 13-oz. can artichoke hearts
1 small head romaine, sliced
1 small head Boston lettuce, torn
1 small head radicchio, torn
4 sun-dried tomatoes, sliced
2/3 c. black olives, halved
1/2 small red onion, sliced
3- 4 oz. crumbled goat cheese

Combine all vinaigrette ingredients in a covered jar. Shake well. Season to taste. Pour over artichoke pieces and marinate 1 hour.

Sun-dried Tomatoes

When purchasing sun-dried tomatoes look for Romas, they're meatier and more intensely flavored than regular tomatoes. They're available packed in oil or in cellophane bags. If the dried tomatoes are not pliable, reconstitute them in boiling water.

We keep a large canning jar in the refrigerator filled with good olive oil and tomatoes. As the supply gets low, we simply add more sun-dried tomatoes.

The oil is great added to pasta sauces, for quick sautés, or mixed with cream cheese for an appetizer.

On a large platter combine lettuces, artichokes, tomatoes, olives, and onion. Drizzle with half the vinaigrette, toss. Add more vinaigrette if needed. Sprinkle with goat cheese and freshly ground pepper.

An unusual but very tasty salad, it happens to be a favorite of both of our brothers: John (Suzanne's brother) and Fred (Marge's brother).

Fennel & Lychee Nut Salad
serves 8-10

Vinaigrette

>9 tbl. vegetable oil
>1/3 c. flavored vinegar (raspberry, pear, blueberry, etc.)
>2 tbl. orange juice
>1 1/2 tbl. honey (or to taste)
>2 tsp. sesame oil
>salt and freshly ground pepper

Combine the vinaigrette ingredients in a jar or bowl and mix well. Taste and adjust the seasonings. Set aside or store in the refrigerator.

Salad Mixings

>2 c. mixed baby lettuces
>1 small head bibb, Boston, or leaf lettuce
>3 c. fresh spinach, washed and deribbed
>1 c. daikon radish or peeled jicama, julienned
>1 small fennel bulb, sliced in thin rings
>10- 12 fresh snow peas, blanched 7- 10 seconds
>2/3 c. canned lychee nuts, quartered
>1 c. toasted walnut halves

Spinach

When choosing spinach make sure the leaves are fresh and not bruised. If leaves are large, fold in half and tear with stem side up, pulling the stem back towards leaf to remove. Submerge in water and wash twice, making sure sand and dirt have been removed.

81

Lychee Nuts

A unique ingredient in this salad is lychee nuts, a Chinese fruit that's small, oval-shaped, with a red outer shell-like skin. The pulp is sweet, milky-white, and translucent. The fresh variety is expensive and difficult to find. We use the canned type that is available in almost every grocery store. It's already peeled, pitted, and packed in a light sugar syrup. Kids find it a great snack to eat right out of the can.

To Assemble:

Place lettuce greens on a large platter. Sprinkle with radish or jicama, fennel, snow peas, and lychee nuts. Add half the vinaigrette and toss to coat evenly. Add more if needed. Sprinkle salad with walnuts and serve.

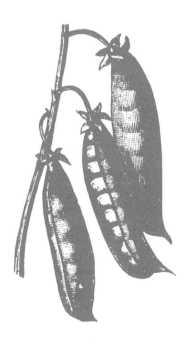

Marge's older daughter, Ryan, requests this salad whenever she visits home. Its unique flavor goes especially well with grilled beef or pork and tastes great even several days later. Vary the colorful vegetables with whatever you have on hand.

Couscous Salad
serves 8-10

4 c. chicken stock
7 tbl. vegetable or olive oil
1/4 tsp. each: turmeric, ground allspice, ground cloves, ground ginger
2 c. couscous
1/2 c. currants or golden raisins
1/2 c. dried apricots, in tiny dice
2 c. zucchini, unpeeled, core removed and chopped
1-1 1/2 c. carrots, chopped
3 1/2 tbl. fresh lemon juice
1/3 c. chopped red onion
1/2 tsp. salt (or to taste)
3 tbl. EACH minced fresh chives and fresh mint
2 tsp. honey
1/2 c. toasted slivered almonds

Bring stock, 4 tbl. oil and spices to a boil. Add couscous and boil over moderate heat 2 minutes or until liquid

Couscous

Couscous is a staple in North African cooking, especially Morocco. It's made of semolina (durum wheat), the same grain used in imported pasta. It's usually sold in this country precooked and instant. The traditional long cooking process uses semolina grains that are flour coated.

It has a cereal-like smell and taste, but with simple additions it becomes a sophisticated side dish to almost any grilled meat, poultry, or seafood. It's a bright change from rice when mixed with butter and freshly grated Parmesan.

Zucchini

When growing zucchini, 2 or 3 plants are enough for an average family. Small, baby zucchini are prized for their tender, delicate flavor. Middle-sized zucchini are great shredded and sautéed with olive oil, garlic, and a sprinkling of fresh herbs.

84

Left unattended, baby zucchini soon become blimp-size, but still good when grated into soups, in quick breads, or stuffed with other vegetables.

is absorbed. Add currants and apricots. Cover and let stand 15 minutes. Chill.

Break up couscous till each grain is separate and add rest of ingredients including remaining oil. Taste and adjust. Chill 4 hours. Taste before serving. If too dry, add more oil and lemon juice. Garnish with toasted almonds.

This is a nice combination of fruit, jalapenos, and peppers. It is exotic and very refreshing.

Tropical Melon Salsa Salad
serves 6

1 cantaloupe, seeded and cut in 1/2" chunks
2-3 jalapenos, finely minced
1 1/2 c. bell peppers (use an assortment of colors—red, yellow, orange, green) cut into 1/2" chunks
1/2 c. chopped sweet onions
1 1/2 c. chopped jicama
3-4 scallions, chopped
3 tbl. lime juice
3 tbl. oil
3 tbl. herbed vinegar
honey (to taste)

Combine all ingredients in a bowl and toss. Adjust sweetness and chill several hours.

Jalapenos

When chopping or mincing jalapenos make sure they are seeded first. The veins in the membranes holding the seeds are the receptacles for the "real heat." The seeds growing next to the veins are also extra hot. If you have sensitive hands, wear rubber gloves during the procedure.

85

Homemade Mayonnaise

Making your own mayonnaise is fun and the end product is delicious. There's no comparison to the store-bought variety, and it can be varied in so many ways. All you need is a blender and good olive oil (but not extra virgin, because the flavor is too intense). The secret to thick, fluffy mayonnaise is the slow addition of oil.

One of our favorites is Curry Mayonnaise (see Index).

Other recipes can include roasted red peppers, garlic, jalapenos, garlic, sesame oil, chili powder, and any flavor that fits your culinary needs.

This is Marge's 85-year-old German Aunt Elfriede's recipe. She's always received compliments for this simple but delicious salad in every restaurant she's owned.

Tante Friedel's Potato Salad
serves 6-8

3 lb. red potatoes, with or without skins
1 c. chopped onion
1/2 c. fresh parsley, minced
1/4 c. olive oil
2 tbl. Dijon mustard (or herbed)
1c. homemade or good quality mayonnaise
salt
freshly ground black pepper

Boil potatoes until fork-tender. Drain and run under cold water. Chop into large chunks and put in a large bowl. Add onions, parsley and half the olive oil. In a small bowl mix the remaining oil, mustard, and mayonnaise. Add to potatoes and blend well. Season to taste. Garnish with additional parsley before serving. Flavors improve the second day, but serve at room temperature.

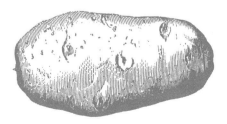

This spring salad can also be a late summer salad with the substitution of green beans for asparagus.

Tuscan Spring Salad
serves 8

10-12 small new potatoes (unpeeled)
1 lb. fresh asparagus
3-4 carrots, sliced thin or on the diagonal
1 tsp. sugar

Vinaigrette

2 garlic cloves, minced
1/4 c. fresh parsley, minced
1 tbl. dried basil or 3 tbl. fresh, minced
2/3 c. olive oil
6 tbl. red wine vinegar
1 tsp. salt and freshly ground pepper
1/3 c. chopped scallions

Cook potatoes in salted water 15-20 minutes or until tender. Drain and chill. Cook asparagus in boiling water until barely tender. Drain and chill. Slice into 2" pieces. Put sugar in boiling water, add carrots and blanch until barely tender. Drain and chill. Set aside.

To Assemble Vinaigrette:

In a blender or food processor with motor running put garlic and whirl. Add the parsley, basil, oil, and vinegar. Whirl until smooth. Season with salt and pepper. Mix in scallions. Pour over vegetables. Lightly toss. Chill and reseason before serving.

Asparagus

When purchasing asparagus make sure the spears are crisp and bright green without shriveled skin. Break off the white "root" end where it naturally snaps and boil in a sauté pan with 2" of water for no more than 2 minutes. Start thicker asparagus before thin ones for even cooking. Immediately rinse in cold water. To transform this salad into a main dish add 1 1/2 c. smoked ham cubes.

87

Corn

We love August and September for the wonderful corn in Wisconsin. Try grilling it.

Just pull back husks and remove the silk. Tear several outside husks into 1/4" strips to use as ties. Replace husks around cobs and tie with the reserved strips. Soak corn in salted water for 5 -15 minutes. Drain well. Roast on grill over hot fire 15-20 minutes, turning frequently. Remove husks and serve with plain or herb butter and salt and pepper.

88

A colorful salad that travels well for picnics or potlucks. When the corn and pepper season is at its height, add any color bell pepper, and if you like a little heat in your food, be sure to mix in a few hot peppers.

Corn Salad
serves 6

3 c. fresh or thawed frozen corn
1 tbl. butter
1/8 tsp. cayenne pepper
salt and freshly ground pepper
1/2 c. EACH red and green chopped peppers
1-2 jalapenos, seeded and chopped
3/4 c. chopped celery
1/4 c. chopped red onion
1/2 c. chopped fresh parsley
5 tbl. oil
2 tbl. vinegar
1 tsp. Creole-style or Dijon mustard
1 tsp. sugar
1 tsp. salt
1/4 tsp. cumin
1/8 tsp. dried thyme
shredded lettuce

Sauté corn in butter until hot. Add cayenne, salt, and pepper to taste. Set aside to cool.

In a bowl add cooked corn, peppers, celery, onion, and parsley. In another bowl add oil, vinegar, mustard, sugar, salt, cumin, and thyme. Whisk and add to salad. Season to taste and serve over shredded lettuce.

Like many salads, the ingredients and amounts are flexible with the season and your pantry. Feel free to add other vegetables like cauliflower, yellow summer squash, whole baby squash, and sliced baby carrots, as well as other types of hard cheese and salami.

Italian Rice Salad
serves 10

Vinaigrette
  1/2 lemon, juiced
  5 tbl. red wine vinegar
  2 tsp. dried basil
  1 1/2 tbl. fresh rosemary, chopped
  2/3 c. olive oil
  salt and freshly ground pepper
  2 tsp. honey (or to taste)

Salad Mixings
  4 c. cooked cold rice
  2 c. cooked garbanzo beans (1 15-oz. can, well drained)
  10 oz. artichoke hearts, chopped
  1/4 c. kalamata or other oil-cured olives
  1 1/2 c. celery, sliced or on the diagonal
  5-8 oz. salami, cubed
  1/2 c. red onion, chopped
  1/2 c. fontinella or mozzarella cheese, chopped
  1 zucchini, chopped (1 1/2 c.)
  10-12 sun-dried tomatoes, sliced (softened or reconstituted)
  1/2 c. fresh Italian parsley, minced

90

Beach Picnic Menu

Seafood Gazpacho

ℰ

*Chicken Giardiniera with Sun-Dried
Tomato Aioli*

ℰ

Italian Rice Salad

ℰ

Triple Ginger Tart

ℰ

*Serve with a Johannesberg Riesling,
or Spanish Rioja wine*

Combine vinaigrette ingredients in a jar and mix. Taste and adjust seasonings.

Combine salad ingredients in a large bowl; add vinaigrette and toss gently. Taste and adjust flavors. Chill overnight. Bring to room temperature to serve.

Every cuisine has a way to use up leftover breads. This recipe uses pita in a delicious salad.

Middle Eastern Bread Salad
serves 6-8

2 pita bread slices
1 head romaine, torn
2 cucumbers, seeded and chopped
2 tomatoes, seeded and chopped
1/2 c. scallions, chopped
1/2 c. fresh Italian parsley, chopped
1/4 c. fresh mint, chopped
1/2 c. green pepper, chopped

Vinaigrette
2 garlic cloves, finely minced
1/2 tsp. salt
1/3 c. fresh lemon juice
1/2 c. olive oil
freshly ground pepper
zaa'tar (if available)*

Toast pita bread in 350° oven until very dry. Break into small pieces. Mix vinaigrette ingredients (except zaa'tar). Toss lettuce and vegetables with vinaigrette and add pita. Toss again and season to taste. If zaa'tar is available, sprinkle on top.
    * Zaa'tar is a Middle Eastern spice.

Middle Eastern Spices

Middle Eastern cuisine is fresh and colorful. It depends a great deal on perfectly ripe fruits and vegetables, and often recipes are variations on themes. What makes them distinctive are some of the unusual spices.

Zaa'tar and sumac are Middle Eastern spices, readily available to American cooks. Zaa'tar is a combination of sesame seeds, oregano, and sumac. It's a salty/sour blend used in soups, marinades, and rice dishes. The sumac is not the same poisonous variety grown in America, but a sour red-colored tasty herb.

91

Make this salad a day ahead, adding tomatoes just before serving. It makes a nice addition to an antipasto dinner.

White Bean Salad
serves 8

1/2 c. dried white beans
1/4 c. olive oil
1/4 c. red wine vinegar
2 ripe tomatoes, cubed
1/2 c. minced fresh parsley
1 tsp. dried marjoram
1 tsp. dried oregano
1/2 tsp. dried basil
1/2 c. sliced black olives
1/2 c. sliced celery
1/4 c. chopped red peppers
1/2 tsp. fennel seeds, crushed
3 scallions, minced
1 clove garlic, minced
salt and pepper
lettuce leaves (optional)

Soak beans overnight and simmer the next day until tender, approximately 2 hours. Drain and cool. Combine all ingredients and refrigerate. Taste and adjust seasonings. Serve cold on lettuce leaves.

Dried Beans

Beans, lentils, and peas—known as legumes—are more versatile than their humble culinary beginnings. A menu mainstay for thousands of years, beans provide nutritious simple meals for pennies. Most dried beans require soaking in water for 8-10 hours before cooking. When in a hurry, substitute canned beans for dried. Remember this easy conversion: 1 lb. of dried beans = approximately 6 c. canned beans.

We especially like this salad for a festive warm summer night buffet. To transform this into a vegetarian dish, just omit the chicken.

Chicken with Black Bean Salad
serves 8-10

2 large whole chicken breasts, skinned and boned
1 tbl. olive oil
2 tbl. commercial or homemade chili powder (mild)
2 15-oz. cans black beans, rinsed well and drained
   (or homemade equivalent)
2 c. cooked corn, cooled
1 c. cubed green and red bell peppers (1/4"-1/2" cubes)
1-2 jalapenos, seeded and finely minced
3/4 c. finely chopped red onion
1/2 c. fresh cilantro, coarsely chopped
1 1/2 c. daikon radish*, peeled, cubed (1/4"-1/2")
6 medium flour tortillas
vegetable oil
salt

Vinaigrette
1 1/2 tbl. honey
2 cloves garlic, minced
3 tbl. sherry vinegar or spicy herb vinegar
1/3 c. vegetable oil
1/8 tsp. cayenne pepper
1/2 tsp. ground cloves

Scoville Unit

Scoville units, developed in 1902 by Wilbur Scoville, offer a way to measure the power of the capsicum (pepper). Scoville needed to measure the heat of peppers used in making the muscle salve "Heet."

Scoville based his units on how much he had to dilute the chile before he could not taste any heat. The scale ranges from 0 for bell peppers to 200,000 for the hottest habaneros. On a scale 0 to 10, bell peppers are 0, jalapenos are 7, serranos are 8 and habaneros are 10.

Tortilla Chips

Fresh flour Tortilla Chips are an easy and special treat. The shapes can vary between the standard strips or wedges, or be as creative as you like. Fry in small batches in a heavy deep pan with 1/2" of very hot vegetable oil, until golden on both sides. For removing chips, we find using a Chinese wok strainer is easiest. The chips cook very quickly so watch carefully. Place chips on paper towel to cool and absorb any excess oil. Then put chips into a large paper bag, add salt, and toss carefully. Store in a covered metal tin until ready to use (within 2-3 days).

2 tsp. dried oregano
1 1/2 tsp. ground cumin
2 tsp. salt
freshly ground black pepper

Rub chicken with oil and sprinkle liberally with chili powder. Marinate for 30 minutes. Grill or broil until done. Set aside. In a large bowl combine beans, corn, peppers, onions, and cilantro. In a jar combine dressing ingredients and pour over bean mixture. Toss well and season to taste. Chill until serving time. Mix in radish before serving.

For garnish: cut tortillas into 6-8 wedges or triangles. Fry in 1/2" hot oil until light golden brown. Turn once. Drain on paper towels and salt lightly. Set aside in metal cookie tins until ready to serve.

Cut cooked chicken in strips. Place bean salad on a large platter. Arrange chicken decoratively on top and scatter tortilla chips around edges of the platter.

*If unavailable, you can substitute jicama—or omit. Daikon radishes are white and very long (like a huge carrot) and mild in taste. They may be found in Asian food markets and large specialty food stores. Don't add the daikon until just before serving or it will turn gray from the black beans.

This unique salad is an adaptation from one of our best cook friends, Donna Taylor. Its surprising taste and colorful presentation make it a perfect dish to serve at summer picnics and potlucks.

Chinese Sausage Rice Salad
serves 8-10

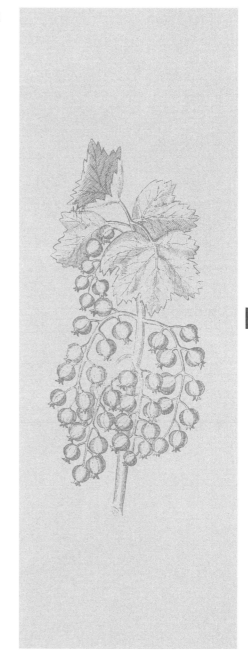

3-4 c. cooked rice, cold
1 c. Tarragon Vinaigrette (see Index)
1/4 c. fresh parsley, minced
3 tbl. fresh basil, minced
3 tbl. fresh lovage, minced
2 tbl. fresh tarragon, minced
1/4 c. fresh cilantro, minced
1/3 c. scallions, minced
1/4 c. red onion, minced
1/2 c. fresh red or green bell peppers, chopped
2 tbl. currants
1/2 tbl. whole coriander seeds, simmer in water
   15-20 minutes to soften
1/2 cup pimento-stuffed olives, coarsely chopped
1 1/2 tsp. salt
freshly ground pepper
5-6 Chinese sausages, boiled 5 minutes and sliced
   on the diagonal *
lemon juice (if needed)
2 tbl. toasted slivered almonds

In a large bowl mix rice, 3/4 of the vinaigrette and

Chinese Sausage

Found in Asian food stores, Chinese sausages are often made of pork and duck and are sweet. When choosing the sausages exercise some care as some are made with liver. We haven't found any of those to have a pleasing taste.

all the ingredients, except almonds. Toss and taste. Add remaining vinaigrette if too dry. Cover and chill 4 hours or overnight. Before serving add salt and a dash of lemon juice if needed. Garnish with almonds.

*Chinese sausages are found in Oriental supermarkets. They're often made of pork and duck and are rather sweet. We use them on pizza with other Asian ingredients.

This salad is especially refreshing in the hot summer months—serve at picnics with cold beer from one of *Wisconsin's* micro breweries.

Seafood Salad with Curry Mayonnaise
serves 8-10

1 lb. fresh shrimp
1/2 lb. fresh scallops
1 slice of lemon
1 bay leaf
1 sprig of fresh thyme or 1/2 tsp. dried
1 1/2 c. chopped onions
1 1/2 tbl. finely minced ginger
1/2 tsp. homemade or commercial curry powder
3 tbl. butter
5-6 c. cooked rice, cold
1/2 c. scallions, chopped
1/2 c. celery, cut on the diagonal
1/4 c. fresh lovage, minced (optional)
1 tbl. fresh thyme, chopped, or 1 tsp. dried thyme
1/2 c. golden raisins or currants
2 Granny Smith or other firm green-colored apples, unpeeled,
  chopped in large chunks
1 green pepper, chopped in large pieces (1")
1 recipe Curry Mayonnaise
salt and freshly ground pepper
1/2 c. salted peanuts
2/3 c. toasted coconut

Coconut

When curry dishes and other Indian foods are served, small bowls of condiments are included: toasted nuts, minced fresh herbs, chutneys, relishes, raisins, yogurt, and coconut. The condiments provide another dimension to the food—some are hot, others crunchy, mild, salty, sour, or sweet. Coconut combines two: sweet and crunchy—but must be toasted first.

This simple process takes just a few minutes. Begin with a preheated 400° oven. Spread the sweetened, raw, or unsweetened coconut on large baking sheets and place in the oven. Bake for about 2 minutes, remove and gently toss. You will notice that the coconut browns on the outer edges first. Return to the oven for another minute or two and remove to a bowl. Coconut burns even faster than nuts, so watch carefully.

Cook shrimp and scallops in water with a slice of lemon, bay leaf, and thyme. Cook over medium heat until shrimp turns orange and scallops are just tender. Remove, peel shrimp and devein. Set aside.

In a skillet, sauté onions, ginger, and curry in butter for 4-5 minutes or until soft. Place in a large bowl. Add rice, scallions, celery, lovage, thyme, raisins, apples, and pepper. Cover and chill until ready to serve.

To Assemble:

Add seafood and mayonnaise to rice mixture. Toss gently and adjust flavorings with salt, pepper, and possibly more curry powder. Garnish with peanuts and coconut.

Curry Mayonnaise

2 garlic cloves
1 1/2 tsp. homemade or commercial curry powder (mild)
2 1/2 tbl. fresh lemon juice
1 tsp. honey
1 egg
1 tsp. Dijon mustard
1 c. vegetable oil
salt

With motor running on a food processor or blender add garlic cloves and process until pulverized. Add curry, lemon juice, honey, egg, and mustard, blend well. With motor running, very slowly add vegetable oil. Season with salt and chill. Chilling will thicken the mayonnaise. It will keep 3-4 weeks in the refrigerator.

If you are making this salad ahead of time, wait until just before serving to mix in the peanuts and coconut—it keeps them from becoming mushy.

Curry Chicken Salad
serves 8

Vinaigrette
2/3 c. vegetable oil
1/4 c. vinegar
2 tsp. Dijon mustard
1 1/2 tbl. honey
2 tsp. curry powder (or to taste) commercial or homemade
1 tsp. salt
freshly ground pepper

Salad
1 1/2 c. chopped onions
3 cloves garlic
2 tbl. vegetable oil
1 1/2 tsp. curry powder, commercial or homemade
1 1/2 tsp. chili oil
2 whole cooked chicken breasts, skinned, boned, and
    cut into 1/2" cubes or shreds
1 c. chopped scallions
1 c. currants
2 green peppers, cut into thin strips (1/3" x 2")
1 1/2 c. celery, cut diagonally
1 c. salted peanut halves
1 c. toasted coconut

Poaching Chicken

When cooking chicken for salads we like to poach them in water with thyme, bay leaves, onion, and parsley stems. Simmer slowly until just done. The chicken becomes flavorful yet moist with this method. Remove the chicken, and keep the liquid as a tasty stock.

2 Granny Smith apples, halved, cored, and cut into 1/2" cubes
4 c. cooked rice
salt and pepper

In a jar, make the vinaigrette by combining oil, vinegar, mustard, honey, and 1 1/2 tsp. curry powder, salt, and pepper, then set aside.

Sauté onions and garlic in 2 tbl. vegetable oil, add 1 1/2 tsp. curry powder and chili oil, continue to sauté 2-3 minutes, until onions are transparent. Add cooked onion mixture to a large bowl, combine with remaining ingredients, reserving 1/2 c. peanuts and coconut. Toss salad ingredients with vinaigrette, season to taste, and sprinkle with reserved peanuts and coconut just before serving.

This main dish salad can be made with leftover grilled beef. Just omit the pre-grilling marinade. Serve with a good crusty bread for a quick meal.

Tortellini, Grilled Beef & Blue Cheese Salad
serves 4-6

Marinade
    8 tbl. oil
    4 tbl. red wine vinegar
    1 tsp. Worcestershire sauce
    6 cloves garlic, minced
    1 tsp. dried Herbes de Provence or thyme
    salt and freshly ground pepper
    1-1 1/4 lbs. beef tenderloin

Vinaigrette
    1/2 c. red wine vinegar
    1/2 c. oil
    1/2 tsp. Dijon mustard
    1/2 tsp. sun-dried tomato paste
    1 tbl. capers
    1 tsp. salt and freshly ground pepper

Salad Mixings
    1 lb. cheese tortellini, cooked and cooled
    2 c. sliced fresh mushrooms
    3 tbl. minced fresh parsley
    1/2 c. red onion, sliced

Graduation Buffet

Chicken with Black Bean Salad

Asian Noodle Salad with Shrimp

Middle Eastern Bread Salad

Tortellini, Beef & Blue Cheese Salad

Serve with an Italian Soave wine

101

Tortellini

We prefer to use fresh or frozen tortellini rather than dried. The flavor is superior and they only take a few minutes to cook. For variety try the multi-color or flavored tortellini that is available at large or specialty grocers.

3/4 lb. fresh asparagus or green beans, blanched and sliced*
4 tbl. blue cheese
tomato wedges for garnish

Combine marinade ingredients, whisk to blend. Slice tenderloin in half lengthwise and place in the marinade. Let sit at room temperature for several hours. Grill or broil. Combine vinaigrette ingredients in a jar and shake well. Taste and adjust seasoning.

To Assemble:

In a large bowl add tortellini, tenderloin cut into 1/4" strips, mushrooms, parsley, onions, and vinaigrette. Mix well and marinade 30 minutes to 2 hours. Just before serving add asparagus and blue cheese and toss to coat. Serve with tomato wedges.

Always add asparagus, green beans, or pea pods last to a vinaigrette dressing salad, because of their tendency to lose color when mixed with acids.

We like this salad for ladies' luncheons, served with small flavorful muffins or quick breads such as zucchini or cranberry.

Wild Rice, Smoked Turkey & Chevre Salad
serves 4

2 c. cooked wild rice
1 c. smoked turkey, cut into cubes
1/2 c. scallions, chopped
2 tbl. fresh chopped chives
1/2 c. chopped celery
1-2 oranges, chopped (rind grated)
1/2 c. peas (if frozen, thaw)
3 oz. chevre (goat cheese)
1 c. toasted pecans
Bibb or leaf lettuce

Tarragon Vinaigrette

1 tbl. orange juice
1/4 c. oil
2 tbl. rice wine vinegar
2 tbl. honey
2 tsp. dried tarragon
grated orange rind
salt and pepper

Combine vinaigrette ingredients in a large bowl and whisk. Add rice, turkey, scallions, chives, celery, oranges,

Rice Vinegar

We use Marukan or Mitsukan seasoned or unseasoned rice vinegar for many of our vinaigrettes, salsas, aiolis, and marinades.

It's made from fermented rice and imparts a delicate, mild, and less acidic flavor than most vinegars. Substitute it in any salad dressing but cut down on the honey or sugar if using the seasoned vinegar.

and peas. Toss and season to taste. Chill. Just before serving add goat cheese and pecans. Mix gently and serve on a platter lined with lettuce.

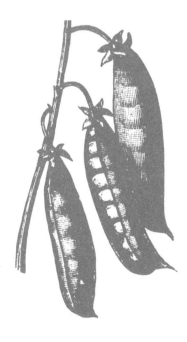

We like to prepare large buffet dinners featuring at least 3 salads of differing ethnic groups, such as Asian Noodle, Black Bean with Chicken, and Seafood Salad with Curry Mayonnaise.

Asian Noodle Salad
serves 6

Marinade
2 tbl. Thai Chili Sauce
1 tbl. oil
1/4 c. water
3/4-1 lb. fresh shrimp, peeled and deveined

Vinaigrette
1 1/2-2 tbl. fresh ginger, finely minced
1/4 c. soy sauce
3 1/2-4 tbl. sesame oil
dash chili oil
1/2 tsp. Chili Paste with Garlic*
juice of 1/2 lime
6 tbl. oil
2 tbl. sugar
1/4 c. rice vinegar

Salad Mixings
1 lb. *Asian* noodles, cooked
4 oz. pea pods, blanched
10 oz. mini corn, drained, cut in half lengths
3 tbl. fresh basil, chopped

Asian Noodles

There are as many Asian noodles as Italian pastas, each with a specific use and unique flavor. Soba (made from buckwheat) is a Japanese noodle—thin, round, and tan-colored (some are flavored with green tea). Udon, also a round noodle, is much thicker and requires a longer cooking time.

§

The popular ramen or somen is pre-cooked and makes a quick lunch—you'll find it with a variety of seasonings in almost every grocery store.

§

Chinese noodles, called mein, are available fresh or dried and resemble sour egg noodles. They come in a variety of shapes, sizes, and flavors.

§

1/2 c. red onion, chopped
1/4 c. scallions, chopped
1 yellow pepper, julienned
2 large carrots (1 1/2 c.), julienned and blanched
1 yellow squash, unpeeled, julienned
1/2 c. chopped cilantro
chopped scallions for garnish
basil for garnish
*available at Asian food stores or specialty grocers

Asian Noodles

Cellophane noodles, which look like transparent fishing line, are made from mung beans. Tasteless by themselves, they absorb the flavor of the liquid they are cooked in.

§

106

Last on our list are rice sticks, or mai fun—a vermicelli made from rice. When deep fried, they puff up to twice their original size. Fun to serve and great to eat as a salad topping or with stir-fried vegetables.

§

Combine Thai Chili Sauce, oil, and water. Mix well and add raw shrimp. Let marinate 30 minutes. Remove from marinade and grill or sauté in a skillet until shrimp turn pink-orange. Place cooked shrimp in a bowl and set aside.

To Make Vinaigrette:

Combine all ingredients in a jar or small bowl and whisk. Taste and adjust seasonings. Add half of the vinaigrette to the shrimp and toss. Cover bowl with plastic wrap and chill 30 minutes to overnight.

Place the remaining vinaigrette in another bowl and add the cooked noodles, pea pods, corn, basil, onion, scallions, pepper, carrots, squash, and cilantro. Toss gently, and taste and adjust seasonings.

To Serve:

Place noodle mixture on a large platter. Scatter shrimp on top and garnish with additional scallions and fresh basil. Serve cold or at room temperature.

When grilling tenderloin for dinner, make extra to use in this next-day salad. You can substitute sirloin or other tender beef.

Beef Tenderloin Salad with Balsamic Vinaigrette
serves 6

1 lb. beef tenderloin
oil for sautéing

Marinade
1/4 c. oil
2 tbl. lemon juice
2 tsp. freshly ground black pepper
salt
1/4 tsp. Tabasco
1/4 tsp. hot chili oil

Vinaigrette
3-4 tbl. balsamic vinegar
2 cloves garlic, minced
1 tbl. Dijon or herbed mustard
4 tbl. fresh parsley, minced
1 1/2 tsp. dried thyme
1/4 c. olive oil

Salad Mixings
3/4 lb. green beans, partially blanched, or asparagus
1 large red pepper, julienned

Summer Picnic Menu

Iced Tomato Cream Soup

Beef Tenderloin Salad

Muffuletta Sandwich

Caramel Nut Tart

Serve with a dry Rose
or *Valpolicella* wine

4 scallions, sliced in 1" lengths
2 small heads of Belgian endive, cleaned
1 small head of romaine or radicchio
1/2 red onion, thinly sliced
2 tomatoes, sliced, or 8-10 patio tomatoes, halved

Place the whole trimmed tenderloin in a shallow bowl. Combine all the marinade ingredients in a bowl and mix well. Pour over tenderloin. Marinate at room temperature 1 hour or overnight in the refrigerator.

Make the vinaigrette by combining the vinegar, garlic, mustard, thyme, and parsley. Gradually whisk in olive oil. Taste and adjust seasonings.

Sauté beef in a small amount of oil for 15-20 minutes or until done. It should be slightly pink inside. The meat can also be grilled. With either method, let beef rest 5-10 minutes, to set juices before slicing. Cut into strips and add with green beans to vinaigrette. Let both marinate for 15 minutes. Add peppers and scallions.

To Serve:

Arrange endive, romaine, or radicchio on a large serving platter—tear into bite-size pieces. Add remaining red onions and beef and toss gently. Decorate with tomatoes.

This recipe is a variation from Marge's Swiss neighbor Trudy Ehrlich, who probably got it from her family in Green County, Wis. Feel free to interchange the herbs—that's what makes it so versatile.

Basic Vinaigrette
3/4 cup

1/2 c. olive oil
3 tbl. vinegar
1-2 tbl. honey
1 tsp. Dijon mustard
1 tsp. dried herbs or 1 tbl. fresh herbs*
salt and freshly ground pepper

Combine all ingredients in a jar and mix well. Taste and adjust seasonings. Store in refrigerator if using fresh herbs.

*Basil, oregano, marjoram, thyme, rosemary, tarragon, Italian parsley, salad burnet, or a preferred combination of herbs.

Vinaigrette Hints

To make vinaigrettes creamy, slowly whisk the olive oil in by hand. A miniature metal or wire whisk is especially handy for this procedure.

Combine leftover vinaigrettes to make marinades for chicken, pork, beef, and vegetables.

109

Vinaigrette Hints

Use good quality olive oils. Bottles labeled extra virgin oil are darker green, strongly flavored, and more expensive. Use sparingly in vinaigrettes, even cutting the total oil with regular olive oil for a milder flavor. Extra virgin olive oil is wonderful with assertive greens.

110

Creole Vinaigrette
1/2 cup

6 tbl. oil
2 tbl. herbed vinegar
2 tsp. Creole style mustard, Dijon, or herbed mustard
1 tsp. sugar (or to taste)
1 tsp. salt
1/2 tsp. EACH dried cumin and thyme
1/2 c. scallions
1 tsp. minced fresh chives
1/2 tsp. red pepper flakes

Combine all ingredients in a bowl or jar and mix well. Taste and adjust seasonings.

Creamy Blue Cheese Vinaigrette
3/4 cup

1 1/2 tbl. tarragon vinegar
1 tbl. low-fat yogurt
2 tsp. honey
1 tbl. fresh tarragon, minced
1 tbl. fresh chives, minced
1 tsp. fresh thyme, minced
salt and freshly ground pepper
1 tbl. blue cheese, crumbled

Combine all ingredients in a jar and mix well. Taste and adjust flavors. Will keep several days in the refrigerator.

Vinaigrette Hints

If using fresh herbs or prepared mustard, store vinaigrettes in the refrigerator. They will keep for 4-5 weeks.

Don't be tempted to discard the vinaigrette when you see that the oil has congealed. Oil hardens in cold temperatures. Simply bring it to room temperature or place in a pan of lukewarm water for 3-4 minutes.

Sage Vinaigrette
3/4 cup

1 large shallot, peeled
6-8 sage leaves, about 2" long
1 tsp. Dijon mustard
2 tbl. balsamic vinegar
salt and freshly ground pepper
1/2 c. oil

In a blender or food processor with motor running, add shallots and whirl. Add sage leaves and process again. Add remaining ingredients and blend well. Season and pour over salads with assertive greens—romaine, escarole, endive, etc.

Soups

We have divided our Soup chapter into three areas: Cold Soups, Dinner or First Course Soups, and Hearty Whole Meal Soups and Chilis. Some are cream soups that are light yet rich tasting, perfect in the most elegant of menus, such as our Cream of Five Onion Soup, Butternut Squash Soup, and the spicy Cream of Red Pepper Soup. There's even a light Fish Soup that features freshwater fish to delight the fisherperson in your house.

The Hearty Soups are meant to be main course entrees. A soup such as Lentil, Leek & Ham may be served as dinner. Chicken Chili can make a fine Sunday night potluck supper. Minestrone can serve as a quick one-dish meal on a busy weekday. We're sure you're going to find them unique and satisfying.

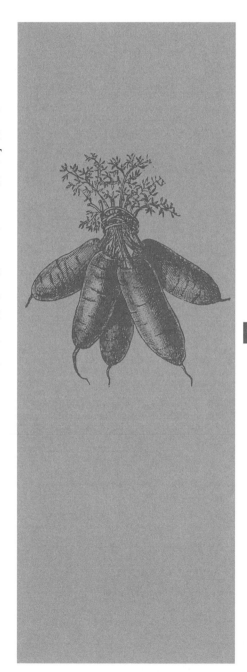

Tomatoes

When using fresh tomatoes we prefer Romas because their flavor is more intense and the texture is meatier. Remove the skin by lowering the tomatoes in boiling water 1 1/2- 2 minutes; cool slightly and peel.

To remove seeds cut in quarters and scoop out with a spoon. If using canned tomatoes, choose Italian plum or Romas, and add a touch of honey to counteract the tin flavor.

This is an elegant first course soup for warm summer evenings. Prepare early in the day when the weather is still cool.

Iced Tomato Cream Soup
serves 6

1 tbl. butter
1 medium onion, chopped
6 fresh tomatoes, peeled, seeded, and chopped or
   1 28-oz. can of Italian-style pear shaped tomatoes and juice
1/2 c. chicken stock
1/2 tsp. sugar
1/2-3/4 tsp. dried thyme (fresh: 1 1/2 tbl.)
1/2-3/4 tsp. salt
3/4 c. heavy cream
1/4 c. sour cream
2 tbl. lime juice
salt and fresh ground pepper to taste
lime slices for garnish
1 tbl. chopped chives

Melt butter in skillet and add onions. Cover and sauté over low heat for 15 minutes, or until soft. Add tomatoes, stock, sugar, thyme, and salt. Simmer uncovered for 10 minutes. Cool. Puree in blender or food processor with heavy cream, sour cream, and a sprinkling of lime juice. Force through a sieve (to remove tomato seeds). Taste and add salt, pepper, and additional lime juice if necessary. Serve chilled with a slice of fresh lime and chopped chives.

This soup is so flavorful and fresh tasting, even those people who aren't fond of cold soups ask for seconds.

Seafood Gazpacho
serves 8

2 cloves garlic, minced
1 small cucumber, peeled, seeded, and cut into 1/4" pieces
1 sweet red pepper, cored, seeded, and finely minced
1/2 medium red onion, finely chopped
1 1/2 c. chicken stock
1 14-oz. can Italian tomatoes, drained and chopped
   (or the equivalent fresh)
1 1/2 c. tomato juice (use some of the drained tomato liquid)
1/4 c. fresh lime juice
1/4 c. good olive oil (mild, not extra virgin)
1 c. fresh bread crumbs (2-3 slices of fresh bread, any kind,
   whirled in a blender or food processor)
1 1/2 tsp. cumin seed, crushed
1 tsp. dried oregano
1 sprig salad burnet (optional)
3 tbl. fresh cilantro, chopped
1 sprig thyme
salt and freshly ground pepper
.1/2 lb. cooked shrimp, cut in large pieces, chilled

In a large bowl mix garlic, cucumber, peppers, onions, stock, tomatoes, and tomato juice. Stir in lime

115

Fresh vs. Dried Bread Crumbs

There is a difference! Dried crumbs refers to bread or rolls that are dried out and whirled in a food processor or blender. Fresh bread crumbs are made from fresh bread or rolls, whirled in a blender till soft and fluffy. Their uses are different. Dried bread crumbs give a hard coating to foods like fried chicken or fish. Fresh bread crumbs give a light coating or thicken foods. When a soup or stew is a little watery you can add a handful of fresh bread crumbs to the base without cooking it. This replaces the often used white sauce or roux.

❧

juice, oil, bread crumbs, and herbs. Puree only half the soup in a blender and stir back into bowl. Season with salt and pepper. Chill 8 hours or overnight. Stir in shrimp just before serving.

❧

Suzanne's family takes this comforting soup on ski trips. The combination of the smoky bacon and nutty flavored rice makes it a hit.

Cream of Wild Rice Soup
serves 6

2/3 c. wild rice
1/2 c. onion, diced
1/2 c. celery, diced
1/2 c. carrots, diced
3- 4 strips bacon, diced
2 tbl. butter
4 1/2 c. chicken stock
1/2 tsp. dried thyme
1 tsp. dried crushed rosemary
1 1/2 c. heavy cream
Beurre Manie (1 tbl. flour and 1 tbl. butter kneaded together)
salt
pepper
fresh parsley

Sauté rice, onion, celery, carrots, and bacon in butter until vegetables are tender and bacon is crisp, 3-4 minutes. Stir in stock and herbs, bring to a boil, reduce heat, and cover. Simmer until rice is tender, 30-40 minutes. Stir in cream, whisk in Beurre Manie until soup thickens. Season. Add more stock if soup appears too thick. Serve hot, and garnish with chopped fresh parsley.

Wild Rice

Wild Rice is a Native American grass, grown in the waters of the Western Great Lakes region. It is indigenous to Wisconsin and harvested by many local tribes. Considered by many a luxury product, we find the price well worth the extra pennies. We use raw wild rice instead of parboiled or instant for a better flavor.

Wild rice should not be overcooked, which is easy, since it is surprisingly more delicate than the other varieties. Remember to prewash the rice in 3 or 4 changes of water to remove small stones, etc.

117

Stock—Homemade vs. Canned

All of us wish we had time to make and freeze our own chicken or beef stock. Not only is it inexpensive, but the flavor is far superior to anything you can buy. But today's busy schedules don't always permit such endeavors, so the only option is canned stock or broth.

There are many varieties of canned, powdered, paste, or liquid stocks and the final decision is up to you. We prefer the low-salt canned beef or chicken stocks or the liquid beef or chicken concentrates (Bovril or Knorr are good). A can of beef or chicken broth is approximately 1 7/8 cup of liquid. Naturally just shy of 2 cups !

118

This is another elegant soup best served as a first course with our delicate homemade crackers.

Cream of Five Onion Soup with Herbed Crackers
serves 8-10

4 heads (not cloves) garlic, unpeeled
3 tbl. olive oil
4 tbl. butter
3 leeks, white part only, chopped
1 onion, chopped
1 bunch scallions, white part only, chopped
6 tbl. flour
4 c. chicken stock
1/3 c. dry sherry
1 c. heavy cream
fresh lemon juice, to taste
salt and pepper, to taste
2 tbl. fresh chives, minced

Cut off top 1/4" of each garlic head. Place heads in a small baking dish and drizzle with 1 tbl. olive oil. Turn to coat. Cover dish with foil. Bake in a preheated 350° oven for 1 hour or until cloves are very, very soft. Let cool. (Can be baked 1-2 days ahead.) Press individual garlic cloves to release the puree. Set aside.

Melt butter and 2 tbl. olive oil in a soup kettle or deep saucepan. Sauté leeks, onions, and scallions until soft, about 8 minutes. Reduce heat to low and add garlic puree.

Add flour and cook 8-10 minutes, stirring occasionally. Stir in stock and sherry. Simmer 20 minutes, stirring occasionally. Remove from heat and let cool slightly. Puree in batches in a blender or food processor. Return to saucepan and add cream. Simmer until slightly thick, about 7-10 minutes. Add lemon to taste and season with salt and pepper. Thin out with chicken stock if soup is too thick. Ladle into bowls and garnish with chives.

Herbed Cheese Crackers

> 1/4 c. butter, at room temperature
> 1/2 c. flour
> dash of salt
> 1/2 c. shredded Swiss, cheddar, or Edam cheese (2 oz.)
> 1-2 tbl. water, if needed
> 1 egg, beaten
> 1/4 c. poppy seeds, caraway, or sesame seeds (singly
>   or in combination)

Grease a large baking sheet and set aside. Preheat oven to 375°. In a food processor or mixer combine butter, flour, salt, and cheese. Whirl or mix well. Add water in small amounts until mixture sticks to itself. Wrap in plastic and chill 15 minutes.

On a floured board (or in between wax paper) roll pastry to about 14" x 10". Cut into strips with a pastry wheel or with decorative cookie cutters. Handle dough carefully, it's quite fragile. Place cut-outs on prepared pan. Brush with egg and sprinkle on seeds. Bake for 10 minutes or until crisp and golden brown. Store in airtight tins.

Stock, continued

So if your recipe calls for 2 cups, simply add the difference in water. The secret to picking the right stock or broth is to read the label. Make sure the first ingredient isn't salt, and the product should contain chicken or beef.

If you have a little time, you can enhance commercial stocks with a few aromatic vegetables and herbs.

❦

120

A great soup to make at the end of the summer when red peppers are inexpensive and plentiful.

Curried Cream of Red Pepper Soup
serves 10-12

1/2 c. onions, chopped
2 tsp. homemade or commercial curry powder (mild)
4 tbl. butter
3 large fresh red bell peppers, chopped
2 1/2 c. chicken stock
3 tbl. raw white rice
1-1 1/2 c. heavy cream
salt and freshly ground pepper
1 recipe salsa

In a large saucepan or Dutch oven sauté the onions and curry powder in the butter until soft, 2-3 minutes. Lower heat, add peppers, and cook 3-4 minutes. Add stock and rice; cover and simmer 15 minutes or until rice is cooked and peppers are very soft. Cool; puree in a blender or food processor. Add cream and season. Chill 8 hours or overnight. Taste and add more curry, salt, and pepper, if needed. Serve with a generous dollop of salsa in each bowl.

Fresh Tomato Salsa

    1 medium tomato, seeded and diced
    1 tbl. red onion, minced
    1 1/2 tsp. jalapeno pepper, minced
    1 tbl. balsamic vinegar
    1 tbl. fresh basil, minced
    1/2 tbl. olive oil
    salt and freshly ground pepper

Combine all ingredients, season. Cover with plastic wrap and chill.

Salsas

Salsas are more than the typical tomato-chili-onion mixture served with chips. Salsas are fresh relishes that can add zip to soups, grilled fish, chicken or beef, homemade tortilla chips, and even omelets.

What's nice about salsas are the varieties you can make or buy. Some commercial salsas are quite good—but check to be sure they aren't too watery. If the flavor seems flat, add some fresh minced chilis, or herbs, or even a dash of herb vinegar.

Making salsa is fun and easy. Use the freshest fruits and seasonal vegetables and don't be afraid to experiment. Cut the ingredients in small similar sizes—usually 1/4"-1/2" dice—and combine only at the last minute.

121

Dried Mushrooms

Dried mushrooms have become very popular recently and are more widely available to the home cook. They're expensive, with an intense flavor, but only a few are called for in recipes. There are many varieties and new ones are appearing on grocers' shelves all the time. Most common are the Chinese shiitakes, chanterelles, cepes, morels, and the Italian porcini. You can buy them singly or in mixes.

Once purchased, store them in a dry place, similar to where you store pasta. Dried mushrooms must be reconstituted to use—a simple process. Place the amount called for in a bowl and cover with 1" boiling water. Let stand for about 30 minutes, or until they are soft. Remove any woody stems (particularly with shiitakes) and slice. Use as your recipe calls for, but don't throw away the liquid. Strain through a coffee filter to remove any grit or small particles and use in your recipe, or freeze for use in other recipes.

122

Sprinkling fresh mushrooms with a little lemon juice keeps them looking white even after cooking.

Cream of Three Mushroom Soup
serves 8

8 dried shiitake mushrooms
1/2 oz. assorted woodland mushrooms (like chanterelles, cepes, morels, or porcini)
1 c. boiling water
10-12 oz. fresh mushrooms, sliced
1 tbl. fresh lemon juice
grated rind of 1/2 lemon
2 tbl. butter
1/3 c. chopped shallots
2 tbl. flour
1 can beef stock
salt
1 1/2 tsp. dried thyme
1/4 tsp. freshly ground pepper
1 tsp. fresh ginger, finely minced
1 c. heavy cream
2 tbl. fresh chives, minced

Soak dried mushrooms in boiling water for 30 minutes. Drain and strain liquid. Reserve. Remove woody stems from shiitakes. Chop all mushrooms and set aside.

Mix fresh mushrooms with lemon juice and grated rind and set aside. In a large saucepan, melt butter and sauté shallots for 2 minutes. Add fresh mushrooms and cook covered for 5 minutes. Sprinkle with flour and stir a few minutes.

Reduce heat to low, add stock, reserved strained soaking liquid, dried mushrooms, salt, thyme, pepper, and ginger. Heat to boiling. Reduce and simmer covered about 25 minutes. Stir in cream and cook until slightly thick. May need to thicken with a Beurre Manie*. Taste and adjust seasonings to taste. Garnish each bowl with chopped chives.

* Beurre Manie is made of equal parts flour and butter kneaded together.

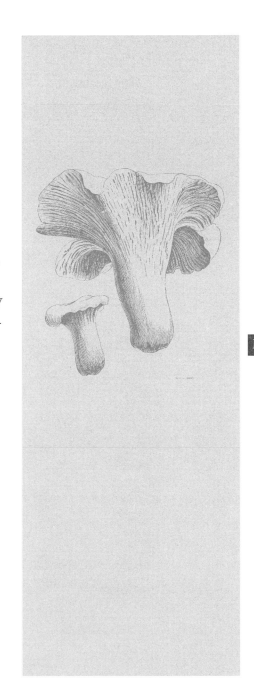

Quick Chicken Stock

1 tbl. oil
1 onion, unpeeled, chopped
2 carrots, unpeeled, chopped
1 celery stalk with leaves, chopped
1 stalk parsley, with stems
3 cans chicken stock, low salt

Sauté in oil the onions, carrots, and celery until slightly brown. Add stock and parsley and cook on low 30 minutes. Strain and use.

§

Squash

When peeling squash use a vegetable parer. Cut off the underlayer of green along with skin.

Peak season for butternuts is October through December. Look for squash that seem heavy for their size, smooth-skinned with hard, tough rinds. Keep in a cool place until ready to use.

§

A beautiful autumn orange-colored soup that would make a grand start to any dinner, or even a casual meal on its own, with a crusty bread and a salad of mixed greens.

Butternut Squash Soup
serves 8-10

4-4 1/2 lbs. butternut squash
2 leeks, cleaned and chopped, or 2 1/2 c. chopped onion
5-5 1/2 c. chicken stock
1 tsp. dried thyme
2/3 c. sour cream
1 tsp. salt
freshly ground pepper
1/8 tsp. cayenne
4 tbl. rum
freshly minced parsley and chives
sour cream

Peel squash, cube, and remove seeds. Place squash and leeks in a stock pot, add chicken stock and thyme. Cook 20 minutes or until tender. In a blender or food processor puree squash mixture in batches adding sour cream (if mixture becomes too thick add additional stock). Return squash to pot, season with salt, pepper, and cayenne; add rum. Reheat, mix well. Serve garnished with parsley, chives, and a dollop of sour cream in the center of each bowl.

124

This soup contains both an herb and a spice from the same plant. Coriander is also called cilantro and Chinese parsley. The leaves are the herb, but when the plant goes to seed, the seeds are a spice used in curry mixes and baking.

Carrot Soup with Two Corianders

4 tbl. butter
2 shallots, minced
2 tbl. ground coriander
5 c. chicken stock
1 1/2 lb. carrots, peeled and chopped (about 1 1/3 c.)
1 large parsnip, peeled and chopped
1/4 c. heavy cream
3 tbl. fresh coriander, chopped
2 tbl. plain yogurt
salt and freshly ground pepper

Melt butter in a deep saucepan over moderate heat. Sauté shallots and 1 tbl. ground coriander 2 minutes. Add stock, carrots, and parsnips. Bring to a boil, reduce heat, cover and simmer 30-35 minutes or until vegetables are very tender.

In batches, puree soup mixture in a blender until smooth. Return to the pan. Add cream, remaining 1 tbl. ground coriander, 2 tbl. fresh coriander, and yogurt. Blend well and heat through. Taste and season with salt and pepper. Just before serving, mix in remaining fresh coriander.

Can be served hot or cold.

Parsnips

This very sweet, underrated root vegetable once had the reputation of being an aphrodisiac! It's easily grown in Wisconsin, much like carrots. In fact, in recipes, they're interchangeable. Choose evenly sized parsnips for uniform cooking. Peel the skin and wax, if they've been dipped. Slice and remove woody stems of the larger parsnips. Steamed, baked, or sautéd, they're a great addition to soups.

Besides the crouton garnish below, other garnishes such as fresh herbs, sprinklings of vegetables, grated cheese, or thin juliennes of fried tortillas can complement soups.

Fisherman's Soup
serves 8

1 1/3 c. chopped onion
1 c. chopped celery
3/4 c. chopped carrots
2 garlic cloves, minced
1 tbl. olive oil +1 tbl. butter
1 8-oz. bottle clam juice
3 c. water
3 tbl. tomato paste
1 c. dry white wine
3 tbl. brandy
1 1/2 tsp. salt
3/4 tsp. freshly ground pepper
1/2 tsp. dried tarragon
1/2 tsp. dried oregano
3 sprigs parsley
1/2 bay leaf
1/8 tsp. cayenne
2 carrots, cut into thin 2" juliennes
1/2 lb. sole filets, cut into pieces
1/2 lb. raw shrimp, cleaned and deveined
1/4 tbl. fresh parsley, chopped
sautéed croutons

In a large pan sauté onions, celery, chopped carrots, and garlic in melted oil and butter until vegetables are soft. Add clam juice, water, tomato paste, wine, brandy, salt, pepper, tarragon, oregano, parsley, bay leaf, and cayenne.

Bring to a boil and simmer 1 hour, stirring occasionally.

Strain broth into a large clean pan, pressing solids with the back of a spoon to extract all juices. Bring broth to a boil and add julienned carrots. Cook 5 minutes, reduce heat to medium-high, and add sole and shrimp. Continue to cook 2 minutes until shrimp are bright orange pink and fish is flaky. Serve in heated bowls with parsley and croutons.

Sautéed Croutons

3 tbl. olive oil
1 tbl. butter
5 thick slices day old French bread cut into cubes (4 c.)
1 tsp. salt
freshly ground pepper
1 tsp. oregano
1 tsp. basil

In a large sauté pan over high heat, melt oil and butter. Add bread cubes, cook while tossing until golden brown. Sprinkle with salt, pepper, oregano, and basil and continue to toss until well coated. Cook until crusty and hard, about 20 minutes over medium heat. Serve immediately or store in an airtight container.

Fish Stock

6 lbs. fish bones, heads, flesh of other fish, and shellfish trimmings

3 qts. water
2 onions, quartered
2 leeks, chopped
1 c. dry white wine
1 tsp. salt
2 tsp. fennel seeds
1 bay leaf
2 tbl. parsley stems
8-10 peppercorns
1 carrot, sliced
1 rib celery, sliced

Place in large stock pot and slowly bring to a boil, skimming often. Lower heat and simmer 45 minutes-1 hour. Strain the stock. Chill overnight and remove fat from top. Use immediately or freeze.

꽃

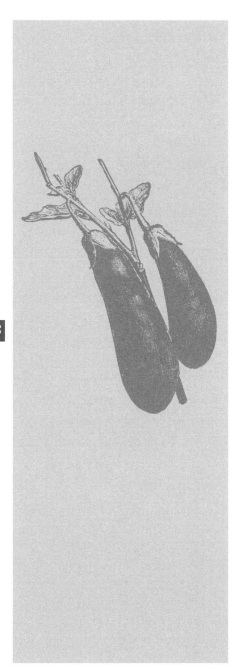

A good way to introduce cooked beans to your family. If you don't have the varieties suggested, use any cooked, canned bean.

Vegetable Chili
serves 10-12

1/2 oz. dried mushrooms (porcini, cepes, shiitake, etc.,
   or a combination)
1 c. boiling water
1 large eggplant, peeled and cut into 1" chunks
salt
3 tbl. oil
4-6 garlic cloves, minced
2 onions, chopped
1 large green bell pepper
10-12 oz. fresh mushrooms, trimmed and quartered
1 28-oz. can Italian tomatoes, chopped with liquid
2 tbl. commercial or homemade chili powder (mild)
1 tbl. ground cumin
1 tbl. dried oregano
1 1/2 tsp. fennel seeds
salt
dash cayenne pepper
2 cans (15-16 oz. each) garbanzo beans, or homemade equivalent
1 can (15-16 oz. each) white or navy beans
1 can (15-16 oz. each) small red beans
1 can (15-16 oz. each) kidney beans
sour cream
cilantro
salsa

Soak mushrooms in boiling water for 30 minutes. Cut into small pieces and save soaking liquid. Place eggplant cubes in a colander and sprinkle with salt. Let drain 30 minutes. Rinse with water and dry well.

Place oil in large kettle or Dutch oven and sauté garlic, onions, and green pepper 1-2 minutes. Add fresh and dried mushrooms, eggplant, tomatoes, herbs, and strained mushroom soaking liquid. Bring to a boil, reduce heat, and simmer 30 minutes or until eggplant is tender. Add beans and water, if too dry. Adjust seasonings and heat through, about 10-15 minutes more.

To serve, garnish each bowl with a dollop of sour cream or yogurt, cilantro leaves, salsa, and Corn Bread.

Growing Shelling Beans

For a real back-to-nature experience, try growing your own shelling beans. The seeds are available from most seed catalogs. One summer we successfully grew black (turtle) beans and Italian red beans with very little effort. You only need a sunny location with a trellis or fence for support and minimum care. The beans are harvested very late in the fall after they've dried out and the pods have shriveled. Then gather your harvest and shell them. That year we made gifts for the holidays of assorted dried beans and packets of herb seasonings. What a hit!

Chicken chili is an intriguing twist on the traditional Texas chili. Serve in the winter or summer with a Jalapeno Corn Bread, our Orange and Black Olive Salad and top the meal off with our Pine Nut Tart.

Chicken Chili
serves 8

4 chicken thighs (1 1/2-2 lbs.) boned, skinned, and cut up into 1/2-1" cubes

2 whole chicken breasts, boned, skinned, and cut into 1/2-1" cubes

1/3-1/2 c. flour

vegetable oil

2 onions, chopped (3 c.)

5 garlic cloves, minced

2 red bell peppers, chopped in 1/2" pieces

4-6 jalapeno peppers, chopped

3 tbl. medium hot chili powder (commercial or homemade, see Index)

1-2 tsp. cumin seed, crushed

1 1/2 tsp. ground coriander

1/8 tsp. ground cloves

salt

2 c. water

1 28-oz. can Italian tomatoes, chopped with liquid

1 1/2 oz. grated unsweetened chocolate

1 tsp. honey (or to taste)

2 cans (15-16 oz.) EACH white and navy beans

3 tbl. ground almonds

2 tbl. *toasted sesame seeds (toast seeds in skillet on medium heat until seeds begin to brown and pop)*
1 lb. *smoked Italian turkey sausage (if unavailable, use regular smoked turkey sausage) sliced in 1/2" rounds*
sour cream
cilantro
lime wedges

Dredge chicken pieces in flour and brown in oil in a Dutch oven. Remove and set aside. Add 2 tbl. oil to pan and sauté onions, garlic, bell peppers, and jalapeno peppers until soft (2-3 minutes). Add chili powder, herbs, water, tomatoes, chocolate, honey, beans, almonds, sesame seeds, and sausage. Cook 30 to 40 minutes at low heat to mellow flavors. Add chicken pieces, then cook 15 minutes at low heat. Adjust seasonings to taste. Add additional water if too thick. Garnish with dollop of sour cream, sprigs of fresh cilantro, and thinly sliced wedges of lime.

Chili Powder

We prefer to use true chili powder, which is made from ground chile peppers. When purchasing chili powder, make sure the color is bright brick red. The aroma should be strong, intense, and earthy. Commercial chili powders are mixes, containing cumin, oregano, garlic powder, cayenne, paprika, black pepper, salt, sugar, and very little real chili powder.

❧

131

132

Sage Corn Bread

2 c. yellow cornmeal
1 c. flour
1/4 c. vegetable oil
1 8 3/4-oz. can creamed corn
1 c. (4 oz.) shredded aged cheddar cheese
1 c. buttermilk
2 eggs, beaten
1 1/2 tbl. chopped onions
1/3 c. canned mild or hot green chilis or fresh equivalent, minced
2 tsp. baking powder
1 1/2 tbl. sugar
1 tsp. salt
2 tsp. rubbed sage

Preheat oven to 350°. Grease a 7" x 11" pan or muffin tins. Set aside. In a large bowl combine cornmeal, flour, oil, creamed corn, and cheese; blend well. Add buttermilk, eggs, onions, chilis, baking powder, sugar, salt, and sage. Mix thoroughly. Pour into prepared pans. Bake 25-35 minutes or until done (wooden pick should come out clean). Crust should be lightly browned.

This soup is a real hit with kids, especially if you use fancy shaped pasta.

Minestrone
serves 8-10

4-6 thick slices bacon, chopped 1/2" pieces
1 1/2 c. onions, chopped
1 c. thinly sliced carrots
3/4 c. celery, chopped
4 cloves garlic, minced
3 cans chicken stock
1 16-oz. can Italian tomatoes, reserve liquid
1/2 c. dry white wine or vermouth
2 tbl. fresh parsley, minced
1 bay leaf
2 tsp. dried basil
1 tsp. dried rosemary
salt and freshly ground pepper
1 c. dry macaroni or other small pasta
1 c. zucchini, unpeeled and sliced
1 20-oz. can white beans, drained, or homemade equivalent
Parmesan cheese, grated
Basil Pesto (see Index)

In a Dutch oven or large stock pot cook bacon until crisp. Remove and reserve. Save 3 tbl. pan drippings or add oil if necessary. Sauté onions, carrots, celery, and garlic until soft. Add stock, tomatoes, wine, and herbs. Cook over

Fresh vs. Dried Pasta

Just because the package says "fresh pasta" doesn't necessarily mean it's best. Dried pasta can actually be better. The secret is in using semolina flour, also called durum wheat or hard wheat. Most imported pastas are 100% semolina, but not all domestic pastas contain very much. If your dried pasta falls apart while cooking, chances are it didn't contain durum wheat.

133

Celery

Celery was first used as a medicinal herb, but the 16th-century Italians began using the stalks raw and boiling the roots as vegetables. Ever since, this vegetable has been very popular. The two varieties are "Golden Heart," a blanched white variety grown under paper to prevent chlorophyll from forming and turning it green, and "Pascal," a slower growing tall green variety. With celery's fresh, crunchy stalks, it's delicious cooked, fried, braised, or with a sauce, and makes an excellent accompaniment to roast meats and poultry.

low heat about 40 minutes. Add pasta and cook another 5 minutes or until pasta is al dente (almost done). Add zucchini and beans, heat through, and remove bay leaf. Stir in bacon and taste to adjust flavors. Serve with Parmesan cheese or a dollop of Basil Pesto.

134

The Granny Smith apples and the mango chutney add a lot of texture and flavor to this soup. Serve with our *Winter Fruit Salad and Pappadums* (lentil wafers).

Chicken Curry Soup
serves 8

2 tbl. butter
1 onion (1 c. finely minced)
1 stalk celery, minced
1/2 c. carrot, finely minced
1 tbl. curry powder or to taste
2 1/2 tbl. flour
3 c. chicken stock
2 whole chicken breasts, cooked and cut into
   1 1/2" x 1/4" strips
1 c. heavy cream
1/2 tsp. salt
freshly ground pepper
2 Granny Smith apples, coarsely chopped
3 tbl. mango chutney (fruit pieces minced)
1 tbl. water mixed with 2 tbl. flour
toasted coconut
minced scallions

Sauté in butter the onion, celery, carrots, and curry powder. Add flour, cook 2 minutes over low heat while stirring. Add stock, raise heat, and bring to a boil, reduce heat and simmer 20 minutes. Add chicken and cream, cook

Thickeners

When making wine sauces for entrees, homemade mayonnaise (aioli), or soups, we often add a handful of fresh bread crumbs to thicken the mixture. Fresh crumbs are made from one slice of fresh bread whirled in a blender or food processor. This quick addition adds body without changing the flavor.

135

Curry Powder

Curry powders vary considerably; grocery store powders often lack intense flavor. Instead, try spice merchants such as the Spice House in Milwaukee or East Indian grocers on Devon Avenue in Chicago.

Add curry powder slowly—you can always add more, but subtracting is difficult!

until it begins to thicken. Add salt, pepper, apples, and chutney and heat through. If soup is thin, add flour and water mixture and cook. Season to taste and serve. Garnish with toasted coconut and scallions.

136

The surprise ingredient here is mustard seed. It gives this hearty winter soup a real kick—almost like peppers!

Lentil, Leek & Ham Soup
serves 8

1 oz. dried mushrooms

1 c. boiling water

2 tbl. olive oil

4 leeks, cut in half, cleaned and sliced in thin rings

2-3 carrots, chopped

2 medium onions, chopped

4 garlic cloves, minced

1/2 c. celery, chopped

6 c. beef stock

2 1/2 c. (1 lb.) lentils, washed and sorted

3 c. smoked or regular ham, chopped

4 tbl. tomato paste

1 tsp. mustard seeds, crushed

3 bay leaves

1 tsp. dried thyme

1 tsp. dried tarragon

Soak mushrooms in boiling water for 30 minutes. Place oil in a large, deep soup kettle. Sauté leeks, carrots, onions, garlic, and celery. Cover and cook about 30 minutes at medium heat or until vegetables are soft. Add remaining ingredients, including mushrooms and strained soaking liquid. Bring to a boil. Reduce heat, cover, and simmer 1-1 1/2 hours or until lentils are soft. Taste, adjust seasonings and serve hot. This soup can be frozen.

Lentils

Lentils come in a variety of colors: red, brown, orange, yellow, green and gray. They're rich in protein and require much less cooking time than legumes.

The colorful red, orange, and yellow lentils (called split lentils) are a common ingredient in Indian curries. Cooked, they're used as thickeners for soups and curries. When ground into flour, they become the basis for pappadums—a spicy tortilla-shaped Indian cracker.

137

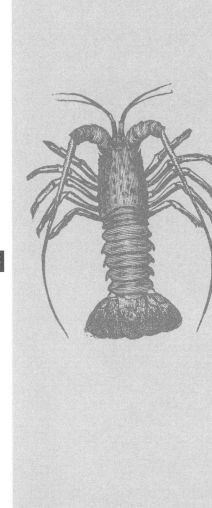

If lobster is unavailable, substitute with all shrimp. When pressed for time, make the soup base ahead of time and refrigerate overnight.

Lobster & Shrimp Corn Chowder
serves 8-10

10-16 oz. lobster tails, cut into 3/4" chunks
1 bay leaf
2 allspice berries
1/2 tsp. peppercorn
1 whole clove

Boil lobster with spices in 1 quart of water for 12-15 minutes or until shell is orange. Cool; remove meat and set aside. Strain stock and set aside 2 cups for use in Soup Base.

Soup Base

4 tbl. butter
2 garlic cloves, minced
1 medium onion, chopped
1 c. chopped celery
1 c. chopped carrots
1 bottle clam juice
1 can (approx. 2 c.) chicken stock
2 c. reserved lobster stock
1 1/2 tsp. dried oregano
1/4 c. brandy

2 1/2 c. chopped potatoes
1-2 jalapenos, chopped (optional)

In a soup kettle melt butter and sauté garlic, onion, celery, and carrots until soft. Add clam juice, stock, oregano, brandy, potatoes, and jalapenos. Cook until potatoes are just tender—don't overcook.

Roux

4 tbl. butter
4 tbl. flour
1 c. heavy cream
2 tbl. Parmesan cheese
dash Worcestershire sauce
dash Tabasco sauce
3 c. corn
1 lb. raw shrimp, peeled and deveined
salt & freshly ground pepper

In a small saucepan melt butter, add flour and cook 1 minute. Add cream and whisk until smooth and mixture begins to thicken. Add to the Soup Base along with the Parmesan, Tabasco, Worcestershire, corn, and shrimp. Heat through (just until shrimp turns orange), then add lobster. Taste and adjust flavors with salt and pepper. Serve with a dollop of salsa.

Christmas Tree Trimming Party

Goat Cheese Torta with Basil
& Sun-Dried Tomatoes

❀

Herbed Pita Chips

❀

Lobster & Shrimp Corn Chowder

❀

Curried Chicken Salad

❀

Chocolate Cranberry Torte

❀

Serve with Brut Champagne

139

The contrasting colors of black beans and a fresh salsa make this soup both attractive and flavorful.

Black Bean Soup
serves 10

1/2 lb. smoked slab bacon
1 1/2 c. onion, finely chopped
1 1/2 c. celery, finely chopped
1 1/2 c. carrots, finely chopped
1 bay leaf
1 tbl. garlic, finely chopped
1 1/2 tsp. dried thyme
2 tbl. ground cumin
1 tsp. freshly ground black pepper
1 tbl. dried oregano, crumbled
3 tbl. tomato paste
10 c. chicken stock
4 c. water (or as needed)
1 lb. black beans, canned or homemade equivalent
6 tbl. fresh lime juice
1/4 tsp. cayenne pepper
salt
salsa (see Index)
fresh cilantro, chopped
sour cream

Cut bacon in 1/4" cubes. Place in heavy kettle and cook, stirring often until well browned. Drain most fat.

Add onions, celery, carrots, bay leaf, garlic, thyme, cumin, black pepper, and oregano. Stir to blend and cover. Cook about five minutes over moderately low heat. Do not burn. Add tomato paste and combine well. Add chicken stock and water. Bring to a boil. Turn down heat and simmer.

Sort, rinse, and drain beans. Add to soup and cook uncovered over medium high heat 2 1/2 hours. Skim surface and remove fat on top. The soup is ready when beans are soft. Remove bay leaf and puree in a blender. Return soup to kettle and add lime juice and cayenne. Taste and adjust seasoning. Serve with salsa, cilantro, and a dollop of sour cream.

Quick Soak Method For Dried Beans

Place beans in a heavy pot and add water to cover by 2". Bring to a boil, and cook, for 2 minutes. Remove from heat, cover, and let stand at room temperature for 1 hour. Discard water and proceed with your recipe as if they had soaked overnight.

141

Quick Fish Stock

2 c. clam juice (2 8-oz. bottles)
1 1/2 c. water
1 c. dry white wine (like vermouth)
1 onion, chopped
6 parsley stems
1/4 c. mushroom stems
6-8 whole peppercorns

Place all ingredients in a pan and simmer 30 minutes, allowing liquid to reduce to 2 c. Strain. Use immediately or freeze.

142

Here in *Wisconsin* we have a large population of people of Scandinavian ancestry. This soup is loosely based on one of their recipes—an old Finnish fish stew called *Solyanla*. It's hearty, inexpensive, quick, and satisfying, especially on a winter's night with warm crusty bread.

Whitefish Soup
serves 8

4 lg. yellow potatoes (Yukon Gold) cut into 3/4" cubes, about 4 c.
1 c. onions cut in large dice
1 c. carrots, sliced on the diagonal
1 1/2 tsp. salt
8-10 whole allspice berries
6 parsley stems, with leaves
6 dill stems, with leaves
freshly ground black pepper
5 c. fish stock or chicken stock
1/2 c. dry white wine
1 1/2 lb. whitefish, walleye, cod, haddock, or combinations
1/4 c. fresh dill, chopped
1/2 c. heavy cream

In a large soup kettle or Dutch oven put potatoes, onions, carrots, salt, allspice, parsley and dill stems (tied together for easy removal), pepper, stock, and wine. Bring to a boil. Reduce heat and simmer 12-15 minutes, covered, until potatoes are just tender. Add fish and dill, cook until fish flakes easily, about 7-10 minutes. Add cream, heat through, taste and adjust seasonings. Serve hot.

Entrees

While developing recipes for this book, Marge and I have never been at a loss for ideas. It seems as if herbs have an endless ability to adapt themselves to any food ingredients, enhancing cheese, vegetables, meat, fowl, fruit, and sweets. They can change plain chicken into a succulent dish, like Lime Marinated Chicken with Green Sauce, or make fish come alive, like our Grilled Swordfish with Spicy Asian Pesto. They can even make pasta jump up, like our Southwest Chicken Pasta.

We've offered our readers quick entrees, those that take less than 30 minutes to prepare, and recipes adventuresome weekend cooks will enjoy, such as our Shrimp Ravioli made with wonton skins.

For your next dinner, thumb through the pages of our Entree section—we're confident you'll be inspired.

143

144

Even with all the ingredients in this dish, once the Cornish hens are stuffed, cooking time is under 45 minutes.

Mushroom Stuffed Cornish Hens
serves 4

2 thick slices of bacon, finely chopped
1 tsp. butter
1/2 c. shallots, minced
8-10 oz. fresh mushrooms (whirl in a food processor until very
    finely chopped, don't puree)
3/4 tsp. dried rosemary, crushed
3/4 tsp. dried thyme
1/2 c. Calvados (apple brandy) or brandy
1 1/2 c. fresh bread crumbs (2 slices fresh whirled in a food
    processor or blender)
1 egg yolk
2 tbl. dried apricots, finely chopped
1 tbl. fresh chives, minced
salt and freshly ground pepper

2 Cornish hens, split in half, wing tips removed*
1 1/2 tbl. EACH butter and oil
apricot jam or other flavored jelly or jam
1/4 c. Calvados
1/2 c. beef stock
1 tsp. cornstarch mixed with 2 tbl. water
salt and freshly ground pepper

To Make Stuffing:

Add bacon, butter, and shallots to a skillet and cook 1-2 minutes. Add mushrooms, rosemary, and thyme and cook until soft. Add Calvados and cook another minute. Remove to a bowl. Mix in bread crumbs, egg yolk, apricots, and chives. Combine well and season to taste.

Gently separate skin from Cornish hen breasts and legs and place 1/4 of the stuffing mixture inside. It will mound slightly. Repeat with other halves (can be chilled, covered with plastic, for several hours.)

In an ovenproof skillet, melt the remaining butter and oil and place the hens skin side down. Brown well, turn over gently. Place in a 400-450° oven and roast 30-40 minutes. Baste occasionally with pan juices. For the last 15 minutes, brush with warmed apricot jam. Remove hens to a serving platter and keep warm.

Over high heat, place the skillet on top of the stove and add the remaining Calvados and beef stock. Scrape up all of the brown bits. Cook and reduce slightly. Add cornstarch mixture and whisk until smooth. Season to taste and pass in a separate bowl along with the Cornish hens.

Use kitchen shears and cut down on either side of the backbone. Remove and use a large butcher knife and cut down the breastbone. It sounds difficult, but using a heavy-duty kitchen shears will make the entire process easy.

Kosher or Coarse Salt

Kosher salt sits in small bowls next to our stove. We use it daily and prefer it to regular salt because we tend to use less and it seems to have a lighter taste.

Coarse salt is the salt used in canning and pickling. The grains are rough and don't melt on contact with other food. It's the same kind that coats rolls, bagels, and pretzels.

Regular salt, available plain or iodized, contains sugar to make it free flowing—a fact most people aren't aware of.

145

146

Fresh shiitake mushrooms, many grown in *Wisconsin*, are a boon to cooks. Their meaty texture gives body to dishes, as well as a distinctive earthy taste. Be sure to discard their tough woody stems before using.

Chicken Marsala with Pancetta & Shiitake Mushrooms
serves 4

1 tbl. oil
1 tbl. butter
1/4 lb. pancetta, shredded or finely minced
2 whole chicken breasts, skinned and boned
1/4 c. flour + 1 tsp. dried rosemary, crumbled
8 oz. fresh shiitake mushrooms, stems removed, cut into
   thick slices
1/2 lemon, juiced
4 garlic cloves, minced
1 tsp. fresh rosemary, minced
3/4 c. marsala (or sherry)
salt and freshly ground pepper
1-2 tsp. Buerre Manie (equal parts flour and butter) if needed

Heat oil and butter in a large skillet and add pancetta. Sauté over low heat until pancetta is cooked. Dredge chicken in seasoned flour and brown in same skillet, 2-3 minutes. Remove chicken and cover.

Toss mushrooms with lemon juice. Add to pan with garlic and cook 2-3 minutes. Add rosemary and marsala. Increase heat and scrape bottom of brown bits. Let mixture reduce slightly. Add chicken and cook 4-5 minutes longer or until chicken is just done. Taste and adjust seasonings. If sauce is too thin, add 1-2 tsp. Buerre Manie and whisk well. Serve immediately with oven-fried potatoes and a colorful salad.

Simple Vegetable Sautés

For quick vegetable side dishes, sauté 1-2 cloves minced garlic in 1-2 tbl. extra virgin olive oil. Toss in your choice of vegetables and cook until just slightly limp. This should take only a few minutes.

Add a dash of coarse salt and freshly ground pepper and sprinkle with 1 tbl. Parmesan or 1 tbl. finely minced fresh herbs such as rosemary, tarragon, basil, dill, thyme, or marjoram.

Vegetables that work well are finely julienned or coarsely grated zucchini or other summer squash, shredded carrots, chopped fresh Swiss chard or spinach, thinly sliced fennel, or any cabbage. With cabbage, we usually add 1 tbl. of heavy cream and a generous amount of freshly grated nutmeg.

147

Valentine's Day Menu

Shrimp Purses

Boston Lettuce & Goat Cheese Salad
with Honey Vinaigrette

Pecan Chicken Breasts with
Dried Cherry Sauce

Herbed Potatoes

White Chocolate Cheesecake with
Fresh Raspberry Sauce

Serve with a Brut Rose Champagne,
California Zinfandel, or
French Red Rhone wine

This recipe is a fine example of how you can use dried cherries in an entree, adding a wonderful flavor and texture.

Pecan Chicken Breasts with Dried Cherry Sauce
serves 4

2 whole chicken breasts, halved, skinned, and boned
3 tbl. minced fresh parsley
3/4 c. ground toasted pecans
2 tbl. flour
salt and freshly ground pepper
1 egg beaten with 1 tbl. water
3 tbl. butter
3 tbl. chopped red onion
1 1/2 tbl. Dijon mustard
1 tsp. dried thyme
3/4 c. dry white wine
1/2 c. chicken stock
1/2 c. creme de cassis
1/2 c. dried cherries
2 tbl. red currant jelly
2 tbl. balsamic vinegar
2 tbl. cornstarch mixed with 4 tbl. chicken stock
salt and freshly ground pepper

In a bowl mix together parsley, pecans, flour, salt, pepper, and chicken breasts. Dip chicken breasts in egg mixture one at a time coating both sides. Toss in pecan mixture. Set aside.

In a large sauté pan melt 2 tbl. butter, cook chicken carefully on both sides. Cover skillet, turn down heat and continue cooking 3-4 minutes (keep chicken warm).

While chicken is cooking, place additional 1 tbl. butter in new sauce pan and sauté red onion until transparent. Add mustard and whisk, add thyme, wine, and chicken stock. Reduce by half and add cassis, cherries and currant jelly. Whisk until jelly has melted. Add balsamic vinegar and whisk in cornstarch mixture. Continue until sauce is thick and transparent. Season to taste with salt and pepper.

Serve warm chicken breasts with sauce poured over the center in a strip, with remaining sauce in a sauceboat.

Dried Cherries

Dried cherries are dried tart cherries (commonly used in cooking), which are grown in the Midwest, not the sweet larger cherries grown west of the Rockies (better known as "eating cherries"). Fructose is usually added to make the fruit more appealing for snacking.

Even though we both have tart cherry trees in our backyards, we enjoy using the dried variety for entree sauces, rice dishes, and cakes, because of its intense flavor and chewy texture.

149

When Marge worked in a local carry-out restaurant, this was one of her most requested dishes. An easy-to-make piquant recipe that's good for family suppers and company dinners.

Chicken Piccata
serves 4

1 1/2 c. onion, halved and sliced
4 large garlic cloves, minced
4 tbl. olive oil
2 c. mushrooms, sliced
1 tbl. lemon juice
1/2 to 3/4 c. sherry
2 whole chicken breasts, skinned, boned, and halved
1/2 c. flour
1/2 tsp. salt
1 tsp. paprika
1/2 to 3/4 c. chicken stock
6 tbl. Mediterranean vinegar or red wine vinegar
1/4 c. fresh parsley, minced (extra for garnish)
2 tbl. minced mixed fresh herbs (basil, marjoram, chives, thyme, or oregano)
2 tsp. honey (or to taste)
1-2 slices fresh bread whirled in a food processor
1 tbl. capers
salt and freshly ground pepper

Sauté onions and garlic in 2 tbl. olive oil until soft. Toss mushrooms with lemon juice and add to pan. Pour in sherry and cook, covered, over low heat 5 minutes. Remove all to a dish and set aside.

Dredge chicken in flour, salt, and paprika. In same pan, add more oil and sauté—browning chicken breasts. Add stock and vinegar and lower heat. Cook until chicken is springy and just tender. Remove to a platter and keep warm.

Add reserved mushroom-onion mixture, parsley, and mixed fresh herbs and cook to reduce liquid by half. Scrape bottom of pan to remove brown bits. Taste and add honey, if needed. To thicken mixture, add a little of the fresh bread crumbs. Taste and adjust. Add capers and pour mixture over chicken. Garnish with additional minced parsley.

Capers

A frequently used Italian and French condiment that should be in everyone's pantry. Capers are the unopened flower buds of a small bush that grows wild in the Mediterranean.

Capers have a sharp, tart flavor that adds crunch to sauces, mayonnaises and salads. The tiny buds are dried and pickled in vinegar. The larger buds often sold as capers are sometimes pickled nasturtium buds.

Marinating

For the past 8 years, we have been marinating meats, fish, and vegetables in plastic bags. It sure has taken the mess and effort out of marinating. Simply take your marinade and the item to be marinated and place in a thick plastic bag (or put two together). Secure tightly. No longer will you have to turn the meat or clean up messy bowls.

For a delightful picnic, serve this entree cold and accompany it with both Couscous and Melon Salsa salads.

Lime-Marinated Chicken with Green Sauce
serves 4

4 whole chicken breasts, halved, (boned and skinned optional) or 1 whole chicken, cut up

Marinade
    3/4 c. salad oil
    1/2 c. fresh lime juice (include squeezed limes in marinade)
    1 small onion, chopped
    3 scallions, chopped
    2 tbl. fresh chives, chopped
    2 tbl. fresh tarragon, chopped or 4 tsp. dried
    1 1/2 tsp. salt
    1 tsp. coarse ground pepper
    1 tsp. Tabasco

Combine all marinade ingredients, place in a double lined plastic bag with the chicken. Toss. Marinate several hours or overnight.

Grill 30-45 minutes, basting frequently. Serve with Green Sauce.

152

Green Sauce

    1 clove garlic
    3 scallions, chopped coarsely
    1/4 c. rice vinegar
    1 egg yolk
    1 1/2 c. assorted fresh herbs (parsley, basil, chives, savory,
       and tarragon or sage)
    6 tbl. butter, melted
    1/2 tsp. salt
    freshly ground pepper

153

While blender or food processor is running, add garlic and mince. Add scallions, vinegar, egg yolks, and fresh herbs. Slowly add butter and blend well. Season to taste and refrigerate until ready to serve with chicken.

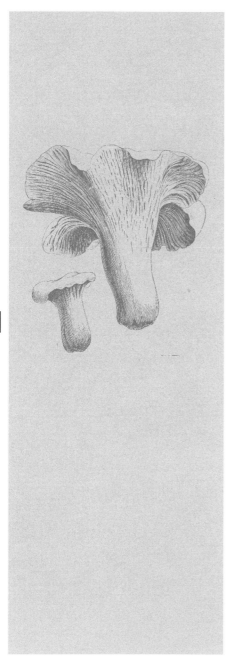

Serve this hearty Italian stew in deep bowls with crusty bread and a good bottle of Chianti. A fruit dessert or sorbet would be a perfect ending.

Chicken, Hunter-Style
serves 8

1/2 to 1 oz. dried mushrooms (porcini, cepes, morels, shiitakes, etc.) soaked in 1 c. water and 3/4 c. Marsala (or brandy)
14-16 oz. fresh mushrooms, halved or quartered
1/2 lemon, juiced
4 tbl. butter
1/4 lb. pancetta, diced (or 3 slices thick hickory bacon, diced)
2 whole boneless chicken breasts, cut in 2" pieces
3-4 boneless chicken thighs, cut in 1 1/2 to 2" pieces
flour mixed with paprika
olive oil
2 very large onions, chopped in large chunks
5 garlic cloves, chopped
1 28-oz. can Italian tomatoes, chopped and drained (or fresh equivalent, 8-10)
1 tbl. capers
1/2 c. pimento-stuffed olives
2/3 c. balsamic vinegar
2 tbl. fresh rosemary or 2 tsp. dried
1 tbl. fresh oregano or 1 tsp. dried
3 carrots, peeled, cut into cubes
1/3 c. Italian parsley, chopped
salt and freshly ground pepper

Soak dried mushrooms in water and wine for 30 minutes. Strain liquid and reserve. Chop mushrooms and set aside. Toss fresh mushrooms with lemon and sauté in butter 1-2 minutes. Remove to dish.

Add pancetta and cook 1-2 minutes. Remove to mushroom dish. Dredge chicken in flour and paprika. Brown in pan, adding more oil if necessary. Add to mushrooms.

Add onions and garlic and cook until soft. Add tomatoes, mushrooms, pancetta, chicken, capers, olives, vinegar, rosemary, oregano, carrots, dried mushrooms, and liquid. Cook 15 minutes.

Remove chicken and reserve. Continue cooking rest of the mixture for 1 hour or until it begins to thicken. Return chicken to pan, add parsley and season to taste. Serve hot.

Balsamic Vinegar

Balsamic vinegar or aceto balsamico is produced in Modeno, Italy. It's a sweet-sour vinegar prized by cooks. The process of fermentation takes approximately 25 years during which the red wine vinegar is steeped in oak, chestnut, mulberry, and juniper kegs to give the characteristic deep-brown color.

The process is as much a family secret as wine, and is as costly. Its marvelous flavor is used sparingly in sauces, stews and vegetables.

155

Pots & Pans

Having the right pan for the right job makes cooking much more fun. Our favorites are ones with aluminum clad outsides and stainless steel insides.

Aluminum is a good conductor of heat, and, with a stainless steel liner, you won't have discoloring from acidic foods like tomatoes.

Copper, of course, is the best. It conducts and distributes heat evenly and maintains temperatures longer. It's beautiful to look at and use, but it does have two obvious drawbacks—namely the prohibitive cost and time-consuming upkeep.

Besides our everyday pans, we also have several non-stick skillets in large sizes. We also own a few heirloom cast-iron pans—indispensable for frying and making Sunday pancakes—and we have several stainless steel stock pots and pasta pans.

A nutritious and delicious entree that takes under 1 hour to prepare and cook—perfect for those busy weekday dinners. It also offers a great chance to experiment with different herbs and herb combinations.

Herbed Yogurt Baked Chicken
serves 4

1 1/2 c. plain yogurt
1/3 c. scallions, minced
2 garlic cloves, finely minced
1 heaping tbl. dried herbs or combination*
1 tsp. sugar
1 tbl. vinegar
salt and freshly ground pepper
2 whole chicken breasts, halved (may remove skin if desired)
flour
paprika

Place in a shallow bowl yogurt, scallions, garlic, herbs, sugar, vinegar, salt, and pepper. Dredge chicken in flour, then dip in a pan, skin side up. Pour on any leftover yogurt mixture. Sprinkle with paprika.

Cover dish with foil and bake at 350° for 25 minutes. Remove foil and bake until brown or starting to brown. Serve with a salad and rice or other cooked grains.

Herbs to choose from: tarragon, dill, curry powder, Mexican herbs, Italian blends, basil, chili powder, and rosemary.

You don't need to have leftover turkey or chicken to make this delicious pie. Poach two large whole chicken breasts with onion, celery, and fresh herbs. Then proceed with the recipe.

Turkey Pot Pie with Fresh Herb Pastry
serves 8-10

Pastry

2 c. flour
3/4 tsp. salt
1 1/4 sticks butter (12 tbl.) cut into tsp. slices
1 tsp. fresh rosemary, chopped
1 tsp. fresh thyme, chopped
3 tbl. water
1 egg, beaten

In a food processor combine flour and salt. Add butter in batches, whirling on and off. Add herbs, whirl until combined. Slowly add water until pastry resembles coarse corn meal and particles stick together when pressed between fingers. Knead a few times with heel of hand and form into a flat disk. Wrap in plastic and refrigerate.

Filling

4 c. cooked turkey or chicken, cut or torn into 1" random pieces
1 tbl. butter
2 tbl. olive oil
2 c. carrots, halved lengthwise, then cut crosswise into 1/2" cubes

157

After Thanksgiving Menu

Turkey Pot Pie

Winter Fruit Salad

Quick Chocolate Mint Mousse

Serve with a Seyval or
French Beaujolais wine

1 parsnip, cut into 1/2" cubes
4 c. potatoes, peeled, cut into 3/4" cubes
1 leek (2 c.) cut into 1/2" slices (white part only)
1 1/2 tsp. fresh thyme, chopped, or 1/2 tsp. dried
1 tsp. fresh savory, chopped
1 tsp. fresh rosemary, chopped
1 1/2 tsp. salt
freshly ground pepper
2 tsp. butter
1/2 lemon, juiced
3 c. mushrooms, cut into 1/3" slices
2 tsp. Dijon mustard
1 c. frozen peas
1/3 c. fresh Italian parsley, chopped

Sauce

1/2 c. flour
4 tbl. butter
2 c. chicken stock
1/2 c. white wine
1/2 c. heavy cream
1/2 c. freshly grated Parmesan or Romano cheese
1/4 tsp. cayenne pepper
1/2 tsp. salt
freshly ground pepper

Egg Wash

1 egg, beaten
2 tbl. water

In a large sauté pan, put butter and oil, cook carrots 2-3 minutes, stir. Add parsnips, potatoes, and leeks. Continue to cook and toss another 5-7 minutes until potatoes are transparent and carrots have begun to soften. Add fresh herbs, salt, and pepper and set aside.

In another sauce pan, melt butter, toss mushrooms in lemon juice, and sauté in butter. Add mustard and continue to cook and toss until most of the liquid has been reduced. Add mushroom mixture to potato mixture, then cooked poultry, peas, and parsley. Set aside in a large bowl.

In a sauce pan whisk together butter and flour over medium heat until melted and golden colored. Whisk in stock, wine, and cream until thick. Add cheese, whisk until melted and smooth. Season with cayenne, salt, and pepper. Combine with filling mixture.

Place filling into a shallow buttered gratin pan, 10" x 14". Roll pastry into shape of pan and seal to edge, crimping dough decoratively. With a knife, make 4-6 slits in center to vent hot air. Paint beaten egg wash with a pastry brush and bake in a preheated 400° oven 45 minutes or until golden.

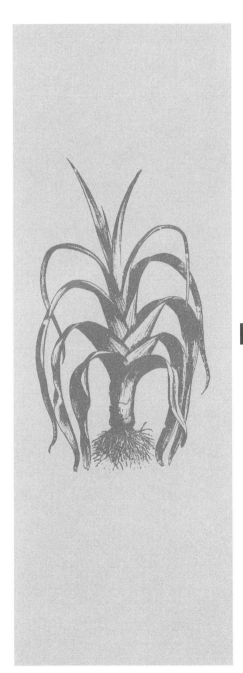

159

Marge's husband Chuck is a die-hard trout fisherman who once used her brand new electric coffee grinder to blend fur for fly-fishing material. Consequently, they are now a two-mill family!

Herbed Stuffed Trout
serves 4

4 whole trout, cleaned (about 14-16 oz. each)

Stuffing
8-10 oz. fresh spinach, de-ribbed and cleaned
7 slices thick hickory bacon
1/2 c. shallots, minced
1 garlic clove, minced
2-3 oz. fresh mushrooms, chopped
1/2 c. fresh sorrel, chopped (optional)
1/2 lemon, juiced (if not using sorrel)
2 tbl. Italian parsley, chopped
1 c. fresh bread crumbs (2-3 slices fresh bread whirled in
    a blender or food processor)
3/4 c. raw shrimp, chopped in large pieces
freshly ground pepper
3/4 c. heavy cream
lemon wedges
oil

Wash trout inside and out, pat dry, and set aside. In a skillet, with the water still clinging to the leaves, cook down the spinach until it's wilted. Remove, chop lightly, and place in a bowl.

In the same skillet, cook 3 slices of diced bacon until almost done—don't let it get crisp. Add shallots, garlic, and mushrooms and cook until soft. Add to spinach bowl along with sorrel (or lemon), parsley, bread crumbs, and shrimp. Mix well with hands. Taste and adjust. Mixture should hold together when squeezed.

In a large baking dish, lightly coat with oil and place all 4 trout next to each other. Divide the stuffing equally and place in the trout cavities. Secure with toothpicks if desired. Place 1 strip of bacon over the stuffing opening. Pour cream on bottom of dish and put in a 375° oven. Lightly cover with foil. Bake for 20 minutes or until trout flakes easily. Place a whole trout on each plate and serve immediately with lemon wedges.

May Wine

May Wine is not an actual type of wine, but a drink made from German wines and sweet woodruff.

May Wine Punch

1 c. dried sweet woodruff

1 c. superfine sugar

1 gal. Rhine or Moselle wine

1 bottle chilled champagne

1 qt. fresh strawberries, lightly sugared

161

In a large container, combine woodruff, sugar, and wine. Cover and let steep overnight in the refrigerator. Strain mixture into a punch bowl or a large pitcher. Add ice cubes or a decorative ice ring, champagne, and strawberries. Mix and serve.

Wisconsin is noted for Friday night fish fries—you can host your own with this recipe. Just add oven-fried potatoes, homemade coleslaw, and a juicy fruit pie. Because the breading on the fish is made from fresh bread crumbs, it will be lighter, and, we think, better tasting.

Lake Perch with Rosemary
serves 4

1 c. flour
salt and freshly ground pepper
2 tsp. paprika
2 c. fresh bread crumbs (5 slices of fresh bread whirled
   in a blender or food processor)
2 tbl. dried rosemary, crushed
1 to 1 1/2 lbs. lake perch fillets
2 eggs, beaten
1/4 c. vegetable oil (as needed)
3 tbl. butter (as needed)
lemon wedges
Remoulade Sauce

Mix flour, salt, pepper, and paprika on wax paper. Mix crumbs and rosemary and place on another sheet of wax paper. Dip each fillet in beaten egg, then in bread crumbs, pressing with your hands to make sure crumbs adhere. (Coated fish can be covered with plastic wrap and chilled up to several hours.)

Heat oil and butter in a deep skillet until hot. Keep temperature consistent. Fry fillets, a few at a time, about 30

162

seconds or until golden brown; turn to brown on both sides. Fish should begin to flake when done. Add more oil and butter as needed. Drain on paper towels and serve immediately with lemon wedges and Remoulade Sauce.

Remoulade Sauce

1 c. mayonnaise—homemade is preferable
1 tbl. finely chopped scallions
1 tsp. dried basil
1 large garlic clove, finely minced
1 tsp. dried tarragon
1 tbl. minced fresh parsley
1 tbl. Dijon mustard
1 tsp. fresh dillweed, chopped
1 tsp. capers, chopped
1 large dill pickle, finely chopped
anchovy paste (optional)
salt and freshly ground pepper

Combine all ingredients in a bowl or blender, adding anchovy paste to your taste. Adjust seasonings and add more herbs or scallions, if needed. Refrigerate 2-4 hours to blend flavors. Serve cold or at room temperature.

Canadian Fisheries

The Fishing Industry of Canada has come up with a simple and foolproof way of determining how long to cook fish (excluding shellfish).

Use a ruler and measure the thickest part of the fish you are cooking (even if stuffed). Calculate 10 minutes total cooking time per inch of fish. It doesn't matter if you bake, fry, or grill the fish, the time is still the same.

163

Mustard

Mustard is an herb cultivated for its pungent seeds or leaves (mustard greens). The greens are easily prepared by washing several times and cooking in a small amount of boiling water with a slice of salt pork or bacon. Cook for 15-30 minutes, drain, and serve.

The seeds are used in pickling mixtures, fish dishes, sauces, vegetable gratins, and as a crunchy garnish.

In powdered form mustard can be transformed into flavorful sauces. Mix the powder with water or champagne and add your choice of dried herbs. To make it crunchy, add a few seeds—whole or crushed.

Remember when cooking any type of fish, either grilling, broiling or pan-frying, cook your fish 10 minutes for every inch of thickness (measuring the thickest part).

Tuna with Garlic Mustard Sauce
serves 2

1 to 1 1/2 lbs. fresh tuna
1/2 c. Dijon mustard
6 cloves garlic, minced
1 tbl. fresh lime juice
1/3 c. olive oil
3 tbl. butter
1 onion (medium) halved and thinly sliced
1 tbl. ginger root, grated or finely minced
1/2 c. white wine or vermouth
2 tbl. sherry
pinch saffron
1 1/2 tsp. fresh thyme or 1/2 tsp. dried
6 tbl. chicken stock
1/2 c. heavy cream
salt and freshly ground pepper

In a bowl, combine mustard, garlic, lime juice, and oil. Pour into a double lined plastic bag, add tuna and marinade for 1 hour. In a sauté pan, cook onion and ginger in melted butter until soft. Add vermouth, sherry, saffron, and thyme. Reduce liquid by half over high heat.

Remove tuna from marinade and broil until done. Add marinade to sauce, along with stock and cream. Cook and reduce slightly. Taste and adjust seasoning with salt and freshly ground pepper. Serve over warm tuna.

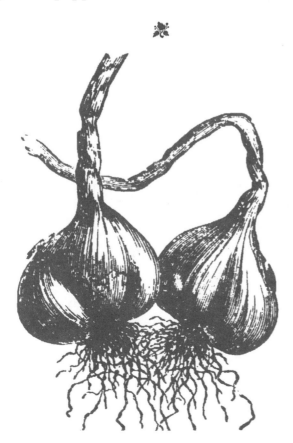

Grilling Tips— Wood Chips

Instead of using chemically treated briquette-type charcoal in your grill, try the different types of wood chips available, commercially or from your own yard.

Fruit Woods: Impart a pleasant sweetness, rather mild opposed to a smoky flavor. Any fruit trees will do: apple, cherry, peach.

Oak: Burns slow and long, food doesn't need to be added until the last minute.

We prefer to grill the swordfish over an open flame, but if weather or time doesn't allow this procedure, the broiler will do just fine.

Swordfish with Spicy Asian Pesto
serves 4

2 lbs. swordfish
1/3 c. oil
3 tbl. *Asian Vinegar (see Index)* or rice vinegar
2 cloves garlic, minced
1 tsp. dried red pepper flakes
1 tbl. ginger root, minced
1/4 tsp. salt
freshly ground pepper
1 recipe Spicy Asian Pesto *(see Index)*

In a bowl combine all the above ingredients except the fish. Pour into a double-lined plastic bag, add fish and marinate at least 1 hour. Broil swordfish until done. Serve with pesto.

A quick entree to make in spring and summer when you find you can't grill outside. Round it out with some South-of-the Border side dishes and icy-cold beer.

Walleyed Pike Veracruz
serves 4

2/3 c. onions, chopped
4 garlic cloves, minced
1 tbl. olive oil
2 jalapenos, cut in slivers
5-6 Italian tomatoes, chopped, or 1-16 oz. can,
    undrained and chopped
1/4 tsp. salt
1/2 tsp. sugar
1/4 tsp. cinnamon
1/8 tsp. ground cloves
dash dried oregano
1 tbl. lime juice, fresh
1/2 c. pimento-stuffed olives, cut in rings
2 tsp. capers
2 tbl. cilantro, chopped
2 lbs. walleye fillets, cleaned
lime wedges

In a skillet large enough to hold the fish fillets, sauté onion and garlic in olive oil until soft. Add jalapenos, tomatoes and their liquid, salt, sugar, cinnamon, cloves, oregano, and lime juice. Cover and simmer 10 minutes. Stir in olives, capers, and cilantro. Add fish. If the fillets are

Grilling Tips— Wood Chips

Mesquite: *A Southwestern and Mexican hardwood that is cured to produce charcoal. It burns hot and long, imparting a distinctive smoky flavor. If using chips, soak in water and add the moment of grilling, since they burn up fast.*

Herbs: *When trimming plants in the garden, save the cuttings and place on the grill at the last moment. Any combinations will add that extra aroma.*

Fish Facts

There are 3 categories of fish: fresh-water, saltwater, and half and half, that is, the fish live in salt water but spawn in fresh water.

That makes thousands of varieties. But in our area, the more commonly available fish are:

Fresh Water: perch, pike, whitefish, bass, herring, catfish, and trout

Salt Water: whiting, cod, haddock, sole, grouper, mahi mahi, marlin, flounder, shark, halibut, turbot and snapper—to name just a few.

Half and Half: sturgeon, mackerel, salmon, swordfish, tuna, pompano, mullet.

different thicknesses, place the largest in first—cook 1-2 minutes, then add the rest. Cover and poach for 10 minutes per inch of thickness.

Remove the cover, place fish on a platter, and keep warm. Turn up heat and reduce sauce until slightly thick, 2-4 minutes. Spoon over fillets and serve at once with lime wedges.

We use pork tenderloin more than any other cut of pork. It's lower in fat, more tender than most cuts, and takes just minutes to cook. When grocery stores have them on special, we stock up and freeze them in plastic bags.

Tequila Marinated Pork Tacos
serves 8

Marinade

1/2 c. tequila (or gin)
1/4 c. olive oil
1 tbl. chipotle chile (optional)
1 1/2 tsp. rubbed sage
2 tsp. cumin seed, crushed
1 1/2 tbl. Dijon mustard or herbed mustard
1/4 c. orange juice
1/2 tsp. cayenne pepper
3/4 c. chopped onion
1/2 tsp. Tabasco
2 lbs. pork tenderloin, trimmed of fat

Garnishes

lettuce, shredded
Asiago cheese, shredded
red onions, halved and sliced
flour tortilla, warmed
salsas (see Index)

Combine marinade ingredients in a plastic bag and add pork. Marinate at room temperature 1 hour or over night in the refrigerator. Grill or broil until done (165°). Cut into long juliennes and serve with Taco garnishes.

Quick Tacos

One of our busy-day dinners, no matter what the season, inevitably features tortillas. We make quick fillings for tortilla from almost any leftover. Sauté onions, sweet peppers and add leftover cooked chicken, pork or beef. Add some hot sauce, tomatoes, tomato sauce, salsa, chili powder, mole sauce, cumin seed, and oregano and you've invented a great fajita.

Serve with shredded garden lettuces, carrots, scallions, grated cheeses, salsa, hot sauces, and olives and your meal is complete.

Vegetarian versions are easily adapted when you have leftover Spicy Eggplant, Roasted Vegetables or Spicy Black Beans.

Experiment and enjoy!

169

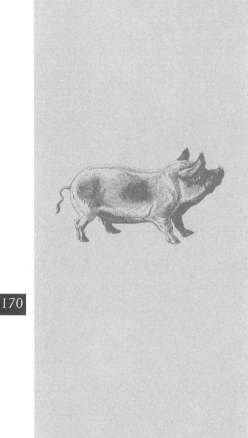

For large gatherings—like graduations or anniversary parties—this dish is perfect. It can be made a day ahead and refrigerated, but wait until just before serving to slice into rounds.

Saltimbocca (Pork Rolls)
serves 4

1 1/2 to 2 lbs. tied boneless pork loin

Filling

3 tbl. oil
3 tbl. butter
6 oz. mushrooms, chopped (squeeze 2 tbl. lemon juice over mushrooms)
1/2 c. onions, chopped
2 garlic cloves, chopped
1/4 c. dry white wine (dry vermouth works well)
6 fresh sage leaves, chopped
1/4 c. toasted pine nuts (toast on a baking sheet in a 400° oven 4-7 minutes)
1/2 c. fresh Italian parsley
1/3 lb. Fontinella cheese, crumbled (or use *Asiago*)
5 slices prosciutto
salt and freshly ground pepper

Separate pork roast and cut into 1/3" slices. Place between wax paper and pound very thin. Set aside. (Don't worry about subsequent holes in flattened pork—the prosciutto will cover.)

170

In a large skillet, place 1 tbl. oil and 1 tbl. butter and sauté mushrooms, onions, and garlic until soft. Add wine and cook 2 minutes more. Remove mixture to a bowl and add sage, pine nuts, parsley and cheese. Mix well. Taste and adjust flavors.

To Assemble:

Place 1/2 slice of prosciutto on each piece of pork and divide filling equally among each. Fold in sides and roll up. Secure with toothpicks, if desired. Place seam side down on a large plate, cover with plastic wrap, and chill 1 hour to overnight.

In same skillet melt remaining butter and sauté the rolls, a few at a time, until lightly browned all over. Remove to a baking sheet, cover lightly with foil, and bake 10-15 minutes at 350°. Cool slightly and slice into 1/2 rounds. Serve with Sage Sauce.

Italian Cheeses

In the Dairy State, we have access to all kinds of cheeses. Besides the usual Swiss, cheddar, and brick, Italian cheeses are nice to serve as snacks or as toppings on food. Here are a few of our favorites:

Fontina—a mild, sliceable, cheese with a buttery-rich taste.

Gorgonzola—a creamy blue cheese with a distinctive piquant taste.

Fontinella—a firm cheese, like a cheddar, but with a little bite. Great with an antipasto platter.

Asiago—a hard, sharp cheese we often use in place of parmesan or as a snacking cheese with red wine.

Provolone—a smoky, creamy cheese with a mild, yet nutty flavor.

172

Prepare this sauce a few days ahead for ease and convenience. Make extra for grilled chicken, or spread on bread with left-over meat sandwiches.

Sage Sauce

15 large fresh sage leaves (or 3 1/2 tbl. dried)
1 large jar pimentos or roasted red peppers (10-12 oz.) or
   2 large fresh red peppers, roasted
1 bunch chopped Italian parsley (1 1/2 c.)
3 cloves garlic, minced
1/2 c. olive oil (more if needed)
3 1/2 tbl. red wine vinegar
1 c. fresh bread crumbs
3/4 tsp. salt
1/2 tsp. freshly ground pepper

Combine all ingredients in a blender or food processor and whirl. Adjust seasonings. Add more oil if too thick. Refrigerate several hours or overnight to blend flavors. Serve at room temperature.

This hearty autumn/winter entree is excellent served with a pinot noir wine. It may also be made with a pork loin roast, sliced 1/2" thick and pounded to a thin 1/4" thickness.

Pork Tenderloin with Calvados-Lingonberry Sauce
serves 4-5

1 1/2 lbs. pork tenderloin or pork loin, cut and pounded very thin
1 tbl. butter
4 shallots or 1/2 c. onion, minced
1 c. beef stock
1/2 c. Madeira
1/2 c. Calvados or pear brandy
2/3 c. port
1/2 tsp. dried thyme or 1 1/2 tsp. fresh
1 bay leaf
5 tbl. lingonberry preserve
1 tbl. balsamic vinegar
2 tbl. cornstarch + 1/2 c. beef stock
1/2 tsp. salt
freshly ground pepper
2 tbl. butter
1 tbl. olive oil
3 Granny Smith apples, peeled, cored, and sliced into wedges

In a large saucepan, melt 1 tbl. butter. Add shallots, sauté until soft and transparent. Add stock, then reduce on high heat 4-5 minutes. Add madeira, Calvados, port,

Deglazing

Deglazing is a sauce-making technique which uses the existing pan juices and particles from roasting meat, poultry, or vegetables.

To utilize the flavors, add your choice of liquid: wine, water, stock, or vinegar to the roasting pan which the food was browned in. Stir over medium-high heat, scraping up browned particles with a whisk, fork, or spatula. Whisk in additional liquid, herbs, or cream, and simmer to reduce. Dissolve cornstarch in cold liquid at a 1 to 4 ratio. Add cornstarch mixture to sauce, whisking constantly. Cook until transparent and thick, season with salt and pepper.

174

thyme, and bay leaf, continue to reduce to half. Mix lingonberries and vinegar into sauce and whisk in cornstarch mixture. Season to taste with salt and pepper.

In a large sauté pan melt butter and olive oil, cook apple slices on both sides until golden. Remove to a warm plate and set aside. Salt and pepper pork slices and with medium high heat, sauté on each side until golden. Serve pork and apple slices decoratively with Lingonberry Sauce on a warm platter.

This recipe uses a liqueur called creme de cassis (black currant liqueur). It's used to make delicious cocktails like Kir (white wine and cassis) or Kir Royale (champagne and cassis), but we find its fruity flavor good for sauces and desserts, too.

Pork Chops with Rosemary-Cranberry Sauce
serves 4

1/2 c. flour
1 tsp. dried rosemary, crushed
salt and freshly ground pepper
2 lb. boneless pork chops, 1 1/2" thick
1 tbl. oil + 1 tbl. butter

Sauce

3/4 c. red onion, chopped
1 garlic clove, minced
1 1/2 tsp. fresh ginger, minced
1/2 c. port
1/2 jalapeno, minced
1/4 c. creme de cassis (or substitute port)
1 c. beef stock
1/3 c. brown sugar
1 1/2 tsp. dried rosemary, crushed
2 c. fresh whole cranberries, sorted and cleaned

Combine flour, rosemary, salt, and pepper and dredge pork chops in the mixture. Melt oil and butter and

Fresh Cranberries

The American Indians named the fruit "craneberries" because its blossoms resembled the crane. They used it in pemmican—a forerunner of beef jerky except it's made from venison.

Wisconsin is the number two state in the production of this popular autumn fruit. The berries are grown in lowlands and boggy areas on evergreen-looking bushes. As they grow, the berries change from white to the distinctive wine-color, but only after the weather cools down.

Cranberries are high in vitamin C, making them a great breakfast juice, and because they have so much natural pectin they thicken when cooked in a matter of minutes.

176

brown chops on both sides. Place in an ovenproof pan; cover with foil and keep warm in a low oven (250°) for approximately 30 minutes. Don't overcook—check periodically.

Make sauce. In same pan in which the chops were browned, add the red onion, garlic, and ginger. Sauté until soft over low heat. Cover to release some of the liquid from the onions. Add port, jalapeno, creme de cassis, beef stock, sugar, rosemary, and cranberries. Cook over low heat until cranberries are soft and begin to thicken, about 20-25 minutes. Taste and adjust seasonings. Return pork to pan and heat. Serve immediately.

Every once and a while we get a craving for beef—and this dish satisfies those cravings.

Beef with Herbes de Provence
serves 6

3 tbl. Herbes de Provence (see Index)
1 tsp. coarsely ground black pepper
1 1/2 to 2 lbs. beef tenderloin, trimmed and cut into
   1"-thick steaks
1 tbl. butter
1 tbl. oil
2/3 c. brandy
1/3 c. beef stock
1 tbl. soy sauce
salt
1 tbl. Buerre Manie (equal parts flour and butter—see Index)

Combine *Herbes de Provence* and black pepper. Press into both sides of each steak. Cover with plastic wrap and let sit for 30 minutes. (Can be done ahead and refrigerated overnight.)

Heat butter and oil in a heavy-bottom skillet and sear steaks on both sides. They should be slightly pink inside. Remove to a platter and keep warm.

Add brandy, stock, and soy to the skillet and bring to a boil. Continue cooking to reduce liquid by half. Scrape bottom to loosen brown bits. Taste and adjust seasonings. Whisk in 1 tbl. *Buerre Manie* to thicken sauce. Pour over steaks and serve immediately.

Baked Tenderloin

On many catering jobs, one of our most requested entrees was baked sliced tenderloin.

To make: trim a 2-4 lb. whole tenderloin (or cut in half) of excess fat. Press a handful of Herbes de Provence all over the tenderloins. Let rest 30 minutes or overnight (cover with plastic and refrigerate.) Preheat your oven to 450°. Put tenderloin (one or more) on a baking sheet and roast for 20-25 minutes.

Remove. Let cool completely. Wrap very well in aluminum and refrigerate overnight. Slice before serving with assorted aiolis and mustards.

❦

One of our favorite meals to make on cold, wintry days. Use a good quality thick-cut hickory-smoked bacon for a rich flavor.

Beef in Beer
serves 4-6

2 1/2 to 3 lbs. lean chuck roast or rump roast
1/4 c. flour mixed with 1/2 tsp. freshly grated nutmeg
6 slices thick hickory-smoked bacon, chopped in 1/2" pieces
oil (if needed)
3 c. halved and sliced onions
1 1/2 c. dark beer
1 1/2 c. water or beef stock
1/8 tsp. EACH ground cloves and freshly grated nutmeg
1/4 c. fresh dill, finely chopped
1 bunch fresh parsley, chopped
1 tsp. dried thyme
6 tbl. red wine vinegar (plain or herbal)
3 tbl. brown sugar
6 parsnips, cleaned, peeled, and cut into 1 1/2" lengths
salt and freshly ground pepper

Cut meat into 1" cubes. Dredge in flour and nutmeg mixture. Place bacon in a Dutch oven and fry a few minutes. Add meat and brown on both sides. Add onions and cook 2-3 minutes.

Blend in beer, water, spices, vinegar, brown sugar, and seasonings. Bring to a boil and place in a 350° oven and cook, covered, for 1 hour. Check level of liquid and add parsnips. Return to oven for another hour or until meat is fork-tender and some of the liquid has evaporated. Remove cover the last 30 minutes of cooking. Taste and adjust seasonings. Serve with boiled potatoes or noodles.

Bouquet Garni

Traditionally a bouquet garni was just a few sprigs of fresh parsley, thyme, and a bay leaf tied with string or placed in a cheesecloth bag. Today we use small reusable muslin bags or tea balls and fill with any combination of dried herbs and spices that fit our needs. We never use dried parsley, although many recipes call for it.

179

Dad's Night

Marinated Roasted Red Peppers
with Herbed Cheese

❧

Marinated Steak with
Gorgonzola Sauce

❧

Garlic Mashed Potatoes

❧

Corn Salad

❧

Chocolate Bourbon Bars

❧

Serve with a Cabernet Sauvignon
or Italian Barolo wine

A very elegant, rich dinner entree that's surprisingly simple to prepare —a sure winner at your next dinner party.

Marinated Steak with Gorgonzola Sauce
serves 2-3

Marinade
>   1/2 c. oil
>   1 tbl. dry mustard
>   1 tbl. honey
>   1 tsp. garlic
>   2 tsp. soy sauce
>   1 tsp. lemon juice
>   dash cayenne
>   2 tsp. freshly ground pepper
>   1 lb. tenderloin steak.

Combine all ingredients in a shallow pan and add steak, turn to coat evenly or place all in a thick plastic bag. Cover with plastic wrap for 1 hour to overnight.

Sauce
>   3 cloves garlic, minced
>   5 tbl. minced scallions
>   2 tbl. butter
>   1 c. chopped mushrooms
>   2/3 c. white burgundy or chardonnay
>   1 c. heavy cream

3 oz. Gorgonzola cheese, crumbled
1/2 tsp. freshly ground black pepper

Sauté garlic and 3 tbl. scallions in butter. Add mushrooms and wine. Lower heat, cover and cook 1-2 minutes. Uncover, add cream and reduce by half. Remove from heat and whisk in cheese. Season to taste and place over broiled steak. Garnish with remaining scallions.

Indoor Grilling

It's possible to have your grill and eat inside too! Cookware shops all over sell several new kitchen tools that enable you to grill indoors—well, almost.

There are several styles of grill. Some are heavy cast-iron flat squares or rectangles, another is a round domed apparatus with grill grooves. All have the distinctive grill patterns so your food will really look authentic.

Most are made of heavy cast iron and usually coated with a non-stick surface. They fit directly over one burner and sometimes over two.

Be sure your kitchen has adequate ventilation because these grills really heat up.

Make the meat patties ahead and refrigerate up to 8 hours. Serve with Tante Friedel's Potato Salad, fresh tomato salad, and Homemade Ice Cream.

Wisconsin Burgers
serves 4

2-3 large slices rye bread (crusts included)
2 tbl. beer
1 lb. ground round beef
1 egg, beaten
3 thick slices bacon, uncooked and chopped finely
1/2 tsp. caraway seeds
Swiss cheese slices
toasted thick-sliced rye or pumpernickel bread
Sauerkraut (optional)

In a large bowl, soak rye bread in beer until beer is completely absorbed. Add beef, egg, bacon, and caraway and blend thoroughly. Shape into patties. Grill until almost done. Add a slice of Swiss cheese on top of each and cook until melted. Place burgers on toasted bread and top with sauerkraut. Serve piping hot.

This dish contains anchovies—an acquired taste for some. We use them in lots of dishes. They're available packed in salt, olive oil, or in paste form. Added to dishes, they give a piquant flavor without the fishiness.

Fresh Tomato Pasta Sauce
serves 4

4 oz. pancetta, cut in large cubes, or 3 thick slices bacon, diced
1 1/2 lbs. Italian tomatoes, peeled or unpeeled, seeded and coarsely chopped in large chunks—about 5 (canned may be substituted, but drain well)
1/2 c. fresh basil, chopped
1 1/2 tbl. sherry vinegar
2 tbl. capers
1/3 c. olive oil
6 oz. marinated artichoke hearts, sliced and drained
salt and freshly ground pepper
12-16 oz. cooked small-shaped pasta
Parmesan cheese
6-8 anchovies (if packed in salt, rinse well and pat dry)

Cook pancetta or bacon until crisp. Remove and set aside. In a large non-reactive bowl, add all ingredients except pancetta and anchovies. Mix gently. Taste and adjust. Pour sauce over hot, drained pasta and mix well. Add pancetta or bacon. Sprinkle with cheese and garnish with anchovies.

Pasta Party

A fun dinner party to host during the winter months is a Pasta Party. Either make your own or buy several flavored ones. Today most grocery stores and specialty shops stock interesting flavors—squid ink. saffron, chile peppers, herbs, wine-flavored, and so on.

Preboil each kind of pasta until almost al dente. Remove, drain, and place in Zip-Loc bags with a little olive oil to prevent sticking. Set aside until ready to use.

Make several kinds of sauces—tomato marinara sauce, a rich seafood sauce, a simple herb sauce, and maybe an unusual vegetable sauce. Grate lots of Parmesan and Asiago and set out in bowls.

Pasta Party

Serve Campari (an Italian aperitif) and soda water with lime slices for a real Italian opener. Make an antipasto platter of pantry items—olives, pickles, marinated artichokes, plus cheese and salami. Have crusty warm bread and a green salad and your party is complete. Just before you're ready to eat, bring a large pot of water to a boil. Place the partially cooked pasta in for just a minute—to reheat.

Drain and serve.

When you first introduce herbs to your family, we suggest you try this dish. It's also a nice accompaniment to grilled steaks instead of the usual baked potato.

Pasta with Fresh Herbs
serves 4

Sauce

    1/2 c. heavy cream
    1 tbl. butter
    1/3 c. Parmesan cheese
    1/3 c. grated *Asiago* cheese
    1/4 tsp. cayenne
    1/4 c. Italian parsley, chopped
    1/3 c. assorted fresh herbs (chives, thyme, basil, marjoram, and oregano)
    pkg. dried fettucine or other pasta, cooked
    salt and freshly ground pepper

Combine all sauce ingredients in a bowl. Mix well. Add to hot pasta and toss. Taste and adjust flavors. Serve immediately.

Suzanne's 18-year-old son Ethan, doesn't think a meal is complete unless it contains some heat, and this dish certainly fits that category. Not being fond of seafood, he prefers that Suzanne to substitute chicken, which is as tasty as this shrimp version.

Shrimp in Black Bean Pasta Sauce
serves 4

Sauce

    1 tbl. Chinese Black Bean Sauce with Garlic*
    1/4 c. jalapenos, chopped or to taste
    1 tbl. sherry
    1 1/2 c. chicken stock
    2 tbl. cornstarch + 3 tbl. water
    1 tsp. sesame oil

    1 to 1 1/2 lbs. shrimp, peeled and deveined
    3 garlic cloves, minced
    1 tbl. fresh ginger, minced
    2 tbl. oil
    6-8 scallions, sliced
    1 red pepper, cut in juliennes
    1/3 c. fresh cilantro, chopped
    hot cooked rice or pasta

    *Available in Asian markets, or the Asian sections of large grocery stores.

Hot Peppers

Size does not always indicate the intensity of heat. Generally smaller varieties are hotter than larger ones, because they have less flesh in proportion to the amount of veins.

Climate also affects the heat level. Peppers grown in cooler, wetter climates tend to be milder than ones grown in hot conditions.

186

Combine sauce ingredients in a bowl and set aside. In a skillet, sauté shrimp, garlic, and ginger in oil. Remove shrimp and set aside. Add scallions and sauce mixture. Heat until thick. Return shrimp and red peppers and heat through—don't cook. Add cilantro and adjust. Serve over warm pasta.

This is a great South-of-the-Border recipe. Serve over pasta for a quick and satisfying dinner.

Southwest Chicken with Chipotle Chile Sauce

serves 6

3 chicken breast halves, skinned, boned, and cut in strips
1 tbl. butter
1 tbl. oil
2 garlic cloves, chopped
1/2 medium onion, chopped
1 tsp. dried oregano
1/2 tsp. cumin powder
2-3 tsp. chili powder
2-3 chipotle chiles with sauce
1 large sweet red pepper, julienned
1 can chicken stock
1 c. white wine
3 tbl. cornstarch mixed with 1/3 c. stock
1 1/3 c. grated queso quesadilla or monterey jack cheese
    mixed with 1/4 c. flour
1/3 c. fresh cilantro, chopped
cooked pasta
grated Asiago cheese

In a sauté pan put butter, oil, garlic, onion and chicken. Sauté 2-3 minutes or until chicken is almost done.

Southwest Supper Menu

Tortilla Rolls

∾

Southwest Chicken with Pasta

∾

Tropical Melon Salsa Salad

∾

Margarita Tart

∾

Serve with a Cabernet Sauvignon,
California Sauvignon Blanc, or
Australian Shiraz wine

187

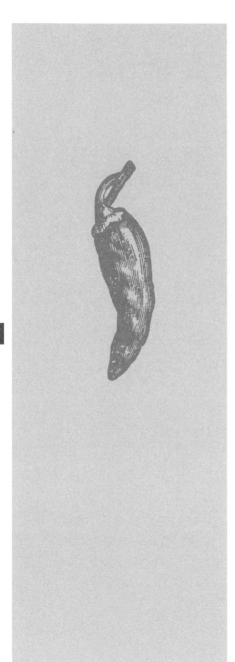

Add oregano, cumin, chili powder, and chipotle. Set aside.

In a saucepan put chicken stock and wine, reduce to 3/4 volume (1 1/2 c.).

Return chicken to heat, add stock, combine well. Stir in cheese, continue stirring until dissolved. Add cornstarch mixture and red peppers, continue to stir until it thickens and smooths. Season to taste, sprinkle in cilantro. Pour over pasta and garnish with Asiago cheese.

You may prepare the sauce ahead of time except for the scallops. When overcooked, they become tough, losing their succulent texture and taste.

Scallops in Green Peppercorn Pasta Sauce
serves 4-6

1 lb. fresh scallops
4 tbl. butter
1 c. minced onions
2 garlic cloves, minced
2 c. chicken stock
2/3 c. white wine
1 1/2 tsp. fresh thyme
3/4 c. heavy cream
12 oz. fresh mushrooms, sliced
2 tbl. fresh lemon juice
2 tbl. green peppercorn mustard
1 tbl. sliced or chopped jalapeno
1 1/2 tbl. chopped mild chiles (canned)
2 tbl. cornstarch mixed with 1/2 c. chicken stock
1/2 tsp. salt and freshly ground pepper
fresh basil cut into thin strips (chiffonade)
finely grated Asiago cheese

In a sauté pan, melt 2 tbl. butter. Add onions and garlic, cook until soft and transparent, about 5 minutes. Add stock, wine, and thyme. Increase heat and reduce mixture to half. Add cream, continue to reduce 3 minutes.

Scallops

Scallops come in many colors and sizes, from the largest, ocean (sea) scallops, to the smallest, bay scallops. Colors range from pure white to pearly pink. When purchasing, look for a good gloss and moist sheen. If the aroma is not sweet, do not purchase.

❦

190

While stock is reducing, toss mushrooms in lemon juice, sauté in another pan with the remaining 2 tbl. butter. Add mustard, combine well, and cook another 1-2 minutes. Add peppers and chiles, continue cooking 1 minute. Combine cornstarch mixture with sauce, stir until thick. Season to taste with 1/2 to 2/3 tsp. salt and freshly ground pepper. Add scallops, cook until just heated through and the scallops have changed from a semi-transparent to an opaque color. (Remember not to overcook scallops or they will become tough).

Taste and adjust seasoning. Serve over hot pasta sprinkled with fresh basil and Asiago cheese.

A very rich and exotic dish that would make an elegant first course. Use any shape of wonton skin—make them into squares, rounds, triangles, or use cookie cutters for festive shapes.

Shrimp Ravioli with Wonton Skins & Saffron Sauce
serves 4

Paste Mixture
    2 tbl. flour
    1/4 c. water

    Mix very well in a small bowl until smooth. Set aside.

    1 pkg. 3" wonton skins, thawed

Filling
    2 tbl. Canadian bacon, minced (could substitute smoked ham)
    3/4 lb. fresh shrimp, shelled, deveined, and chopped into
       large chunks
    2 tbl. scallions, minced
    1 tbl. fresh chives, finely minced
    1 tsp. fresh ginger, very finely minced
    3 tbl. Parmesan cheese
    1 egg white
    1/2 tsp. EACH salt and freshly ground pepper
    1/2 fresh jalapeno, seeded and cut into tiny slivers

Saffron

The most expensive spice in the world comes from the dried stigmas of a crocus grown in Southern Europe and Asia. It takes thousands of stigmas to make a pound. Harvesting is very labor intensive and can only be done by hand—hence, the high prices.

Fortunately saffron has a powerful flavor—very little is needed for most dishes. The flavor is earthy and pleasantly bitter, the color a rich golden yellow and highly prized.

Saffron is sold powdered or in what is called "threads." Keep it in tightly covered glass jars away from the sun. The flavor and color is released when the threads are added to a liquid and heated. Use in soups, rice dishes, breads, rolls and sauces.

❦

191

Combine all filling ingredients in a bowl and set aside. Place about 1 tbl. of filling on each wonton skin. Brush two sides with the paste mixture. Fold over and seal. Place on wax paper-lined baking sheets. Cover with plastic wrap and use immediately or refrigerate for a few hours.

Sauce

> 1 tbl. butter
> 3 tbl. shallots, minced
> 1 c. dry white wine
> 1 1/4 c. chicken stock
> a few saffron threads
> 1/2 tsp. sugar
> 3 sun-dried tomatoes, cut in slivers (reconstitute if dry)
> 2 tbl. heavy cream
> salt and freshly ground pepper

Melt butter in a small pan and sauté shallots until soft. Add wine and chicken stock and reduce by 1/3. Add saffron threads, sugar, sun-dried tomatoes, and cream and cook until slightly thick. Taste and adjust. Serve hot.

To Cook:

Bring a large pot of water to a boil. Add 1 tsp. oil and place 8-10 raviolis in at a time. Cook 2-3 minutes or until they rise to the top. Don't overcook. Remove with a slotted spoon. Drain briefly on paper towels (they will stick to the paper towels if left too long). Place on one large platter or individual plates and top with Saffron Sauce. Serve immediately.

A truly versatile dish. Either prepare the recipe as indicated and serve with a colorful pasta, or use halved chicken breasts and serve with our Wild Rice Pilaf (see Index) as an elegant entree for 6.

Chicken Chardonnay
serves 6

Sauce

1/2 oz. dried mushrooms (assorted)
1 1/2 to 2 c. boiling water
1 to 1 1/2 lbs. fresh mushrooms, sliced
1 lemon, juiced
4 tbl. oil
4 tbl. butter
3- 4 shallots, finely minced (1/2 c.)
1 1/2 to 2 c. chardonnay
1 tsp. dried rosemary or 1 tbl. fresh, chopped
2 tsp. curry powder (hot)
3/4 c. chicken stock (+ 1/4 c. mixed with
    1 1/2 tbl. cornstarch)
3 tbl. honey
2 tbl. Dijon mustard
1/4 c. cream
salt and freshly ground pepper

3 whole chicken breasts, halved, boned, and cut into 1/2" strips
Seasoned Flour (1 c. flour, 1 tsp. salt, 1/2 tsp. EACH paprika
    and rosemary, 1 tsp. curry powder—hot)
cooked hot pasta
parsley, chopped for garnish

Chicken Safety

In recent years we have become more aware of the dangers of salmonella and how to prevent the contamination. Raw chicken is one of the biggest culprits in carrying salmonella, but any poultry or fish is suspect. Items that come in contact with raw poultry, including juices, must be washed with a mixture of hot soapy water and bleach. Cutting boards, especially in the crevices and seams, are a depository for salmonella.

New research recommends wood cutting boards rather than plastic, suggesting that wood counteracts salmonella. We suggest having separate boards for poultry and the rest of the foods you chop.

Make sauce first. Soak dried mushrooms with boiling water for 30 minutes. Remove, chop mushrooms, and set aside. Strain liquid and reserve. Toss fresh mushrooms with lemon juice and set aside.

Melt 2 tbl. butter and 2 tbl. oil in a skillet and sauté shallot until soft. Add fresh mushrooms, chardonnay, rosemary, curry, chicken stock, dried mushrooms, and their liquid and cook 5-8 minutes until slightly thick.

In a bowl mix honey, Dijon, and cream and add to sauce with stock and cornstarch mixture. Whisk until smooth. Taste and adjust seasonings. Keep on low and prepare chicken.

Melt remaining butter and oil in another skillet. Dredge chicken strips in seasoned flour and sauté until just tender. Add to sauce and heat through. Serve over pasta and garnish with parsley.

This sandwich serves quite a crowd. We usually make it for special TV sporting events, like the Rose Bowl!

Muffuletta Sandwich
serves 12

1 8" or 10" round loaf of bread
1/2 lb. Genoa sausage
6-8 slices prosciutto of Copa
1/2 lb. very thinly sliced provolone
1/2 lb. very thinly sliced mozzarella
10-12 oz. marinated artichoke hearts, halved
1 large sweet red pepper, roasted
1/2 red onion, very thinly sliced
Olive Salad

Olive Salad

8 oz. Giardiniera, chopped (*see Index*)
10 oz. Spanish or salad olives, chopped
1 1/2 tsp. dried oregano
2 tbl. Dijon mustard
2 tsp. Creole seasoning (*see Index*)
2 tsp. horseradish
2 tsp. paprika
2/3 c. olive oil
3 tbl. parsley, finely minced
1/2 c. scallions, finely minced
2 garlic cloves, finely minced

Marinated Olives

You can make your own oil-cured marinated olives without owning an olive orchard! Add your favorite herbs or spices to store-bought olives and cover with olive oil. Packaged in small decorative canning jars, these marinated olives make a wonderful holiday or hostess gift.

Italian Herbed Olives

1 1/2 lb. green olives
4 cloves garlic, peeled and placed
    on a skewer
4 sprigs EACH fresh thyme and
    oregano
1 small sprig rosemary
2 slices lemon
1/2 tsp. whole allspice berries
peppercorns
olive oil to cover

Place all in a glass jar and refrigerate
2 days. Remove the garlic and discard.
Taste and add more herbs if needed.
Keeps for months in the refrigerator.

Make olive salad first. Combine all the ingredients in a large bowl and mix well. Taste and adjust flavors. Chill for several hours. Retaste and season again, if necessary.

To Assemble:

Take a slice off the top of the round bread. Scoop out most of the inside; save for another use. With a pastry brush, paint some of the Olive Salad vinaigrette all over the exposed bread—and at the top.

Begin by layering Genoa, then provolone, Olive Salad, mozzarella, prosciutto, artichoke hearts, roasted pepper, Genoa, provolone, prosciutto, and mozzarella. Press down firmly after each addition. Replace top slice of bread and press firmly. Wrap in plastic wrap and chill or let sit out at room temperature for several hours. (Can be done the day before).

Replace the plastic wrap with aluminum foil and bake at 350° for 20-30 minutes until bread is soft and cheese begins to melt. Remove. Cool slightly and slice into wedges.

When stuffing turkeys, roasting chickens, and Cornish hens, allow 1/2 c. of stuffing per pound of bird.

Dried Fruit & Sausage Stuffing
enough for an 18-20 lb. turkey

1 lb. Italian sausage, crumbled
4 tbl. butter
2 c. onions, chopped
1 c. celery, chopped
1/2 c. port
1 lb. bread (with or without crusts) torn
1 1/2 c. chicken stock
1 1/2 c. dried cranberries
1/4 c. EACH golden raisins and cut up dried apricots
3 tbl. fresh rosemary, minced or 1 tbl. dried
1/4 c. fresh parsley, chopped
2 Granny Smith apples, unpeeled, cored, and cut into 1/2" cubes
2 eggs, beaten
salt and freshly ground pepper

In a large skillet cook sausage until no longer pink. Remove to a paper towel-lined dish. Drain off all oil from pan. Add butter and sauté onion and celery until soft. Add port and cook 1-2 minutes.

In a large bowl add the bread and the remaining ingredients including the onion and sausage. Mix with hands or large wooden spoon. Taste and add additional salt, pepper, or rosemary. For roasting times and temperatures, consult your poultry package directions.

197

A perfect stuffing for turkey, other poultry, pork, or beef.

Savory Stuffing
enough for a 20-lb. turkey

1 lb. hot Italian sausage, or other pork sausage
1 c. minced onions
2 large cloves garlic, minced
1 c. green pepper, chopped
1 c. celery, chopped
1 1/2 c. toasted walnuts, chopped
1 1/2 c. mushrooms, chopped
2 tbl. lemon juice
4 hard-cooked eggs, chopped
3/4 c. currants
3/4 c. chopped fresh parsley
6 c. cubed bread (oatmeal, wheat, cornbread, white
    or combination)
2 c. wild rice, cooked until almost done
3 apples, cored but not peeled, cubed
1-2 tbl. salt
1 1/2 tsp. freshly ground pepper
1 tsp. dried thyme
1 tsp. dried rosemary
broth or boiling water

In a large sauté pan, fry the sausage, break up into small pieces, and remove. Add onions to the pan drippings; continue to sauté 2 minutes. Add garlic, green pepper, and celery and continue to sauté 5 minutes. Add the walnuts; toss the mushrooms in the lemon juice and add to the mixture along with the eggs, currants, parsley, bread, wild rice, apples, salt, pepper, thyme, and rosemary. Mix well and add enough broth to bring dressing to the desired consistency.

Harvesting Herbs

Choose a sunny morning to harvest herbs, and wait until the dew is off of the leaves. Cut flowers or leaves with a sharp knife, but be sure to leave enough foliage so the plant can continue to grow.

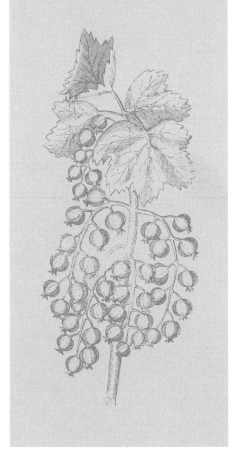

Vegetables & Side Dishes

Wisconsin has been blessed with wonderful Farmers' Markets and Community Cooperative Farm Organizations that provide fresh produce (much of it organic) to its members for 8-9 months out of the year. Both Marge and I joined one of the local farm groups that sold membership shares in weekly fruits, vegetables, and herbs. The produce was outstanding and the variety of vegetables was staggering. Often we would receive produce that normally wouldn't have been on our shopping list, but it did give us an opportunity to expand our usual green bean and broccoli recipes to include new dishes such as Parsnip & Potato Gratin, Acorn Squash Spoonbread, and Turkey Pot Pie with Root Vegetables.

We also discovered that many of our vegetable recipes served double duty. Not only were they delicious side dishes and accompaniments to our meals, but when served at room temperature with crusty bread they became notable appetizers—including our Spicy Eggplant, Braised Leeks, & Caramelized Onions. See if you don't agree!

201

202

A wonderful side dish to serve in the heat of the summer. We find it also tastes great in omelets or as a sandwich filling in pita bread.

Green & Red Tomato Ratatouille
serves 6

1 large eggplant, peeled and cut into 1/2" cubes
1 tbl. salt
1/4 c. oil
water
1/2 lb. (about 2-3) firm green tomatoes, very coarsely chopped
1 red or green pepper, chopped
1/2 lb. (about 2 large) onions, chopped
2 large garlic cloves, minced
1 lb. (about 3-4) ripe red tomatoes, peeled and coarsely chopped
1/2 tsp. freshly ground black pepper
dash cayenne pepper
1 tsp. dried basil
1 tsp. dried oregano
1 small can tomato paste
1 tbl. honey
1 medium zucchini, unpeeled, cut in thin rounds (optional)
2 tbl. balsamic vinegar
1/3 c. fresh Italian parsley, chopped

Sprinkle eggplant with 1/2 tbl. salt and let stand 30 minutes. Rinse, drain, and pat dry. Place 2 tbl. oil in a very large skillet or Dutch oven and sauté eggplant. Add a small amount of water to the pan, reduce heat and cover. Cook until eggplant is still firm, yet tender. Remove from pan with a slotted spoon.

Add green tomatoes, pepper, onion, and garlic and sauté until wilted, about 5 minutes. Add the remaining oil if needed. Add red tomatoes and cook another 4-5 minutes. Add black pepper, remaining salt, cayenne, basil, oregano, tomato paste, and honey, and increase heat. Scrape bottom of pan often to prevent sticking or scorching. Add zucchini, cover, and cook until firm yet tender. Return eggplant to pan and heat through. Add balsamic vinegar and parsley. Taste and adjust. Serve cold or at room temperature. Flavor improves if prepared one day ahead. Use as a side dish, omelet filling, or in pita bread sandwiches.

Honey

During the summer in Madison, the Farmers' Market is packed with honey stands. They're from all over the state—and the honey varies in color from dark amber to almost white with flavors to match.

For one pot of honey, bees have to visit more than 2 million flowers, and the honey taste depends on the flowers they choose. Clover is the mildest, but some prefer exotic choices like basswood, lavender, fruit blossoms, herb flowers, alfalfa, and mixtures from different fields.

Honey keeps for months in a cool cupboard. When refrigerated, it crystallizes and thickens, but placing in a pan of hot water will bring it back to spreading consistency.

203

Shallots

Shallots are a member of the onion family and like leeks are also classified as herbs. They range in color from orange-copper to the French gray cylinder-shaped ones. Mild in taste, but more flavorful than scallions, they're an expensive item and don't keep as well as onions. We use them in vinaigrettes, fish dishes, and in sauces (particularly butter, vinegar or wine sauces).

In Cajun and New Orleans Creole cookbooks, the shallots referred to in recipes are actually scallions.

These are best made from firm, not overly ripe tomatoes. But, we have to admit, we have even used those hockey-pucks they call winter hothouse tomatoes and have had great results!

Baked Tomatoes
serves 8

4 tomatoes
salt
4 tbl. oil
1/2 c. minced shallots
2 tsp. minced garlic
1 1/2 c. fresh bread crumbs (place 1-2 slices or bread in a
    blender or food processor and whirl)
1/4 c. chopped fresh herbs or 1 tbl. dried herbs or herb mix*
1 tbl. minced fresh parsley
1/3 c. Parmesan cheese
salt and freshly ground black pepper

Preheat oven to 400°. Halve the tomatoes and remove the seeds. Lightly salt and drain upside down on paper towels 5 or 10 minutes. Meanwhile, heat 3 tbl. oil in a skillet and sauté shallots and garlic until soft. Add crumbs and sauté until golden. Remove from heat and add herbs, cheese, and salt. Mixture should not be dry—add more oil to bind, if needed. Spoon mixture into tomatoes, pressing gently. Drizzle with a little more oil.

Place in buttered or foil-lined pan and bake for 10 minutes or until heated through and skins start to shrivel. Don't overcook or the tomatoes will collapse.

*Herbs to choose from: basil, dill, thyme, tarragon, Italian mix.

This is the best way we've found to get kids to eat green beans and carrots! Roasting vegetables isn't a new technique, but it's effective in bringing out their natural sweetness.

Roasted Green Beans & Carrots
serves 4

1 1/2 tbl. garlic-flavored olive oil or regular olive oil
1 lb. green beans, trimmed
1 lb. carrots, peeled, cut into 1" chunks
1 tbl. butter
2 large garlic cloves, finely minced
1 tsp. EACH fresh savory and thyme, minced
salt freshly ground pepper

Preheat oven to 475°. Add oil to large 10" x 15" baking sheet. Add green beans and carrots and turn to coat completely with oil. Roast in oven for 30-35 minutes, turning frequently. Continue baking until almost tender.

Meanwhile, melt butter in a saucepan and sauté garlic until soft. Toss with the vegetables and the herbs. Season to taste. Serve hot or at room temperature.

Green Beans

Living in the city, we have very small backyard vegetable gardens, but we use intensive gardening techniques to get the maximum use from small spaces. One of those vegetables that fits into this type of gardening is French green beans or haricot vert (pronounced ary ko VERT). We grow both bush varieties such as Finaud, Astrelle, and Fin des Bagnols and pole types such as Emerite.

With just a few plants, the bush beans produced more than we could use for our families. Unfortunately, haricot vert do not freeze well, so our season is brief, but oh so good.

(See Sources for Seed Catalog addresses)

205

Vinegar

In French, "vinaigre" means sour wine—which is where it originally came from—either intentionally or accidentally. Vinegar is made from fermented liquids such as apple cider, rice wine, malted barley, sherry, and red wine (balsamic) with the addition of a bacteria called a "mother."

A dash of herbed vinegar or balsamic after gently steaming or sautéing broccoli, carrots, asparagus or green beans brings out their sweet flavors.

When a pasta sauce or entree dish seems to lack sparkle, add a dash of red wine vinegar while it's simmering.

The secret to this pesto is the cider vinegar—we've tried others as substitutes, but the flavor is never quite the same.

Fresh Green Beans with Dill Pesto
serves 4

Pesto

3/4 c. scallions, including green tops, chopped
3 tbl. fresh parsley, chopped
3- 4 tbl. fresh dill weed, chopped
3 tbl. cider vinegar
3 oz. walnuts, coarsely chopped
1/2- 3/4 c. olive oil
salt and freshly ground pepper

1 1/2 lb. fresh green beans, trimmed and cleaned
dill sprigs

In a blender combine scallions, parsley, dill, vinegar, walnuts, and 1/2 c. oil. Whirl until the mixture is smooth, adding more oil as needed. Pesto should be smooth but with a slight coarse texture. Season with salt and pepper and set aside. (Can be frozen.)

Cook green beans in a large skillet in 1"-2" water. When tender-done, not limp, drain and remove to platter. Pour enough Dill Pesto on green beans just to coat them. Toss gently. Chill mixture for several hours or overnight.

To Serve: Bring back to room temperature. Taste and adjust seasonings—you may have to add a little more pesto. Garnish with dill sprigs.

This dish is so subtle, sweet, and earthy tasting, it reminds us of what dining in Tuscany must be like. See if you don't agree. Include it in your menu when grilling marinated chicken or whole pork roasts.

Braised Leeks, Italian Style
serves 4

5 large leeks
2 tbl. pine nuts
1/4 c. olive oil
1/3 c. currants
14 oz. can Italian tomatoes, chopped (reserve liquid)
   or about 6 fresh tomatoes
salt & freshly ground pepper
1/4 c. red wine vinegar
2 tbl. brown sugar

Trim leeks, leaving only 1"-2" of pale green tops. Cut lengthwise and clean well. Slice in 1/2" pieces. Sauté pine nuts in 2 tbl. oil in a deep skillet. As they begin to color, add the currants and tomatoes. Sauté a few minutes and add the leeks. Add remaining oil and water, enough to come halfway up the sides of the leeks.

Bring to a boil and simmer, partially covered, and braise for about 15 minutes or until the leeks are tender when pierced. Remove leeks gently and place on serving dish. Increase heat on pan and begin to reduce the pan juices. Add vinegar and sugar, tasting to adjust to your liking. Add salt and pepper. Continue to reduce until slightly thick. Pour over leeks. Chill. Remove and bring to room temperature and adjust seasonings.

Pine Nuts

Pine nuts actually come from a type of pine tree—the Stone-Pines that grow in the Mediterranean. Pine nuts are small and delicate and shaped like a corn kernel. They are delicious in pesto, pasta sauces, and tarts, but their price tag usually prohibits frequent use. They're found in Italian delicatessens or Asian markets. Store them in the freezer because their resinous oils spoil easily.

In New Mexico and Arizona a variety of the pine nut is also cultivated called pinon. They grow on low bushy pinon trees and are less sweet and drier tasting than the Mediterranean kind. However, they can be used interchangeably.

Julienning Vegetables

Juliennes are matchstick-size strips of food, such as carrots, leeks, turnips or other foods. We use juliennes in salads, soups, vegetable dishes and as little strips of color in garnishes.

This is a light and healthful way to showcase and enjoy your home garden produce. Different herbs and vegetables may be substituted, including green beans, julienned zucchini, and sliced fennel.

Leek, Asparagus & Carrot Sauté
serves 6-8

1/4 c. chicken stock
5 large carrots, in 4" juliennes and matchstick widths
2 leeks, split, cleaned, and julienned
3/4 lb. thin asparagus, trimmed and julienned
1 recipe Mustard Butter (see below)

Place stock in skillet and bring to a boil, add carrots and cook 4 minutes. Add leeks and cook 2 additional minutes. Add asparagus, cover, and cook 1 to 1 1/2 minutes longer. Drain vegetables, add Mustard Butter, and toss. Place on platter. May be served warm or at room temperature.

Mustard Butter

5 tbl. butter
2 tsp. herb or Dijon mustard
1 tsp. fresh lemon juice
1 tbl. fresh dill weed, chopped
1 tbl. fresh chives, minced
1/2 tsp. salt
freshly ground pepper

Cream butter with mustard, add lemon juice, and mix well. Add dill, chives, salt and pepper.

Marge's 11-year-old daughter, Dana, requests this colorful dish at Halloween because it looks just like candy corn!

Gingered Corn & Carrots
serves 6

1 tbl. butter
1 tbl. fresh ginger, very finely minced
6-8 garlic cloves, finely minced
2 1/2 c. carrots, peeled and cut into 1/4" cubes
1/3 c. chicken stock
1 tsp. sugar
2 1/2 c. corn
salt and freshly ground pepper

Melt butter in a deep saucepan. Add ginger and garlic and cook 1-2 minutes or until beginning to soften. Add carrots, stock, and sugar and bring to a boil. Reduce heat, cover, and cook 6-8 minutes. Add corn and heat through. Taste and season. Serve hot.

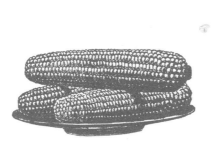

Sweet Corn

In the Midwest sweet corn celebrations are annual events, reminding us that we grow probably the best corn around.

There are so many varieties it's hard to choose a favorite. Sweet, extra sweet, white, yellow, or bi-colored—you pick.

If you want to grow it yourself, you'll need plenty of room—this isn't a plant for intensive or container gardens, even if all you want is the newest food fad—baby corn. Actually baby corn isn't a special variety. It's really only sweet corn that is picked when it's very immature.

Allspice

An interesting spice native to the Caribbean, sometimes called a Jamaican pepper. Although it's grown on the evergreen pimento tree, it's not to be confused with the pimento pepper. The whole berry, round and hard, is like a peppercorn and tastes faintly like a mixture of cinnamon, cloves, and nutmeg—hence the name "allspice."

Available whole or ground, allspice is used in patés, pickling spices, cakes, cookies, steamed puddings, sweet rolls, and as a mulling spice ingredient.

A quick side dish that rounds out a Mexican, Southwestern, or Caribbean meal. Serve with Sangria or cold beer.

Spicy Black Beans
serves 8

2 tbl. vegetable oil
1 1/2 c. minced onion
2 large cloves garlic, minced
1 1/2 tsp. cumin seed, crushed
1 1/2 tsp. dried oregano
1/2 tsp. EACH ground allspice and ground cloves
1 chipotle chile, minced with seeds or 2 jalapenos, minced*
2 cans black beans (reserve some liquid)
salt
1/4 c. scallions, minced for garnish

Place oil in a deep skillet and sauté the onion and garlic over low heat until soft. Add herbs, spices, and chilies and mix well. Add beans and cook over low heat until most of the liquid is absorbed. Try not to smash beans. Taste and adjust. Serve hot with scallions sprinkled on top.

Chipotles are smoked jalapenos. They're available either dried or canned in a tomato sauce called Adobo.

Fennel is a not-so-common vegetable often mistakenly labeled anise in grocery stores. Sliced in salads and pureed in velvety cream soups, the licorice flavor is refreshing and delicious.

Braised Fennel
serves 4

3 fennel bulbs
1 tbl. butter
2 tbl. oil
1 tbl. pancetta* diced or 1 slice thick hickory bacon, diced
4 large shallots, cut in large chunks
1/2 c. white wine or vermouth
2 tbl. fennel leaves
3 tbl. balsamic vinegar
1 tsp. sugar
water (if needed)
freshly ground pepper
fennel sprigs for garnish

Trim fennel. Cut off ends and any brown areas. Chop into large chunks, reserving sprigs for garnish. Place butter and oil in a large skillet and add pancetta, shallots, and fennel. Heat over low flame and cook until shallots begin to soften, about 4-5 minutes. Add rest of the ingredients and raise heat slightly.

Cover and braise until fennel is tender, but still has a crunch. If liquid begins to evaporate, add a little water.

*Pancetta is an Italian bacon.

Anise

Anise is of Mediterranean origin, and is one of the first aromatic plants to be written about. The Greeks, Hebrews, and Romans valued anise for its reputed medicinal properties. Anise belongs to the parsley family, and is very similar to fennel—so much so that they are often interchanged and mislabeled in grocery stores.

Known for its distinctive licorice flavor, anise grows to reach 2' and has long, feathery leaves. The fruit of the plant, when dried, is called aniseed. It's used in liquors in Italy and breads in Germany and Scandinavia. We also use the seeds in baking and candy making, especially licorice confections. Remember to crush the seeds to release their flavor.

211

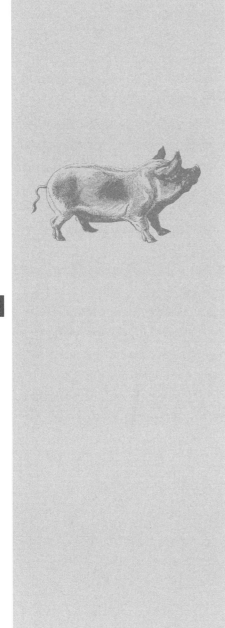

212

Turn and mix often. When fennel is done, remove with shallots and set aside. Reduce liquid to 1/4 c. and pour over vegetables. Sprinkle with freshly ground pepper and serve hot or at room temperature. Garnish with fennel sprigs.

A versatile and aromatic dish. Instead of combining herbs, try using just one each time and see which flavors you like best.

Herbed New Potatoes
serves 6

1 1/2 to 2 lbs. small red potatoes, unpeeled
4-6 tbl. butter
3 tbl. fresh assorted minced herbs—tarragon, chives, mint, dill,
    chervil, or parsley, or 1 tbl. dried
salt and freshly ground pepper
lemon juice

Partially cook new potatoes. Remove from heat and drain. Cool slightly and slice with peels on. Melt butter in skillet and add potatoes. Cook until almost done and add herbs. Turn gently to coat—do not cook herbs. Season and sprinkle with lemon juice, if desired.

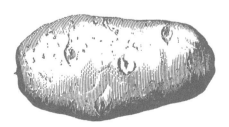

Potatoes

Buy or grow a specific potato for your specific purpose. Low starch or waxy potatoes are best for boiling or frying—Norland, Early Ohio, or Red Pontiac. They'll hold up in salads or just boiled and tossed with herbed butter. Tiny new potatoes, by the way, aren't a variety of potato, but simply the earliest crop. For baking, try Kennebec or russets—the potato sometimes referred to as Idahos.

All potatoes, no matter what kind, should be stored somewhere cool, layered between newspapers so that if one turns bad the rest won't spoil. Refrigeration should be avoided—cold temperatures cause the starch in the potatoes to turn to sugar. With proper storage, potatoes will keep for months.

213

Suzanne's sister Mary lives in Texas and serves Wisconsin Burgers and Parmesan-Rosemary Potatoes to all her Texan friends.

214

Parmesan-Rosemary Potatoes
serves 6-8

4 tbl. olive oil
1/2 c. chopped green onions
3 garlic cloves
2 tbl. fresh rosemary, minced
2 1/2 to 3 lbs. potatoes, cleaned, cut in wedges or
    large chunks, unpeeled
1/2 c. Parmesan
salt and pepper

Combine oil, green onions, garlic, and rosemary. Place potatoes on a baking sheet and pour oil mixture over. Toss to coat. Place in a 450-500° oven for 15 minutes. Remove and toss. Sprinkle on half the cheese and return to oven to bake an additional 10-15 minutes. Remove and toss again. Potatoes should be crispy. Add remaining cheese and salt and pepper. Toss and serve.

An easy potato dish to make for Thanksgiving and Christmas—best of all it can be prepared hours ahead and reheated.

Garlic Mashed Potatoes
serves 6-8

3 lbs. boiling potatoes, peeled and quartered
1 bulb of roasted garlic*
4 oz. goat cheese (plain or herbed)
1/2 c. warm milk (or more to reach desired creaminess)
2 tbl. lowfat cream cheese
2 tbl. butter
1/8 tsp. freshly grated nutmeg
salt and freshly ground pepper
fresh chives

Boil potatoes until soft. Drain and return to pan. Add roasted garlic, goat cheese, milk, cream cheese, and butter. Mash, using a hand masher, and add more milk as needed. Season well with nutmeg, salt, and pepper. Garnish with chives. Serve immediately.

Can be prepared ahead of time. Place in a glass oven-proof dish, cover with foil, and chill several hours. To serve: Place in a preheated 350° oven and bake 30-35 minutes or until heated through.

Once garlic is roasted, squeeze the cloves to release the puree. Cover and set aside until ready to use.

Roasted Garlic

An appetizer that's become popular in homes and restaurants across the country is roasted garlic. In its raw state, garlic is strong and very pungent, but when slow-roasted in an oven it becomes sweet and succulent.

Roasted garlic is served with French bread, salt, and freshly ground pepper. Guests pull apart the cloves and press the soft interior onto a slice of bread, season well and then eat. Yum!

Here's how to prepare:
On a 12" square of heavy duty aluminum foil place an entire bulb of garlic (be sure there are no soft spots or bruised cloves). Don't peel, but either separate the cloves or leave the bulb intact with 1/2" of the top cut off. Pour in about 2 tsp. of extra virgin olive oil all over and toss to coat evenly. Gather the foil into a ball and place on a small pie plate. Bake in a 400-450° oven for 30-35 minutes. Toss occasionally. Remove from foil and serve immediately or cool and store in the refrigerator for later use.

216

The parsnip is a much overlooked root vegetable that looks like a large white carrot and has a semi-sweet flavor. Parsnips are a great addition to soups and stews, or simply julienned and sautéed in butter with a dash of lime juice.

Potato & Parsnip Gratin
serves 6

1 medium onion, chopped (2 c.)
3 cloves garlic, minced
1 tbl. butter
1 tbl. olive oil
4-5 medium russet potatoes, peeled and sliced thinly (6 c.)
4 parsnips, peeled and sliced thinly
1/2 lb. Swiss cheese, grated (or monterey jack or other medium soft cheese)
4 tbl. fresh minced scallions
2 tbl. minced fresh chives
1/2 c. heavy cream
2/3 c. chicken stock
1/4 c. flour
salt and freshly ground black pepper

Sauté onions and garlic in butter and oil until soft and translucent. Butter a 9" x 13" gratin pan. Place half of the potatoes in a thin layer in the pan. Salt and pepper the potatoes and spread half of the onions and 1/3 of the cheese in a layer over the potatoes. Sprinkle top with scallions and chives. Add parsnips in a layer to the top. Salt and pepper top. Add remaining onions, 1/3 of the cheese, scallions, and the chives. Lay the remaining potatoes on the top, season with salt and pepper, and sprinkle with the remaining cheese.

In a small bowl combine cream, stock, and flour, then pour into gratin dish. Cover with foil and bake 30 minutes at 400°. Uncover and continue to bake an additional 30 minutes or until crusty, brown, and tender in the center. Let sit 5 minutes before serving.

Gratins

Gratins are both a baking method and a type of cookware, French in origin. They're prepared and served in the same dish. Choose a shallow pan so that everyone gets a healthy share of the crusty top. Heat-conducting materials are best, such as earthenware, porcelain, or Le Cruset-type pans (i.e. cast iron enamel). When baked, the top should be crusty golden brown, with almost burnt edges for a rustic look, and the inside soft and creamy.

217

Hazelnuts

Also known as filberts, hazelnuts are prized as one of the supreme dessert nuts by pastry makers. Grown in the Northwest and Midwest (including Wisconsin), they are widely available.

Since hazelnuts are perishable, store in the freezer as you would other nuts. Remove the skins before using.

When toasting hazelnuts, bake at 350° for 10-12 minutes, until flesh is golden brown and skin is a dark brown color. Cool. Rub together or put in a cloth towel and rub to remove skins.

218

The interesting addition of hazelnuts and dried cranberries to wild rice makes this dish flavorful and truly a Wisconsin treat.

Wild Rice Pilaf with Hazelnuts & Dried Cranberries
serves 4

3 scallions, chopped
3/4 c. wild rice, washed
2 tbl. butter
2-3 c. chicken stock
2/3 c. white rice
1/2 c. dried cranberries
1/2 tsp. dried rosemary or 1 tbl. fresh, minced
1/2 c. toasted (and skinned) hazelnuts, chopped coarsely
1/4 c. parsley, minced
1/2 tsp. salt
freshly ground pepper

Sauté scallions and wild rice in butter 3-4 minutes. Add 2 1/2 c. stock and bring to a boil, reduce heat, and cover, simmering 20 minutes or until rice begins to soften. Add white rice and cook for 10 minutes. Add cranberries and rosemary and cook until rice is tender. You may not use all the liquid—don't overcook wild rice. Add nuts and parsley and heat through. Season to taste and serve hot.

Lemon rice is easy to make and goes with practically any meal. We particularly like its tart-sweet flavor with curries, Caribbean, Thai, and spicy Southwestern foods.

Lemon Rice
serves 4

2 tbl. oil
1 garlic clove, minced
2 large shallots, minced
1 1/2 c. long grain rice
3 c. chicken stock
1 tbl. grated lemon rind
2 tbl. fresh parsley, chopped
1/3 c. assorted fresh herbs, chopped (basil, chives, dill,
    tarragon, marjoram, mint, oregano)
salt and freshly ground pepper
1/3 c. toasted coconut (place on a baking sheet in a 400°
    oven for 5 minutes or until just starting to turn golden)

Melt oil in a deep skillet and sauté garlic, shallots, and rice for 2 minutes. Add stock and bring to a boil. Add lemon rind and parsley and lower heat. Cover and simmer 25 minutes.

Remove cover and mix in other herbs. Taste and adjust seasonings. Just before serving, sprinkle with coconut.

Summer Grill Out

Curried Cream of Red Pepper Soup

Grilled Swordfish with
Spicy Asian Pesto

Lemon Rice

Tomato & Sweet Onion Salad

Chocolate Ginger Torte

Serve with Chardonnay, Australian
Semillon, or Alsatian Riesling wine

219

Lemons

Lemons are a must in everyone's pantry—store at room temperature to obtain the most juice, but refrigerate if you're planning to keep them for some time.

Lemons provide a tart accent to sauces, vegetables, salad dressings, marinades and seafood. A little squeeze will intensify and perk up flavors. It also keeps freshly sliced mushrooms, cut-up apples, pears, avocados, and bananas from turning brown.

Freeze leftover juice in ice cube trays or small plastic containers—they'll add sparkle to ice tea, lemonade, club soda, and wine spritzers.

Try lemon juice as a substitute for vinegar in dressings—the taste is clean and refreshing.

Risotto has become a popular dish in recent years. An Italian comfort food, it's great with pork roasts, lamb, or baked chicken. We usually make this recipe in place of an entree on cold winter nights, often substituting sautéed spinach, greens, or mashed winter squash for the mushroom mixture.

Wild Mushroom Risotto
serves 6-8

1/2 oz. dried wild mushrooms, assorted
1/2 c. boiling water
5 c. beef stock*
2-3 tbl. olive oil
2 oz. pancetta, cut in cubes (or use 1 slice of very thick bacon)
3 tbl. butter
10-12 oz. assorted fresh mushrooms, sliced
1/2 lemon, juiced
1/2 c. heavy cream
1/3 c. onions, minced
1 1/2 c. Arborio rice
1/2 c. dry white wine
1/3 c. freshly grated Parmesan cheese
salt and freshly ground pepper
1/4 c. fresh Italian parsley

Soak dried mushrooms in the boiling water for 20-30 minutes or until soft. Cut up in strips, set aside, and strain soaking liquid. Reserve. Heat beef stock in a large saucepan and keep warm over a low flame.
*Keep the stock constantly hot. Cold liquids chill the mixture and make the risotto mushy.

220

Add 1 tbl. oil and 1 tbl. butter to a deep skillet and cook the pancetta until crisp, 3-5 minutes. Remove to a bowl and set aside. Sprinkle fresh mushrooms with lemon juice. Add another tbl. of butter to same skillet and cook the fresh mushrooms until soft. Add dried mushrooms and cream and cook until mixture is slightly reduced. Place in bowl with pancetta.

In same skillet, add 1 tbl. butter and the remaining oil and sauté onions 1-2 minutes. Add rice and stir with a wooden spoon about 1 minute. Add wine, 1/2 c. hot stock, and the reserved soaking liquid. Cook over medium heat. Add broth, 1/2 c. at a time, stirring frequently and waiting until most of the liquid is absorbed before adding more. This should take 18-20 minutes. When rice is tender, but firm, add reserved mushroom mixture, remaining butter, Parmesan, salt, pepper, and parsley. Mix and taste to adjust seasonings. Serve at once.

Arborio Rice

To make a perfect risotto, it's essential to use the correct kind of rice. Not just any rice, but a short grain rice that can absorb a great deal without becoming mushy. That's Arborio.

Italian-grown Arborio has a distinctive flavor and texture that's ideal for the long gentle-cooking risottos. It's more expensive than the regular short grain rice, but worth it. At one time it was only available in Italian markets, but today we can find it in any large grocery store.

It's also a good rice to use in paellas and jambalaya. Follow the package directions and add your own flavorings—saffron, shellfish, and sautéed vegetables.

221

Spoonbread

Spoonbread is a Southern specialty, a baked dish made with white or yellow cornmeal, milk, eggs, and shortening, which is served with a spoon. Historically, spoonbread is an adaptation of an Indian method of preparing native white cornmeal, called "Suppawn." This porridge-like dish was cooked in pots, and later refined by the English colonists, who added milk and eggs. Then, some unknown cook left the mixture too long in the oven by mistake—spoonbread was the result.

222

Even though this is called a bread, you should think of it more as a side of mashed potatoes—moist and served with a spoon.

Acorn Squash Spoonbread
serves 6

1 c. cornmeal
1 tsp. salt
1/2 tsp. paprika
1 c. cooked acorn squash, pureed
1 1/2 c. water
3 tbl. butter
1 jalapeno, halved, seeded, and chopped
4 eggs
1 c. milk
1/2 c. grated Swiss or Parmesan cheese
1/4 c. fresh chives

Preheat oven to 425°, grease rectangular oven pan (9" x 12"). In a small saucepan, combine cornmeal, salt, and paprika. Add squash and water, stir well. Cook over medium heat, stirring constantly 3-5 minutes or until thick. Remove from heat, add butter and jalapenos.

In a mixer beat eggs until frothy and lemon colored. Add milk, cheese, and chives, stir to blend. Add cornmeal mixture and mix until smooth. Pour into pan, smooth even and bake 25 minutes or until tip of knife inserted in center comes out clean.

We usually double this recipe since the earthy mixture tastes great the next day on toasted Italian bread—like a Crostini.

Caramelized Onions with Sun-Dried Tomatoes & Walnuts
serves 4

2 lb. small pearl or baking onions, peeled*
3 tbl. good olive oil
1 1/2 tbl. fresh rosemary, coarsely chopped
salt and freshly ground pepper
1/3 c. walnut halves
2 tbl. sun-dried tomatoes, cut into strips

Place onions in a 9" x 13" pan. Drizzle with olive oil and sprinkle with rosemary. Bake uncovered in a 375° oven for 25-34 minutes. Remove, toss occasionally, until onions are soft and caramelized—about 30 minutes more. Don't let them burn. Serve warm or at room temperature.

*Place onions in boiling water 2-3 minutes. Remove and cool, and the peels will slip off easily

Drying Tomatoes

During the late summer when the markets are flooded with tomatoes, we oven-dry a few of our own for snacking.

Here's how:
4 lbs. Italian or plum tomatoes, core-end cut off and halved lengthwise
1 to 1 1/2 tbl. good olive oil
coarse salt and freshly ground pepper

Lightly brush the skin side of the tomatoes with oil and place skin side down on large baking sheets. Sprinkle with salt and pepper. Place in a 200° oven to bake to about 1/4 of their original size. This takes 5-6 hours. Be sure they remain a little soft. Remove pan from the oven and let cool completely. Store in covered containers in the refrigerator.

223

224

Every Christmas, Marge's family shares dinner with their good friends Sally and Mike Miley. Each family has two daughters who love broccoli—but this is the only recipe all four girls agree on.

Broccoli with Garlic & Sun-Dried Tomatoes
serves 4

1 lb. broccoli, broken into florets
3 tbl. sun-dried tomatoes, chopped with the oil they were packed in
1 tbl. olive oil
6 garlic cloves, minced
freshly ground pepper

Cook broccoli in your favorite way. We just fill a large skillet with about 1" water and let it come to a boil. Add the broccoli, turn so each floret turns bright green, reduce the heat, cover, and cook 2-3 minutes. Drain and keep warm.

Heat sun-dried tomato oil plus olive oil in same skillet and sauté garlic until soft, 1-2 minutes. Add sun-dried tomatoes, cut into slivers, and heat through. Pour over broccoli and toss gently. Sprinkle with fresh pepper and serve.

We like to use this recipe for a quick appetizer. Serve the spicy eggplant, roasted garlic, and goat cheese in small bowls with thin slices of baguette. Let your guests make interesting and creative appetizers with different combinations.

Spicy Eggplant
serves 8-10

3 tbl. olive or vegetable oil

1 tbl. sesame oil

1 to 1 1/2 lbs. eggplant, peeled (or 4 Japanese eggplants, unpeeled) cut in 3/4" chunks

2 garlic cloves, minced

2 tbl. fresh ginger, minced

1-2 tsp. Chili Paste with Garlic

2 tbl. sherry

2 tbl. soy sauce

1/2 tsp. sugar

1-2 tbl. seasoned rice vinegar

1/2 c. chicken stock

2-6 scallions, sliced thin

In a large skillet heat oils and add eggplant. Stir-fry 3- 4 minutes or until slightly browned. Add garlic, ginger, Chili Paste, sherry, soy sauce, sugar, vinegar, and stock. Reduce heat, cover, and cook 10 minutes or until eggplant is tender. Remove cover. Taste and adjust seasonings with salt and pepper. Add scallions. Serve cold or at room temperature.

Sesame

Sesame is an annual tropical/sub-tropical herbaceous plant. It reaches up to 4' high, and has been grown for its tiny grayish white or black seeds.

The seeds were brought to the American South by African slaves who called it "benne" or "bene" seeds. Sesame is still known by those names and is still popular in Southern cooking. Toast them to bring out flavor. The crunchy texture is good as a garnish for appetizers, salads, and almost any dish which requires nuts. If not toasted, use in baked dishes such as chicken, over bread before baking, in cakes and cookies, over noodles and vegetables, or crushed to make sesame oil.

225

Desserts

It's hard to imagine any meal, especially a dinner party, that doesn't include dessert. Yes, it's the last course to be served, but often the one by which the meal is remembered. We love desserts; who doesn't? But making them does take some time. With almost any other course in a menu you can adjust a little of this and a little of that in your recipe and still produce a great-tasting dish. But with desserts, there's more accuracy and precision involved. It's basic kitchen chemistry. To compound that fact, cooking desserts with herbs is even more of a challenge.

Suzanne and I are quite at home inventing dessert recipes with spices or other flavorings, but to use our kitchen herbs in desserts was new. How would we transfer the basil that's used in aromatic pestos to a pie, or pungent rosemary in potatoes and lamb dishes into a cake? Our families did raise their collective eyebrows; well, we experimented and experimented and found that indeed herbs did marry well with desserts, and the recipes that follow are proof.

Use a mortar and pestle to crush the lavender buds. We have several kinds—ceramic and wooden. They both do a good job of pulverizing spices and herbs.

A Perfect Cup of Tea

Bring fresh cold water to a full rolling boil and pour over loose tea (1 tsp. per cup plus 1 tsp. for the pot). Cover and let steep 3-5 minutes; longer for herb tea. Don't judge the tea by color—taste it. You can always add water if it's too strong. Strain and serve with honey or sugar.

228

Lavender & Candied Ginger Shortbreads
makes 36

1/2 c. butter
1/2 c. sugar
1 1/2 tsp. dried lavender buds, crushed
1 1/4 c. flour
dash of salt
1-2 tbl. water
3 tbl. very finely minced candied ginger (also called crystallized ginger)
additional sugar for sprinkling

In a mixer bowl beat butter and sugar until well creamed. Add lavender, flour, and salt. Beat until combined. Mixture will be dry. Slowly add water until slightly moistened. (The mixture should stick together slightly.) By hand, mix in the candied ginger.

Press evenly into a 9" square pan. Bake in a 325° oven for 30 minutes. It will still be light, but beginning to turn brown on the edges. Remove from oven and sprinkle with sugar. While still warm cut into 36 squares. Let cool completely before removing. Store in cookie tins or freeze for up to several months.

Marcel Proust is credited for making madeleines such a popular dessert—we're not disputing that, rather applauding it. They're in between a cookie and a small cake and make a great dessert to serve with punch or tea. We make several flavors besides Rose—including chocolate, lavender, and ginger.

Rose Madeleines
makes about 18

Butter and flour for molds*
2 eggs
1/3 c. sugar
1/2 tsp. vanilla
2 tsp. rosewater
3/4 c. cake flour
1/3 c. butter, melted and cooled
powdered sugar for garnish

Brush molds with soft butter and dust with flour.

In a bowl beat together eggs, sugar, vanilla and rosewater with an electric mixer until light colored and triple in volume—about 10-15 minutes. By hand, fold in cake flour. Fold in cooled melted butter.

Spoon into prepared pans, filling to top. In a 375° degree oven, bake 10-12 minutes or until cookie springs back when touched with finger tips.

Remove from molds and cool on a rack. While warm, sprinkle with powdered sugar. Store in cookie tins. Before adding batter, butter and dust molds each time.

Madeleine molds are small tin sheets with an indented scallop design. They can be found in most cookware shops.

Rosewater

Rosewater is a liquid flavoring distilled from fragrant rose petals. In Middle Eastern and Indian cooking it's used for pastries and drinks. In its purist form, rosewater is used as a basis for perfume—oil of rose. When diluted with water, it gives off a faint hint of roses—that's the type used in cooking.

It can be found in Asian and Indian grocery stores and through mail-order gourmet catalogs.

Add a dash to ice water for your next dinner party or in a simple syrup to be poured over pound cake for dessert.

229

Kathy's* Mint Julep Southern Style

Into a silver mug or collins glass, dissolve one teaspoon powdered sugar with two teaspoons of water. Then fill with finely shaved ice and add 2 1/2 oz. of Old Kentucky Tavern Bourbon Whiskey.

Stir until glass is heavily frosted, adding more ice if necessary. (Do not hold glass with hand while stirring.) Decorate with 5 or 6 sprigs of fresh mint so that the tops are about 2" above rim of mug or glass.

Use short straws so that it will be necessary to bury your nose in the mint. The mint is intended for aroma rather than flavor.

*(Suzanne's sister-in-law)

230

These are definitely adult brownies and not for the Cub Scout meeting. Enjoy them either plain or with the chocolate glaze.

Bourbon Brownies with Coriander
2 dozen

8 oz. unsweetened chocolate
1 c. butter
5 large eggs
1 1/2 tbl. vanilla
2 tsp. almond extract
3 tbl. instant coffee
3 3/4 c. sugar
pinch of salt
3/4 tsp. ground coriander
5 tbl. bourbon (optional)
2/3 c. semi-sweet chocolate chunks
1/3 c. bourbon (for brushing)
2 c. flour
2 c. coarsely chopped pecans

Using a greased 9" x 12" pan lined with foil, butter and flour lightly.

Melt 8 oz. chocolate and butter in a small saucepan over low heat. Set aside. With an electric mixer beat eggs, vanilla, almond extract, coffee, and sugar on high for 2-3 minutes until light and fluffy. Mix in chocolate/butter mixture, salt, coriander, and bourbon. Blend in flour, pecans, and chocolate chunks. Pour into prepared pan. Bake in a preheated 350° oven 35-40 minutes. The brownies, when tested, should be moist and sticking somewhat to the toothpick or tester. Cool to room temperature. Invert brownies on a board, remove foil, and brush with additional bourbon. Coat with glaze.

Glaze

> 2/3 c. sugar
> 1 tbl. instant coffee
> 1/2 c. heavy cream
> 2 1/2 oz. unsweetened chocolate, finely chopped
> 2 oz. butter
> 1 tsp. vanilla

Combine sugar, coffee, and cream in a small heavy saucepan. Bring to a boil while stirring. Reduce heat and simmer 6 minutes without stirring. Remove from heat, add chopped chocolate, stir until melted and smooth. Add butter and vanilla, whisk. Cool to room temperature, spread on brownies.

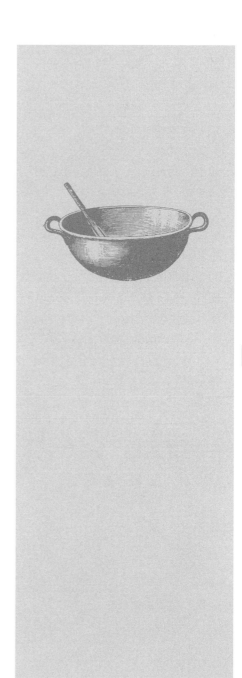

Strawberry Butter

1/2 c. butter, room temperature
3-4 tbl. powdered sugar
8-9 ripe strawberries
dash freshly grated nutmeg
1/4 tsp. fresh rosemary,
    finely minced

Place all ingredients in a food processor, and blend until very smooth. Taste and adjust. Place in a small bowl, cover with plastic wrap, and chill until 30 minutes before serving. Pass with slices of cake.

This cake has the texture of a quick bread. For something different, bake it in small loaf pans and give it as gifts.

Fresh Strawberry Rosemary Cake
serves 10-12

1 1/2 pints fresh strawberries, rinsed and hulled
1 1/3 c. oil
2 c. sugar
4 eggs
grated rind from 1 orange
3 c. cake flour
1 1/4 tsp. baking soda
1 tsp. salt
1 1/2 to 2 tbl. fresh rosemary, very finely minced
1/2 c. coarsely chopped walnuts
Strawberry Butter (optional)

Grease an 8-c. tube pan and set aside. Whirl strawberries in a food processor until coarsely chopped—don't liquefy. Set aside.

In a mixer bowl, place the oil and sugar and beat well. Add eggs and mix well. Combine strawberries and orange rind and blend. Add dry ingredients, rosemary, and walnuts. Beat until a smooth batter.

Pour into prepared pan and bake for 1 to 1 1/2 hours in a 325° oven, or until toothpick inserted in cake comes out clean. Cool in pan on a rack for 20-30 minutes. Remove and cover with plastic wrap. Keep in refrigerator several days. Bring to room temperature to serve. (Can be frozen.)

The apricot, brandy, and rum transforms this cake from the traditional pound cake into holiday splendor.

Apricot Pound Cake
serves 14-15

2/3 c. dried apricots, chopped
1/2 c. apricot brandy
2 sticks (1 c.) unsalted butter, softened
3 c. sugar
6 large eggs
1 c. sour cream (can use low fat)
1 tsp. vanilla
1 tsp. orange extract
1 tsp. rum extract or 1 tbl. dark rum
grated zest (peel) of 1 orange + grated zest of 1 lemon
3 c. sifted all-purpose flour
1/2 tsp. salt
1/4 tsp. baking soda
1 recipe Fresh Thyme Glaze

In small bowl, soak chopped apricots in 4 tbl. of apricot brandy. Set aside for 15 minutes.

In large bowl, cream butter, add sugar a little at a time, beating well, until light and fluffy. Add eggs, one at a time, beating well after each addition. Beat in sour cream, soaked apricots, remaining apricot brandy, vanilla, orange extract, rum extract, orange, and lemon zest. In bowl, sift together flour, salt, and baking soda. Stir dry mixture into

Fresh Thyme Glaze

1/3 c. fresh lemon juice
2 tsp. fresh thyme, chopped
1 tbl. apricot brandy
2 c. powdered sugar

In a small saucepan heat lemon juice, add thyme, and bring to a boil. Remove from heat. Cool. Add brandy and sugar, mix well until smooth. Spoon over cake 4 or 5 times.

233

Mother's Day Dessert Tea

Chocolate Mint Tart

Lavender Candied
Ginger Shortbread

Rose Madeleines

Apricot Poundcake with
Lemon Thyme Glaze

Serve with a German Riesling,
Spatlese, or Seyval wine

234

butter mixture. Transfer batter into well-buttered and floured 2 1/2 qt. bundt pan and bake cake in preheated 325° oven for 1 hour and 15 minutes, or until cake tests done. Let cake cool in pan on rack for 45 minutes; invert on plate and brush on Fresh Thyme Glaze.

When you're invited for dinner or luncheon, and there is a request for a dessert, take this cake. It's a winner! Not only does it travel well, but you can make it the day ahead.

Almond Ginger Torte with Fresh Raspberry Sauce
serves 12

3/4 c. sugar
1 stick unsalted butter, room temperature
8 oz. almond paste
3 eggs
2 tbl. Kirsch
1/4 tsp. almond extract
3 tbl. crystallized ginger, chopped into small pieces
2 tbl. minced fresh ginger
1/3 c. flour
1/3 tsp. baking powder
powdered sugar

Preheat oven to 350°. Butter an 8-1/2" round cake pan, line with wax paper, butter again, and dust with flour. With a mixer combine sugar, butter, and almond paste, and blend well. Beat in eggs, Kirsch, almond extract, and gingers. Add flour mixed with baking powder, combine well. Pour into prepared pan and bake 30-40 minutes until lightly golden brown and knife inserted in the center of the cake comes out clean. Cool in pan. Invert on serving platter, remove wax paper, and dust lightly with powdered sugar.

Raspberry Sauce

1 pint (2 c.) fresh raspberries or
    1 10-oz. bag frozen berries
4 tbl. sugar or to taste
3 tbl. Kirsch, Grand Marnier or
    other fruit-flavored liqueur
2 tbl. cornstarch, dissolved in
4 tbl. water
lemon juice

Combine raspberries with sugar in a food processor or blender, puree. Press through a sieve to remove seeds. Add liqueur and corn starch mixture. Heat until raspberry mixture turns transparent and thickens.

235

A very chocolatey dessert that freezes beautifully. Cut into quarters and wrap each section in plastic. Freeze for up to 1 year. Next time unexpected guests arrive, thaw one section for an hour and serve. Even one-quarter of this cake will serve 6 guests easily.

Chocolate Cranberry Torte
serves 12-14

1 1/2 c. fresh cranberries
1/3 c. sugar
2 tsp. grated orange rind
1/2 tsp. coriander seeds, crushed
3 tbl. creme de casis or sweet vermouth
8 oz. semi-sweet chocolate
8 oz. butter
3 large eggs, separated
1/2 c. sugar
1/4 tsp. almond extract
1/2 c. ground toasted almonds
1/3 c. flour
1/8 tsp. salt

In a small saucepan put cranberries and sugar, orange rind, and coriander seeds, and cook until semi-soft, about 5 minutes. Don't be alarmed when you hear a popping noise—that's just the cranberries. Add the liqueur and set aside to cool slightly.

Melt chocolate and butter in a small saucepan and cool to room temperature.

In a large mixer bowl, beat egg whites with a pinch of salt until stiff. Set aside.

In another mixer bowl, beat egg yolks and sugar until thick and light. Add chocolate mixture and combine well. Add almond extract and almonds. Combine and add cranberry mixture. Fold in flour and salt then continue to gently fold in egg whites. Pour into a greased and floured 9" spring-form pan and bake 40-50 minutes at 350°. Cool on a rack.

Glaze

2/3 c. sugar
1 tbl. instant coffee or espresso
1/2 c. heavy cream
2 1/2 oz. unsweetened chocolate, chopped
2 oz. butter
1 tsp. vanilla

Prepare Glaze:

Combine sugar, coffee, and cream in a heavy saucepan. While stirring, bring to a boil. Reduce heat and simmer 5-6 minutes without stirring. Remove from heat and add chocolate. Stir until melted. Add butter and vanilla. Whisk well. Chill until mixture begins to thicken.

Place cake on a serving plate and pour glaze over top. Let it drip down the sides. Spread to cover all exposed areas. Pour more glaze until all is used. Place in the refrigerator until ready to serve—at least 2 hours. Keep chilled. Remove 30 minutes before serving. Serve with whipped cream or a Cranberry Dessert Sauce.

Cranberry Dessert Sauce

Here's a rich dessert sauce that's great with chocolate cakes, pound cakes, ice cream, and bread puddings.

2 c. cranberry juice
3/4 c. sugar
1 1/2 tsp. orange rind, grated
1 1/2 c. fresh cranberries (coarsely chopped in a food processor)
dash of salt
1/4 tsp. coriander seeds, crushed
1 tsp. cornstarch + 1 tbl. cranberry juice or water
1/4 c. orange liqueur or creme de casis

In a large saucepan reduce the cranberry juice to 1 1/2 c. Add sugar, orange rind, cranberries, salt, and coriander seeds and cook 5-7 minutes. Mixture will thicken. Combine cornstarch with juice and add to mixture. Cook until glossy, 1-2 minutes. Remove from heat and add liqueur. Can be frozen and reheated.

Ginger

Ginger is a plant cultivated in the tropics, although many people grow it indoors in this country. Dried or ground ginger is used in curry powders and pastry making. Ginger contains a volatile oil called gingerly that gives fresh ginger that sharp, piquant flavor. In other forms—dried, powdered, candied, or crystallized— the fire diminishes.

We keep fresh, unpeeled ginger in glass jars refrigerated and covered with sherry. It will keep for months with only a very faint hint of sherry transmitted to other foods. The sherry acts as a preservative. Candied or crystallized ginger is best kept in plastic containers to prevent drying out.

238

Suzanne is the chocoholic and loves ginger equally well. This torte was invented to satisfy both those passions.

Chocolate Ginger Decadence Torte
serves 12-16

12 oz. semi-sweet chocolate
1 1/2 sticks butter
1 c. sugar
2 tbl. grated orange rind
5 eggs
3/4 c. cake flour
1 tsp. ground ginger
1 c. chopped toasted almonds (toast in 400° oven for
   5-7 minutes)
3/4 c. candied or crystallized ginger, minced
3 tbl. finely minced fresh ginger
ginger marmalade (about 1/2 c.)

Butter a 10" cake pan. Line the bottom with wax paper or parchment paper. Butter again and dust with flour.

In the top of a double boiler, melt chocolate. Remove from heat. Add butter, 1 tbl. at a time, and whisk in. Add sugar and orange rind. Beat in eggs, one at a time. Add flour, ginger, toasted almonds, candied ginger, and fresh ginger. Stir well.

Pour into prepared pan and bake at 350° for 1 hour and 5 minutes, or until just springy to the touch. Cool on rack. Cut cake in half horizontally. Heat ginger marmalade and spread on layer. Cover with top. Pour on glaze and chill or freeze.

Glaze

>   1/2 c. whipping cream
>   2 1/2 tbl. orange liqueur
>   11 oz. semi-sweet chocolate
>   1 tsp. corn syrup

Scald cream and liqueur. Remove from heat and add chocolate and corn syrup. Whisk until smooth. Cook till thick and spreadable.

Bruce, Suzanne's husband, lived in New York for many years and loves cheesecake. He never found any that he liked outside "The City" until Suzanne invented this one.

White Chocolate Cheese Cake with a Dark Chocolate Basil Crust
serves 12-16

Crust
> 1 1/4 c. chocolate wafer cookie crumbs, ground
> 3 tbl. ground pecans or walnuts
> 3 tbl. melted butter
> 4 tbl. sugar
> 1/4 tsp. cinnamon
> 1 tsp. dried basil
> dash nutmeg

Preheat oven to 350°. Combine all the above ingredients in a food processor or bowl until well mixed. Pat crumb mixture on the bottom of an 8" springform pan. Bake 5-7 minutes until set and hard. Cool. Lower heat to 315°.

Filling
> 8-10 oz. fine white chocolate
> 1/4 c. heavy cream
> 2-8 oz. pkg. cream cheese, room temperature
> 7 tbl. sugar
> 2 eggs

1/2 tbl. *vanilla*
1 1/2 tbl. *Amaretto or Frangelico (or any other flavored liqueur)*
2 tbl. *flour*

In a small saucepan melt chocolate with cream. Stir to keep smooth. Cool. With an electric mixer beat cheese and sugar together until smooth—4-5 minutes. Add eggs, one at a time, beating well after each addition.

Beat in white chocolate mixture, vanilla, liqueur, and flour into cheese mixture until just blended. Carefully spread into baked crust, place on baking sheet, bake 40 minutes until lightly golden. Turn off heat, cool in oven, and refrigerate overnight. Garnish with fresh fruit and white chocolate curls. Serve with Door County Cherry Sauce.

Door County Cherry Sauce

4 c. *fresh or frozen tart cherries, pitted*
1 c. *sugar*
2 tbl. *corn starch mixed with 5 tbl. cherry syrup*
2 tbl. *lemon juice*
4 tbl. *orange flavored liqueur*

In a saucepan put cherries and sugar; bring to a boil. Add cornstarch mixture. Mix and cook until transparent and thick. Cool slightly; add lemon juice and liqueur. Can be served warm or cold.

Cheesecakes are great to serve at dinner parties—they can be made days ahead or even frozen. Most bakeries cut their cakes while frozen with a clean, hot knife for perfect slices.

Cranberry Cheesecake with a Rosemary Crust
serves 16

Crust

> 1 c. flour
> 1/4 c. sugar
> 1/8 tsp. salt
> 1/2 tsp. grated lemon rind
> 3/4 tsp. grated orange rind
> 1 tsp. fresh rosemary, minced
> 7 tbl. butter, cut into small pieces
> 1 egg yolk mixed with 1 tbl. water
> 1/2 tsp. vanilla

In a food processor, combine flour, sugar, salt, grated rinds, and rosemary. Add butter and combine until pastry resembles coarse corn meal. Add egg yolk mixture and vanilla, combine well. The pastry should just hold together when pressed with the finger tips. Knead together with the heel of your hand a few times, forming into a flat disk. Wrap in plastic wrap and refrigerate 30 minutes or more. Roll out to fit a 10" springform pan. Freeze, prick crust with a fork and bake in a pre-heated 400° oven 20-25 minutes or until golden brown.

Filling

1 c. dried cranberries
3 tbl. orange liqueur
2 lbs. cream cheese at room temperature
1 c. sugar
2 tbl. fresh orange juice
1 1/4 tbl. orange rind
1/2 tsp. lemon rind
4-5 tbl. orange liqueur
large pinch salt
5 eggs

In a ceramic or plastic bowl, put cranberries and 3 tbl. orange liqueur, place in a microwave on high 45 seconds to 1 minute (to plump cranberries). Cool.

With an electric mixer, beat cream cheese and sugar together on medium speed 3-4 minutes, until very smooth. Beat in orange juice, orange and lemon rind and any excess orange liqueur from the cranberries plus orange liqueur to measure 5 tbl. Add salt, then one egg at a time, beating well after each addition. With a rubber spatula, fold in cranberries. Spoon mixture into cooled crust. Bake in a pre-heated 325° oven until just set, about 65-80 minutes.

Turn oven off, cool in oven until room temperature. Remove, cover, and refrigerate overnight. Serve with fresh fruit or Door County Cherry Sauce (see Index).

One of our favorite pies. The clean lemon taste seems even better the second day. If pie crusts or pastry worry you, roll them out between pieces of plastic wrap. It's easier and you use less flour.

Lemon Basil Buttermilk Pie
serves 6

Pastry
    1 1/2 c. flour
    1/2 tsp. salt
    2 tbl. sugar
    1/2 tsp. grated lemon rind
    1/4 c. Crisco
    1/4 c. cold butter, cut in bits
    4 tbl. ice water

Place flour, salt, sugar, and lemon rind in a food processor. Add shortening and butter and whirl. Add ice water 1 tbl. at a time, till soft dough forms. Don't over-mix. Form into a flat circle, wrap in plastic, and chill 1 hour before rolling out. Fit into a 9" metal or glass pie pan and flute edges decoratively.

Filling
    1 c. sugar
    3 tbl. flour
    1/2 tsp. salt
    1 tbl. fresh lemon basil, minced
    2 tsp. grated lemon rind

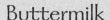

1/4 c. butter, melted and cooled slightly
2 1/2 tbl. fresh lemon juice
2 c. buttermilk
4 eggs
freshly grated nutmeg

In a mixer, combine sugar, flour, and salt. Add lemon basil, lemon rind, butter, lemon juice, buttermilk, and eggs. Beat until smooth. Pour into prepared pie shell and sprinkle generously with freshly grated nutmeg. Bake 10 minutes at 400°. Reduce heat to 325° and bake until custard is puffy and just starting to set—about 50 minutes. Insert knife 2" or 3" from edge and it should come out clean if pie is done.

Cool on rack. Can be made 8 hours ahead. Refrigerate when cool, but remove 1 hour before serving.

Buttermilk

Today's buttermilk is a type of skim milk readily available in almost every grocery store. Originally it was made from the sour liquid left over when butter was churned. It contained small bits of butter fat and children loved to drink it.

Today's version of this tart milk is cultured. A lactic-acid bacterial culture is added to skim or partly skim milk.

Buttermilk has a refreshing, slightly acidic taste, almost lemony. We use it in desserts, salad dressings, pancakes, muffins, and bread. It's available in powdered form—a real help for cooks—or fresh in the dairy case.

245

Herb Honey

1 pint clover honey

2-5 tbl. fresh herbs or 1 tbl. dried
(choose from mint, lemon balm, rose
geranium or lavender)

Heat honey in a pan over low heat.
Pour into a large jar with the herbs on
the bottom. Let sit on the counter
overnight. Strain out herbs (if
desired) and label. Store on pantry
shelves and use for biscuits, muffins,
pancakes, and toast.

This tart is rich and almost brownie-like in texture. Besides the mint flavor, we've made this tart with Grand Marnier and orange peel, Kahlua and espresso, and Framboise and raspberries.

Chocolate Mint Tart
serves 12

1 Paté Brisee pastry recipe (see Index)

Prebake in a 400° oven for 10 minutes. Remove to a rack.

Filling

    2 oz. unsweetened chocolate, melted
    4 oz. semi-sweet chocolate, melted
    1/2 c. butter, soft
    1 1/2 c. sugar
    3 eggs
    1/4 c. fresh mint, finely minced or 1 1/2 tbl. dried
    1/2 tsp. peppermint extract
    1/2 c. chopped nuts (optional)
    3/4 c. flour

In a food processor or mixer, add melted chocolates and butter and blend well. Add sugar and mix well. Add eggs, one at a time, blending well after each addition. Mix in mint, extract, and nuts. Gradually add flour and mix. Pour into prebaked pastry shell and bake until center is set (20-25 minutes). Don't overcook. Cool on rack. Sprinkle with powdered sugar and garnish with fresh mint sprigs.

When fitting the pastry dough into a tart pan, remember to compress the dough several times with your fingers against the side ring. This will help to keep the sides from shrinking while baking.

Apple-Orange Coriander Tart

Pastry

2 c. flour
1/3 c. sugar
1 1/2 sticks butter, cut into bits
1 egg yolk
1 tsp. grated orange rind
1 tbl. ice water (or as needed)

Combine flour, sugar, and butter in a food processor and whirl. Add butter in batches with egg yolk and rind, whirling until the mixture resembles coarse meal. Slowly add water, until pastry particles adhere when pressed together with finger tips. Add water as needed to make dough smooth and pliable.

Form dough into a ball and knead lightly with heel of your hand on a smooth surface for a few seconds to distribute butter evenly. Form into 2 flat circles, one slightly larger than the other. Chill 1 hour. Roll out and fit larger circle into a tart pan with removable bottom (10" or 11"). Reserve smaller circle.

Filling

5-6 Granny Smith or golden delicious apples, peeled, cored, and thinly sliced

Fruit & Herbs

Herbs have a remarkable natural affinity for desserts—especially fruit-based desserts. Basil with its clove-cinnamon flavor is wonderful with lemon or wherever cinnamon is used. Lavender is good in sugar cookies, custards, and with berries, peaches, and apricots. Coriander seed is sparkling with citrus fruits with its orange-like flavor, and also blends well in spice combinations for poaching fruit. Ginger tastes just great with chocolate and pears. Scented geraniums add an exotic perfumey taste to simple cakes, custards, muffins, cookies, sweet rolls, and jellies. Rosemary tames apples and cranberries, and mint is great with everything. Keep these flavor facts in mind and try substituting some in your favorite recipes.

247

Coriander Seed

Coriander seed is the dried fruit of a foot-tall herb which belongs to the parsley family.

Coriander is one of the first spices to be used in cooking. Native to the Mediterranean and Orient, seeds have been found in Egyptian tombs of 960 to 800 B.C. and mentioned in the Bible. The Romans introduced coriander into England and it remained a favorite of the herb garden.

It has a pleasant flavor similar to that of aniseed, cumin seed, and orange. Like many spices, it can be used in a variety of foods. Ground, it flavors cookies, candies, soups, Danish pastries, gingerbreads, cheeses, and meats—even salads.

1/3 c. sugar
1/2 tsp. ground cloves
1/2 tsp. ground coriander
2 tbl. grated orange rind
1 tbl. Grand Marnier or other orange flavored liqueur
1 tbl. flour
1 tbl. heavy cream

Toss apples with sugar, cloves, coriander, orange rind, Grand Marnier, flour, and cream. Let sit while making pastry. Arrange in pastry shell (in circular pattern). Place reserved pastry circle on top of tart, pressing upper and lower pastry edges together. Bake in a 400° oven 45-50 minutes.

Glaze

3 tbl. powdered sugar
1 tsp. orange rind
1 tbl. orange juice
1 tbl. Grand Marnier

Combine all and blend until smooth. While tart is warm, spread glaze in strips across surface.

When making tarts, we use "flan" pans, otherwise known as tart pans, with removable bottoms. They are 1" deep metal pans that come in different sizes and shapes. These pans are easy to use and transport, and to serve from when the outer ring is removed.

Cinnamon Caramel Nut Tart
serves 12-14

Pastry

1 c. flour
2 tbl. sugar
1/8 tsp. salt
1/2 c. butter
1/2 tsp. almond extract
2 tbl. milk

Preheat oven to 425°. In a food processor, combine flour, sugar, and salt. Add the butter in batches and whirl until the pastry resembles coarse corn meal. Mix almond extract with the milk and slowly add to the pastry mixture until particles adhere when pressed together with finger tips, adding more liquid if needed. Knead with the heel of your hand several times, forming a flat disk. Seal in plastic wrap and refrigerate 30 minutes or until ready to use. Roll out dough to fit a 10" flan pan. Prick bottom several times with a fork and freeze until ready to use. Bake in a preheated 425° oven for 10-15 minutes, or until golden. Cool.

Herb Teas

Grow your own herbs for later use in teas. You don't need many and they can be harvested anytime. Brew the dried herb teas singly or mix with black tea for unusual combinations. Create other blends with combinations of herbs such as sage-rosemary-mint. Plants to grow would be: mint, lemon balm, lemon verbena, chamomile, bergamot, anise, hyssop, sage, and rosemary.

249

Nutmeg

Ground nutmeg straight from the jar is a rarely used spice—in demand only at Christmas for hot drinks and cookies! But once you discover the aromatic flavor from grating your own fresh nutmeg, you'll be adding it to all sorts of dishes.

250

There are two types of nutmeg graters or grinders. One is like a pepper mill with a crank handle, and the other is a small tin gadget with teeth or grates that produce a fine dust when whole nutmegs are rubbed over it. Either device is good. The flavor is so fresh and intense you'll be using it in ways you never thought of.

Filling

1 c. heavy cream
3/4 c. packed brown sugar
2 c. coarsely chopped pecans, hazelnuts, macadamia nuts, almonds, pine nuts (a combination)
1 tsp. almond extract
1/4 tsp. ground cinnamon
1/8 tsp. ground coriander

While shell is baking, place cream and sugar in a heavy saucepan and cook over medium heat. Bring to a boil. Stir and continue boiling 1 minute. Add nuts, flavoring, and spices. Cook 2 minutes longer, stirring occasionally. Pour into shell and bake 15-20 minutes or until top is set and nuts start to turn golden brown.

Be sure when laying cranberries in pastry with the apples that they do not poke to the top of streusel. They have a tendency to burn.

Apple Cranberry Tart with Rosemary Streusel
serves 12

Pastry

> 1 1/4 c. flour
> 1/4 tsp. salt
> 2 tbl. sugar
> 2 tsp. minced fresh rosemary
> 8 tbl. butter, cut in 1 tbl. slices
> 3 tbl. water

In a food processor combine flour, salt, sugar, and rosemary, whirl until well combined. Add butter, whirl until the pastry resembles cornmeal. Add water slowly until crumbs just start holding together when pressed between fingers.

Knead a few times with the heel of hand, form into a flat ball. Wrap in plastic and refrigerate 30-60 minutes. Roll out to fit a 10" flan pan. Prick with a fork and freeze until ready to use.

Prebake at 425° for 10-15 minutes until lightly golden.

Streusel

> 1/2 c. + 1 tbl. flour

Baking Apples

When baking, choose the type of apples that are suited for baking and not just eating. Select apples that are firm and tart such as Greening, Jonathan, Cortland, or Granny Smith. Eating apples such as delicious or McIntosh soften too much when baked.

To keep fresh apples on hand in all seasons, they may be sliced, seasoned, and frozen in individual pie-sized packages, ready for use in baking a pie at any time.

251

1/8 tsp. salt
4 tbl. oatmeal
2 tbl. white sugar
3 tbl. brown sugar
4 tbl. melted butter
1/3 c. coarsely chopped toasted hazelnuts

In a bowl combine all dry ingredients except nuts. Add butter, mix with a fork, add nuts and continue mixing until crumbs form. Set aside.

Filling

5 Granny Smith or other baking apples, peeled, cored, and sliced
2/3 c. dried cranberries
3 tbl. brown sugar
4 tbl. white sugar
2 tbl. flour
1/8 tsp. salt
2 tsp. grated orange rind
4 tbl. orange flavored liqueur
1/2 tsp. cinnamon

In a large bowl combine all ingredients. Pour into pastry shell. Sprinkle with Streusel topping and bake at 350° for 30-40 minutes until apples soften and juice forms. Watch crumbs so they don't burn.

A savory, full-flavored pie with nuts and rum. Serve with whipped cream for a spectacular finale.

Drunken Pumpkin Pie
serves 8-10

pastry for a 10" bottom crust (see Margarita Tart)
1/4 c. butter, melted
1/4 c. brown sugar
1/2 c. chopped pecans
2 c. cooked pureed pumpkin
1 c. brown sugar
4 eggs, lightly beaten
1/3 c. + 1 tbl. dark rum
1 1/4 c. heavy cream
2 tbl. crystallized ginger, chopped
2 tsp. ground cinnamon
1/2 tsp. ground ginger
1/2 tsp. ground cloves
1/2 tsp. ground allspice
1/4 tsp. salt
1/8 tsp. freshly grated nutmeg

253

In a small bowl, combine melted butter, brown sugar, and pecans. Pour mixture into prepared crust, prick crust edges with fork, and bake in preheated 425° oven for 5 minutes or until brown sugar mixture bubbles. Remove from oven.

Clove

Clove is the dried, unopened flower bud of the evergreen clove tree, belonging to the myrtle family; grown mainly on the islands of Zanzibar and Madagascar.

First references to cloves are found in Oriental literature of the Han period in China, under the name "Chicken-tongue Spice."

254

It takes between 5,000-7,000 dried cloves to make 1 lb. of the spice after preparation and drying.

Clove oil is an essential ingredient in many perfumes, soaps, toothpastes, and mouthwashes, in medicines, and as a synthetic or artificial vanilla, as well as a widely used culinary ingredient in recipes from entrees to desserts.

In large bowl, combine pumpkin, sugar, eggs, rum, cream, crystallized ginger, cinnamon, ginger, cloves, allspice, salt, and nutmeg. Mix well, pour into crust, and bake in a preheated 350° oven for 40 minutes or until filling is firm in center.

This is a great make-ahead tart. Its shelf life is 1-2 days. Cut into small slices. It's dense and rich—a little goes a long way.

Pine Nut Tart
serves 12-14

Pastry

> 1 1/4 c. flour
> 1/8 tsp. salt
> 1 tbl. sugar
> 8 tbl. butter (1 stick) cut into thin slices
> 1 egg, beaten

In a food processor, whirl flour, salt, and sugar. Add butter in 2 batches, whirling after each addition until mixture resembles coarse cornmeal. Add 1 tbl. water, whirl, adding more water if necessary to hold mixture together when pressed between fingers. Knead with heel of your hand a few times; form into a flat disk. Wrap in plastic and refrigerate. Roll out and fit into a 10" flan pan. Freeze 10 minutes. With a fork, prick bottom and bake in a preheated 425° oven 10-15 minutes or until pastry starts turning golden. Cool.

Filling

> 1/2 c. apricot preserve, warm
> 8 oz. almond paste (we use Solo in an 8 oz. can)
> 4 oz. butter
> 1/3 c. sugar
> 1/2 tsp. almond extract

256

Almond Paste

Almond paste is a blend of ground almonds and sugar. It's available in specialty food stores in an 8 oz. can or 7.5 oz. soft bars or tubes. It should be kept in a cool place, stored in the refrigerator if opened. Almond paste may be used to make marzipan, macaroons, Danish pastry, coffee cake, and many of our desserts. We enjoy the taste, as well as the moist texture that almond paste provides to the desserts we created. It blends well with many flavors and is distinctive on its own.

1/8 tsp. anise extract
4 eggs
1/4 c. flour
1/2 tsp. baking powder
3/4 c. pine nuts

Spread apricot preserve over bottom of pastry. Set aside.

With mixer, combine until smooth the almond paste, butter, sugar, and extracts. Add eggs, one at a time. Mix until well combined. Mix flour and baking powder together, add to almond paste mixture, beat until smooth. Pour into pastry and sprinkle with pine nuts. Bake in a 425° oven for 10 minutes. Reduce heat to 375° and continue to bake 10-15 minutes until dark golden brown.

This is a fun dessert to serve at a Southwestern dinner. We don't consider it a children's dessert, but more like a Margarita in a crust.

Margarita Tart
serves 12-14

Pastry

>1 1/4 c. flour
>1/3 c. powdered sugar
>1/3 tsp. salt
>1/4 tsp. ground cinnamon
>1/3 c. ground pecans
>9 tbl. butter, cut into bits
>2 tbl. water (optional)

In a food processor, mix flour, sugar, salt, cinnamon, and pecans; whirl. Add butter in batches and blend until it resembles coarse meal. Sprinkle with 1 tbl. water; whirl. Add additional water if needed to hold pastry together. Knead with the heel of your hand a few times. Form into a flat ball, seal in plastic wrap. Refrigerate 1/2 to 1 hour. Roll out to fit a 10" removable bottom flan pan. Prick bottom with a fork several times and freeze until ready to use. Bake completely in a 425° oven until dark golden, 15-20 minutes. Cool.

Filling

>1 1/4 c. sugar
>4 1/2 tbl. cornstarch

257

Tequila

Tequila is a Mexican liquor distilled from the fermented juice in the stem of the century plant.

Traditionally, tequila is drunk straight. While holding the glass in the left hand, one places salt in the crevice between the thumb and forefinger; a lime wedge held in the right hand is sucked immediately before licking the salt and downing the small glass of tequila. In the USA tequila is best known as the main ingredient in margaritas.

5 tsp. grated lime rind
8 tbl. fresh lime juice
1 c. half-and-half
pinch salt
6 tbl. tequila
5 tbl. triple sec
1/4 tsp. dried mint
1/2 c. sour cream
1 pint fresh strawberries
whipped cream (optional)

In a saucepan add sugar, cornstarch, lime rind, juice, half-and-half. Combine well and bring to a boil while stirring. Remove from the heat, stir in salt, tequila, triple sec, and mint. Cool and combine with sour cream. Place in baked pastry shell, smooth with a spatula. Decorate with whipped cream and sliced strawberries.

This is a great summer dessert, decorated with fresh sliced fruit such as strawberries, kiwis, or raspberries. Prepare with a ginger preserve glaze or serve plain.

Triple Ginger Tart
serves 14

Pastry

    1 1/4 c. flour
    1/2 c. ground pecans
    3 tbl. powdered sugar
    1 tsp. powdered ginger
    1/8 tsp. salt
    9 oz. cold butter (1 stick + 1 tbl.), cut into thin slices
    1-2 tbl. water

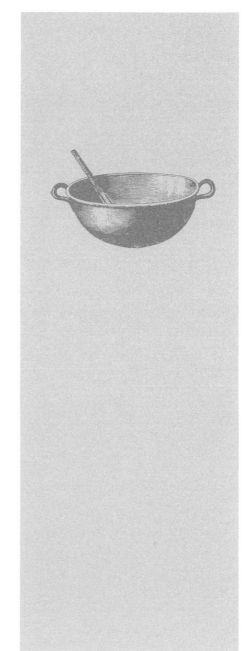

In a food processor whirl flour, pecans, sugar, ginger, and salt. Add butter in 2 batches, whirling after each addition until the mixture resembles coarse cornmeal. Add 1 tbl. water, whirl, adding more water if necessary to hold mixture together when pressed between fingers. Knead with heel of hand a few times, form into a flattened disk. Wrap in plastic and refrigerate. Roll out and fit into a 10" flan pan. Freeze 10 minutes, prick bottom with a fork and bake in a preheated 425° oven 10-15 minutes or until pastry turns golden. Cool.

Filling

    16 oz. cream cheese, room temperature
    2/3 c. sugar

259

Dressing up a Tart

Instead of just placing the tart or torte on a plate, we place it on an attractive doily. We also decorate tarts with chocolate lace—which is melted chocolate placed in a pastry bag fitted with a small plain tip and randomly drizzled on top. We also decorate with fresh fruit either on the dessert or plate. A slice of dessert can look very lonely on a plate. Try a light dusting of powdered sugar or fine cocoa on the plate or on the tart. Remember, do your dusting just before serving.

260

2 eggs
6 tbl. chopped crystallized ginger
1 tbl. fresh ginger, grated
1 tsp. vanilla extract
4 tbl. ginger preserve, warm
fresh fruit for garnish
ginger preserves, melted for glaze (optional)

In a large bowl, combine cheese and sugar with a mixer until smooth. Add eggs one at a time, beat in ginger and vanilla. Spread preserve on the bottom of the prebaked crust. Pour cheese filling on top. Spread and bake in a preheated 375° oven 30 minutes or until set and golden. Cool. Serve as is or arrange fresh fruit on top. Slice thin.

The poaching liquid for this tart is sublime. Sometimes we skip the pastry part and merely poach the pears and serve them with a Fresh Raspberry Sauce (see Index). If your time is short, omit poaching the pears. Instead, peel, core and slice thinly and arrange. They taste just as wonderful.

Glazed Pear Tart
serves 10

Pastry

        1 1/4 c. flour
        1/4 c. sugar
        1 stick butter, in bits
        1 tsp. grated lemon rind
        1 egg yolk
        1-2 tbl. ice water

Combine flour, sugar, butter, and lemon rind in a food processor and whirl until just crumbly. Add the egg and ice water and toss mixture with the on-off switch until just incorporated. (Can be done in a bowl with a pastry blender.)

Knead pastry lightly with the heel of your hand for a few seconds to distribute the butter evenly. Form into a flat disk, cover with plastic wrap, and chill for 1 hour.

Roll out on a floured surface and fit into a 10" flan pan with removable bottom. Prick bottom with a fork and freeze for 20-30 minutes. Prebake pastry in a 400° oven for 10 minutes, or until golden. Remove and cool slightly.

Cinnamon

Cinnamon, known as sweet wood, is the oldest spice known to man. Cinnamon is a reddish-brown spice that comes from the dried bark of shrub-like evergreen trees from the laurel family. This is one of the very few spices not obtained from the seeds, flowers, or fruits of a plant, but rather from the bark.

The kinds of cinnamon most commonly used are cassia and Ceylon cinnamon. Cassia is a native of China, and is lower in quality and price. Now imported from Indonesia and Vietnam, it has an aromatic odor, pungently sweet flavor, and is mainly used in America. Ceylon cinnamon is used more in other parts of the world.

261

Glazes

Glazes turn ordinary desserts into show-stoppers with very little effort. Use good jams and jellies, usually preserves, currant, raspberry jelly, black currant jelly, or marmalades. Put 1/2- 3/4 c. of desired preserves in a small saucepan and heat. Heating thins the mixture.

Add lemon juice or a tsp. of a liqueur if extra flavor is desired. If you don't like the small pieces of fruit in some of the preserves, press the mixture through a sieve.

With a pastry brush, lightly brush the top of your cake, tart, or fruit slices. Be sure to cover everything. Let it dry a few minutes and reglaze. The effect will make your dessert glossy and shiny.

Poaching Liquid
    1 c. sugar
    4-6 c. water
    juice of 1 lemon
    2 sticks of cinnamon
    8 whole cloves
    1/8 tsp. whole coriander seeds
    1/4 tsp. whole allspice berries
    3-4 firm Bartlett pears

Bring sugar, water, lemon, and spices to a boil and simmer 10 minutes. Peel the pears and simmer in the syrup until just tender, 20-30 minutes. Cool. Cut in half, core and slice. Set aside.

Almond Creme
    1/2 c. butter
    1/2 c. sugar
    1 egg
    1 c. finely ground toasted almonds
    3 tbl. amaretto
    1 tbl. flour
    1 tsp. almond extract

3 pears, peeled, cored, and sliced thinly
2 tbl. sugar
1/2 tsp. ground coriander
1/2- 3/4 c. apricot preserves (heat and press through sieve)

In a food processor or mixer, cream butter and sugar until fluffy and light yellow. Add eggs, almonds, amaretto, flour, and almond extract. Combine.

To Assemble:

Pour creme into pre-baked pastry shell, spread evenly. Place pear slices in a circular pattern, covering entire filling.

In a small bowl combine sugar and coriander, sprinkle over pear slices, and bake in a preheated 425° oven for 40-50 minutes or until golden brown and pears are tender.

Cool slightly and brush with apricot preserves.

Because of the natural pectin in cranberries, this chutney thickens quickly. It's such a hit at Thanksgiving, we often give some in festive jars as gifts.

Pear Chutney
makes 2-3 c.

2 lbs. fresh cranberries
3 apples, pared, cored, and diced in 1/2" cubes
3 pears, pared, cored, and diced in 1/2" cubes
1 c. golden raisins
1 c. currants
2 c. sugar
1 c. fresh orange juice
2 tbl. grated orange peel
2 tsp. ground cinnamon
1/4 tsp. coriander seeds, crushed
1/2 tsp. freshly ground nutmeg
1 1/2 c. walnuts, coarsely chopped
2/3 c. orange-flavored liqueur

In a large non-aluminum saucepan, combine all ingredients except walnuts and liqueur. Bring to a boil, reduce heat, and simmer uncovered, stirring frequently until mixture thickens—about 45 minutes. Stir in walnuts and liqueur. Refrigerate covered 4 hours or overnight. Keeps 2 weeks refrigerated.

Flavored Ice Cubes

Freeze mint leaves, lemon balm, rosemary flowers, anise hyssop flowers, or unsprayed rosebuds in ice cube trays. Add them to iced tea, lemonade, water, and sparkling wine spritzers. Don't use tap water for these cubes or for decorative ice rings—the minerals in the water make them cloudy. Bottled distilled water works best.

Finally, a dessert that can be prepared in under one hour and still be impressive. Try substituting pears for the apples when your supply is low.

Quick Apple Turnovers
serves 4

1 sheet frozen puff pastry—purchased or homemade
2 golden delicious apples, chopped
1/2 lemon, juiced
1/4 c. golden raisins
1/2 c. sugar (or to taste)
3 tbl. rum or brandy
1 1/2 tbl. flour
1/4 tsp. aniseed, crushed
1/2 tsp. ground allspice
1/4 tsp. cardamom, crushed
powdered sugar
Flavored Whipped Cream

265

Remove one sheet of dough from package. Rewrap remaining dough and refreeze.

Place apples, lemon juice, golden raisins, sugar, liquor, flour, aniseed, allspice, and cardamom in a bowl and mix well. Taste to adjust.

On a floured board, roll pastry out into a 16" square. Divide into fourths. Place about 3-4 tbl. of the filling in the middle, plus a little of the juice. With your fingers, wet the pastry edge on two sides. Fold over to form a triangle. Press to seal edges. Prick top 1 or 2 times with a fork for air vents.

Cardamom

Cardamom is a spice native to India, and a member of the ginger family. The hard brown seeds are the prized feature and often sold in the pod. It is an expensive spice, with a flowery, aromatic, subtle taste.

Cardamom is used in Indian curry powders as well as in Scandinavian pastries, coffee cakes, and cookies. We use it with fruits such as plums, apples, and peaches, and even to flavor coffee.

Place on parchment paper or aluminum-lined baking sheet. Bake at 400° for 20 minutes or until golden. Remove and sprinkle with powdered sugar. Serve with a dollop of Flavored Whipped Cream.

Flavored Whipped Cream

1/2 c. whipping cream
2 tbl. powdered sugar
1/4 tsp. cardamom, crushed

Whip cream with sugar and cardamom. Chill till serving time.

For a nice surprise, place a few fresh raspberries in the bottom of each ramekin. Cover with the mousse mixture and chill as directed.

Quick Chocolate Mint Mousse
serves 6

5 egg yolks
pinch of salt
1/4 c. sugar
4 oz. semi-sweet or bittersweet chocolate
1 c. heavy cream
1/4 tsp. mint extract*
mint sprigs for garnish
Whipped cream topping (1 c. heavy cream, 3 tbl. powdered
   sugar and 1/4 tsp. mint extract)

In a mixer bowl beat egg yolks, salt, and sugar at high speed until eggs thicken—about 5 minutes—and are twice their volume.

Combine the chocolate and cream in a heavy saucepan and bring to a boil over medium heat, stirring frequently to blend. Keep very hot.

Very slowly add the scalded chocolate/cream mixture to the egg yolks, beating well to avoid curdling. Add mint and pour into 6 ramekins. Chill or freeze.

Whip cream for topping and add powdered sugar and extract. Place cream in a pastry bag and pipe rosettes on top of each chilled ramekin, or serve in a bowl and pass with dessert.   *Change the flavor of this rich dessert by adding different flavorings, such as 1 tbl. Grand Marnier or other orange-flavored liqueur, coffee-flavored liqueur, or raspberry liqueur.

Mint Syrup

1 qt. cider or malt vinegar (or
   half-and-half)
1 c. sugar
2 c. fresh spearmint or peppermint
   leaves, packed

Place vinegar in a non-aluminum pan and bring to a boil. Add sugar and mint. Stir and crush leaves. Boil 3-5 minutes. Strain and cool. Place in bottles and store in refrigerator.

Use as a base for iced tea, punch, or with mineral water.

267

Condiments & Little Extras

In this chapter we've added what we call staples. They're in the form of dried herb blends, flavored vinegar blends, salsa recipes, aiolis (flavored-garlic mayonnaise) and pestos.

The herb blends are fresh and vibrant versions of the common grocery store types. Use them whenever you want to add a unique flavor to just about anything—or package them as gifts. The salsas are our favorites. We use them in place of relishes or chutneys. They're always fresh and the ingredients are flexible, so that if you don't have one fruit or vegetable, you may substitute another.

The aiolis are the closest we get to a restaurant's "signature dish." We have more fun with inventing new flavors and we serve them with all kinds of dishes—from appetizers, to soups, to entrees.

Last is pesto, our all-purpose recipe. Not only do pestos stand alone with just crusty bread, but adding any one of them to a simple salad vinaigrette will transform yesterday's leftovers into a delicious main dish salad or an accompaniment to grilled fish, meats, poultry, even over flavored hot pasta.

In a word, or words, we couldn't do without this chapter. Once you try some of the recipes, you'll be saying the same thing.

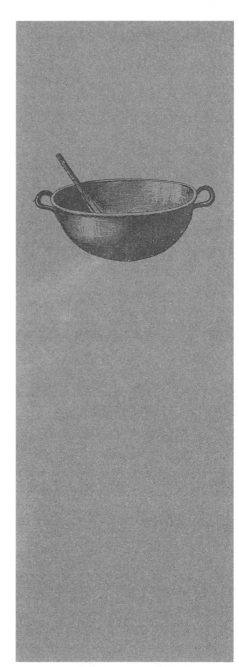

Herbes de Provence #1

2 bay leaves, crushed
1 tbl. EACH: basil, rosemary, and thyme
1/8 tsp. EACH: ground coriander, nutmeg, savory, cloves,
and white pepper

Combine and store in glass or ceramic jars.
Use in patés, omelets, meatloaf, and breads.

Herbes de Provence #2

Equal portions of the following: thyme, sage, fennel seeds,
rosemary, basil, oregano, lavender, and mint

270

Combine and store in glass or ceramic jars.

Paté Seasonings

1/4 c. salt
2 tsp. ground cinnamon
1 tsp. EACH crushed bay leaves, thyme, rosemary,
and basil
3/4 tsp. paprika
1/2 tsp. ground cloves
1/2 tsp. ground pepper
1/4 tsp. ground allspice

Combine and store in a glass or ceramic jar.

Homemade Chili Powder

4 large dried ancho or other mild chiles
2-4 small hot dried peppers
4 tsp. cumin seeds
1/2 tsp. whole cloves
1 tsp. coriander seeds
1/2 tsp. whole allspice berries
1/4 c. dried oregano
2 tbl. garlic powder
1 tbl. salt
1/2 tsp. sugar

Remove stems from peppers and break into
small pieces. Place in cast-iron or other heavy
skillet. Add cumin, cloves, coriander and allspice.
Stir over low heat until it begins to crackle and
gives off an aroma. Cool to room temperature
and put with the rest of the ingredients in a
grinder or blender and whirl until it becomes a
fine powder. Store in glass or ceramic in a cool,
dry place.

Red Chili Seasonings

12 dried hot chiles
9 dried ancho or mild chiles
3 tbl. cumin seed
1 tbl. ground coriander
1 tbl. garlic powder
1 1/2 tsp. whole cloves
2 tsp. dried basil

1/2 tsp. ground pepper
1/4 tsp. ground allspice

With rubber gloves, remove seeds from dried chiles and place in a blender or spice mill. Whirl until mixture is a fine powder. Add rest of ingredients and whirl again. Store in glass or ceramic jars in a cool, dry place.

Italian Blend

3 tbl. EACH: oregano, marjoram, savory, and basil
1 tbl. EACH: thyme and sage
2 tbl. rosemary

Combine all and store in glass or ceramic jars. Use with meatballs, salad dressings, tomato sauces, eggplant dishes, rice, cheese, vinegars, and butters.

Creole Seasonings

8 tsp. salt
2 tbl. ground black pepper
2 tbl. garlic powder
8 tsp. sweet paprika
8 tsp. cayenne pepper
4 1/2 tsp. onion powder
1 tbl. dried thyme

Combine all and store in glass, ceramic, or tin jars away from heat. Use in gumbos, rice, sauces, cheese dips, and marinades.

Curry Powder #1

12 cardamom pods, seeds removed
2 tbl. coriander seeds
1 tbl. EACH: turmeric and ground ginger
1 1/2 tsp. EACH: cumin seeds, ground allspice, ground cinnamon, ground pepper, and ground cloves

Crush with mortar and pestle or in a spice grinder or blender until powdery. Store in airtight glass or ceramic jars.

Curry Powder #2

6 whole cloves
1 tsp. EACH: cumin seeds, whole peppercorns, mustard seeds (black or yellow), ground ginger, and ground cardamom
1 tbl. coriander seeds
6 bay leaves
2 tsp. EACH: chili powder and turmeric
1/2 tsp. EACH: ground cinnamon and cayenne

Toast on a hot heavy skillet until some of the seeds pop. Cool and grind to a powder. Store in airtight glass or ceramic jars.

Poultry Spice Blend

1 1/2 tbl. dried basil
1 tbl. EACH dried marjoram, tarragon, and rosemary
1 tsp. EACH dried thyme, lovage, paprika, and sage
1/2 tsp. garlic powder

Combine all the ingredients, store in a glass, ceramic, or tin jar.

Jerk Spice Blend

1 tbl. EACH dried thyme and chives, ground cinnamon, allspice, ginger, and sugar
2 tsp. EACH ground nutmeg, coriander, cloves, and salt
1/2 tsp. EACH ground garlic powder, pepper, and dried grated lemon peel
2 bay leaves, crushed

Combine all of the ingredients, store in a glass, ceramic, or tin jar. Use on chicken, pork, or fish.

Garam Masala

1/4 c. coriander seeds
1/3" cinnamon stick
1 tbl. black peppercorns
2 tbl. cumin seeds
1/2 tsp. turmeric

1 small dried hot red chile or red pepper flakes
1/4 tsp. ground ginger
1 whole allspice berry
2 tsp. cardamom seeds
6 bay leaves

Combine all in a spice grinder or blender and whirl until finely blended. Store in glass, ceramic, or tin jars. Use whenever curry powder is called for.

❦

Tandoori Masala

1 tsp. homemade or commercial chili powder
1 tsp. cumin seeds, ground
1 tsp. ground coriander

Combine all. Store in glass, ceramic, or tin jars. Used to season chicken, beef dishes, and other curry foods.

❦

Southwest Spice Blend

3 tbl. ground coriander
2 tbl. ground cumin
1 tbl. EACH dried oregano, ground red chiles, and chili powder
1 tsp. dried basil
1/2 tsp. garlic powder
1 bay leaf, crushed

Combine all ingredients, store in a glass, ceramic, or tin jar. Use on chicken, pork, fish, or rice.

❦

Dried Herb Vinegar

1 qt. white vinegar
1 1/2 tbl. dried herbs (assorted)

Bring vinegar to an "almost" boil. Pour over herbs, cover, and let stand 2 weeks. Shake daily, strain, and decant with a sprig of fresh herbs, if desired.

Combinations: tarragon, basil, chives, Italian mixes, fill, fines herbes, rosemary-thyme.

❦

Fresh Herb Vinegar

1 gal. white vinegar
2 c. crushed fresh herbs*

Pour cold vinegar over crushed fresh herbs. Cover and let stand in a warm place for 2 weeks. Check periodically for strength and aroma. Decant in glass bottles with fresh herb sprigs.

*Combinations: same as in previous recipe.

❦

Asian Vinegar

3 sprigs marjoram
3 sprigs sweet woodruff
1 tbl. sliced fresh ginger
1/2 tsp. peppercorn
4 c. rice vinegar

Combine all ingredients and place in glass jars. Let sit for 3-5 weeks. Shake or stir periodically. Check for strength and aroma. Decant into more decorative bottles with fresh sprigs of herbs.

❦

Provençal Vinegar

2 sprigs EACH rosemary, lavender, thyme, and marjoram
2 bay leaves
2 garlic cloves
2 hot chiles, dried
3 1/2 c. white vinegar

Combine all ingredients and follow directions for Asian vinegar recipe. Place in glass jars.

❦

Mediterranean Vinegar

5 hot chiles, dried
3 garlic cloves
2 sprigs EACH basil, thyme, and lemon thyme

273

1 sprig rosemary

3 1/2 c. red wine vinegar

Combine all and follow directions for Asian vinegar recipe. Place in glass jars.

French Blend Vinegar

1 clove garlic, peeled and coarsely chopped

2 sprigs fresh tarragon

2 sprigs fresh thyme

1 sprig fresh rosemary

2 bay leaves, broken

1 shallot, peeled and chopped

2 1/2 c. white wine vinegar

274

Place garlic, herbs, and shallot in a stainless steel pan. Heat half the vinegar to a boil, pour over the herbs and steep until cool. Mix with the remaining vinegar. Pour into a wide-necked bottle, seal tightly, and keep for 2 weeks. Shake every few days. Pour through a strainer, rebottle with fresh tarragon and rosemary sprigs.

Italian Blend Vinegar

1 clove garlic, peeled and chopped

3 sprigs fresh basil

2 sprigs fresh oregano

1 sprig fresh rosemary

1 small sage sprig

1/2 tbl. black peppercorns

2 c. red wine vinegar

Place garlic and herbs in a stainless steel pan. Heat the vinegar to a boil, pour over the herbs, and steep until cool. Mix with remaining vinegar, pour into a wide-necked bottle, seal tightly, and keep for 2 weeks. Shake every few days. Pour through a strainer, rebottle with fresh basil and rosemary sprigs and a small garlic clove.

Spicy Asian Oil

2 garlic cloves

2 small hot dried chiles

1 slice, 1/4" thick, fresh ginger

1/2 cinnamon stick

1/4 tsp. star anise

1/4 tsp. coriander seeds

1/4 tsp. whole allspice berries

grated rind of 1/4 orange

1 c. flavorless oil—canola, safflower, etc.

Combine all in a glass jar and let sit 2-3 weeks. Discard garlic after 4-5 days. Use oil to marinade pork, chicken or for stir-frys.

Herb Butter

1/2 c. room temperature butter
1/2 tbl. fresh lemon juice
1 tbl. fresh parsley, minced
2-3 tbl. fresh herbs or 1-2 tsp. dried*
salt and freshly ground pepper

Cream the butter in a bowl. Add lemon juice slowly. (Can also be made in a food processor or blender.) Mix in herbs and season. Place on foil and roll into a cylinder. Label, chill or freeze until needed. Use in vegetables, fish, omelets, baked potatoes, pita triangles, etc.

* Suggested herbs: dill, tarragon, basil, savory, Italian mixes.

Quick Herbal Mustard

1 1/2 c. Dijon, coarse Dijon, or Dusseldorf mustard
1/4 c. chopped fresh herbs or 2 tbl. dried, crushed herbs*
3-4 tbl. mild flavored honey

Mix all ingredients in a non-aluminum bowl. Taste and adjust seasonings. Store in refrigerator. Serve with hot pretzels, patés, sausages, on sandwiches, or package as gifts in small fancy bottles or jars.

*Suggested herbs: basil, mint, thyme, chives, rosemary, tarragon, or combinations.

Melon Salsa

1 cantaloupe, diced
2-3 jalapeno, minced
1/2 c. chopped onion
1 1/2 c. EACH chopped red and green peppers
     and jicama
1/2 c. chopped cilantro
3 tbl. lime juice
3 tbl. oil
3 tbl. vinegar
1/4 tsp. salt
honey (to taste)
salt and freshly ground pepper

Combine all in a bowl and adjust seasonings. Use within a day of preparation.

275

Tangerine Salsa

2 tangerines, peeled, seeded, and diced
1 yellow pepper, finely diced
1 red pepper, finely diced
1-2 jalapenos, finely chopped and seeded
1 tbl. rice vinegar or mild herb vinegar
3 scallions, finely diced
1-2 tbl. oil
1 tbl. fresh ginger, finely chopped
2-3 tbl. cilantro, finely chopped
honey (if needed)
salt and pepper

Combine all ingredients in a bowl and adjust seasonings. Keeps in refrigerator for several days.

Cucumber Salsa

1/2 c. rice vinegar
1 stalk lemon grass, cut into small pieces
1/4 c. sugar
1/2 c. water
1/2 tbl. red pepper flakes
2 cucumbers, peeled, seeded, and diced
1 red pepper, diced
3 jalapenos, minced
3 tbl. fresh basil, minced
2 tbl. fresh mint, minced

In a small saucepan, bring vinegar, lemon grass, sugar, water, and pepper flakes to a boil. Boil down to 1/2 c. Strain and cool. In a bowl add cooled liquid and remaining ingredients. Taste and adjust flavors.

Fresh Herb Salsa

1/2 c. red onion. minced
1/8 tsp. chile oil
1 large green pepper, minced
1/4 c. scallions, minced
6 tbl. oil
1 1/2 tsp. lime juice
2 tbl. fresh basil, minced
1/4 c. fresh parsley, minced
1 jalapeno, minced
2 tbl. tarragon vinegar
1 tsp. honey

Combine all in a bowl and taste to adjust seasonings. Cover and chill 1 hour.

❦

Fresh Tomato Salsa
(See Index)

❦

Cilantro Relish

1/2 c. fresh cilantro
2 tbl. fresh basil
2 tsp. fresh ginger, minced
1-2 jalapenos, minced, or other fresh hot chile peppers
2 garlic cloves, minced
1/2 c. pine nuts, walnuts, or peanuts
1/2 lime, juiced
1/4 c. oil
salt
1 tsp. brown sugar

Put cilantro, basil, ginger, jalapeno, and garlic in food processor. With motor running, add nuts and lime juice and whirl. Add oil, salt and sugar. Chill until serving time. Mixture should not be watery.

Cranberry-Jalapeno Salsa

1 1/2 c. fresh or frozen cranberries, picked over
1 orange, grated, peeled, and coarsely chopped
4 tbl. sugar
salt
2-3 jalapenos (or to taste), chopped
1/4 c. vegetable oil
1/4 c. scallions, minced
1/4 c. cilantro, chopped
1 tbl. fresh ginger, finely minced

In a good food processor chop cranberries and orange. Do not liquefy; mixture should be coarse. Remove to a bowl and add sugar, jalapenos, oil, scallions, cilantro, and ginger. Taste and adjust. Keeps in refrigerator for up to 3 weeks.

Aioli

2-3 large cloves garlic, chopped
1 large egg or 3 egg yolks
1 tsp. Dijon mustard
3 tsp. lemon juice
1 c. oil (olive, vegetable, corn, or a combination)
salt and freshly ground pepper

In a food processor or blender with motor running, whirl garlic until very finely minced. Add egg, mustard, and lemon juice and whirl

until smooth. Keep motor running and very, very slowly drizzle the oil into the mixture until thick. Taste and adjust seasonings. Store in glass jars in the refrigerator.

Chipotle Aioli

3 garlic cloves
1 chipotle chile (drained)
1 tsp. EACH dried oregano and ground cumin
1 tbl. chili powder (homemade or commercial)
1 tbl. lime juice
1 large egg
1 c. oil
honey
salt and freshly ground pepper

In a food processor or blender with motor running, whirl garlic and chipotle until finely minced. Add oregano, cumin, chili powder, lime juice, and egg and whirl until smooth. With motor running very, very slowly add oil as needed. Taste and add honey if too acidic. Add salt and pepper. Store in glass jars in the refrigerator.

❦

Jalapeno Aioli

3-4 garlic cloves
2 fresh jalapeno, chopped
1 egg

277

1 egg yolk
2 tbl. lime or lemon juice
salt
1 tsp. Dijon mustard
1 tsp. dried oregano
1 c. oil (approximate)
honey (if needed)

In a blender or food processor with motor running, whirl garlic and jalapenos. Add eggs, juice, dash of salt, Dijon, and oregano and whirl until smooth. While motor is running add oil to desired thickness. Taste and add honey if too acidic. Adjust seasonings, store in glass jars, and chill.

278

Sun-Dried Tomato Aioli
(See Index)

Red Chili Aioli
4 garlic cloves, chopped
1 tbl. chili powder, homemade or commercial
1 large egg
1 1/2 tbl. lime juice
3/4 c. olive oil
honey (if needed)
salt and freshly ground pepper

In a food processor or blender with motor running, whirl garlic until finely minced. Add chili powder, egg, lime juice, and whirl until smooth. Keep motor running and very, very slowly drizzle in olive oil until desired thickness. Taste and add honey if too acidic. Add salt and pepper to taste. Store in glass jars in the refrigerator.

Soy Aioli
2 cloves garlic, chopped
2 tbl. fresh ginger, chopped
1 egg
1 egg yolk
2 tbl. rice vinegar
3 tbl. soy sauce
3 tbl. sesame oil
3/4-1 c. vegetable oil
honey (if needed)
salt and freshly ground pepper

In a food processor or blender with motor running, whirl garlic and ginger until finely minced. Add eggs, vinegar, soy sauce, sesame and whirl until smooth. With motor running very, very slowly add oil until desired thickness. Taste and add honey if too acidic. Salt and pepper to taste. Store in glass jars in the refrigerator.

Roasted Red Pepper Aioli

2 garlic cloves, chopped
1 small roasted red pepper, patted dry
1 jalapeno, chopped
1 whole egg
1 egg yolk
3 tbl. rice vinegar
1/3-3/4 c. oil
honey (if needed)
salt and freshly ground pepper

In a food processor or blender with motor running, whirl garlic, red pepper, and jalapeno until finely minced. Add egg, egg yolk, vinegar, and whirl. With motor running, very, very, slowly drizzle in oil until desired thickness. Taste and add honey if too acidic. Season with salt and pepper. Store in glass jars in the refrigerator.

Basic Basil Pesto

2 garlic cloves
2 c. packed fresh basil
2 tbl. pine nuts or walnuts
1/2 c. Parmesan cheese
1-1 1/2 c. olive oil
salt and pepper

In a food processor or blender with motor running, put garlic and pulse until minced very fine. Add basil, nuts, and cheese and whirl until smooth. Slowly add olive oil until desired consistency has been reached. Taste and season. Store in refrigerator with a little film of oil on the top (this prevents the mixture from turning black). The blackening doesn't affect the flavor—just the visual appeal! The pesto can also be frozen for up to one year.

Winter Basil Pesto

2-3 cloves garlic
2 tbl. dried basil
2 c. parsley, stems removed
1/4 c. Parmesan cheese
2 tbl. pine nuts or walnuts
1-1 1/2 c. olive oil
salt and pepper

279

In a food processor or blender with the motor running, pulse garlic until minced very fine. Add basil, parsley, nuts, and cheese; whirl until smooth. Slowly add olive oil until the desired consistency is achieved. Taste and season. Store in refrigerator with a little film of oil on top. May also be frozen.

Sun-dried Tomato Pesto

(See Index)

Tarragon Pesto

2 garlic cloves
2 c. packed fresh tarragon
1/2 c. parsley
3 tbl. walnuts
1/4 c. Parmesan cheese
1/2-3/4 c. olive oil
salt and freshly ground pepper

In a food processor or blender with motor running, whirl garlic. Add tarragon, parsley, walnuts, and cheese. Add 1/2 c. oil and whirl until smooth. Add more oil if a looser consistency is desired. Adjust seasonings. Store in glass jars—can be frozen. Use with chicken, fish, and potato salads.

Dill Pesto

3/4 c. scallions, including tops
3 tbl. fresh parsley
1/4 c. minced fresh dill or 2 tsp. dried
3 tbl. cider vinegar
3-4 oz. walnuts, chopped
1/2 to 3/4 c. olive oil
salt and freshly ground pepper

Place scallions, parsley, dill, vinegar, walnuts, and 1/2 c. oil in a blender or food processor and whirl. Process until mixture is smooth. Add more oil if too thick. Season. Serve over cooked green beans, asparagus, carrots, or potatoes. Can be refrigerated or frozen.

Red Chili Pesto

2 cloves garlic, chopped
2 tbl. homemade chili powder or commercial brand
1/4 tsp. ground cumin
1/4 c. walnuts
1/4 c. Parmesan cheese
1/2-3/4 c. olive oil
salt and freshly ground pepper
1/4 c. cilantro, chopped

With motor running, put garlic into a food processor or blender. Add chili powder, cumin, walnuts, and Parmesan. Slowly add oil and process until a desired thickness. Taste and season. Mix in cilantro by hand. Good with grilled fish and chicken, fajitas, or fresh tortilla chips. Refrigerate or freeze.

Cilantro Pesto

2-3 garlic cloves, chopped
2 c. fresh cilantro, chopped
dash chili oil (optional)
1 tbl. lime juice
3 tbl. walnuts
1/4 c. Parmesan cheese
1/2-3/4 c. olive oil
salt and freshly ground pepper

With motor running, put garlic into a food processor or blender. Whirl until very fine. Add cilantro, chili oil, lime juice, walnuts, Parmesan, and 1/2 c. oil. Whirl until smooth. If too thick, add more oil. Taste and adjust seasonings. Store in glass jars in the refrigerator. Can also be frozen. Use on pasta salads, potato salads, with fresh tortilla chips, on grilled chicken, fish or pork, and fajitas.

Rosemary Pesto

    2 large garlic cloves
    1/4 c. fresh rosemary, chopped lightly
    1/4 c. pine nuts or walnuts
    1/4 c. Parmesan cheese
    1/2-3/4 c. olive oil
    salt and freshly ground pepper

With motor running, put garlic in a food processor or blender. Whirl until finely minced. Add rosemary, nuts, Parmesan, and 1/2 c. oil. Whirl until smooth. Add more oil if too thick. Taste and adjust seasonings. Store in glass jars in the refrigerator. Can also be frozen.

Use with beef, lamb, chicken, or potato salads.

Thai Pesto

    2 garlic cloves
    2 tbl. fresh ginger, chopped
    2 tbl. fresh basil
    1/2 c. fresh coriander

    1/4 c. fresh mint
    2 hot chiles, chopped
    1/2 c. walnuts
    1/2 lime, juiced
    1/2-3/4 c. olive oil
    salt

With motor running put garlic and ginger in a food processor or blender. Add rest and whirl until smooth. Add more oil as needed. Use with grilled fish, chicken, or Asian noodles.

Spicy Asian Pesto

    2 garlic cloves, minced
    3 tbl. fresh ginger, chopped
    2 tbl. jalapeno, chopped
    2 large bunches fresh cilantro, chopped
    1/2 c. walnuts or pine nuts
    1/4 c. Parmesan cheese
    1 tsp. sesame oil
    1/2-3/4 c. oil
    dash of honey
    salt and freshly ground pepper

In a food processor or blender with motor running, put garlic, ginger, and jalapeno. Whirl until very fine. Add cilantro, nuts, Parmesan, sesame oil, and 1/2 c. olive oil. Whirl until smooth. Add more oil if too thick. Taste and add honey if too acidic. Add salt and pepper to taste.

281

Store in glass jars in the refrigerator. Can be frozen.

Use on grilled seafood, or as a dip with homemade tortilla chips or Indian Pappadums (lentil crackers).

Mulling Spice

4 sticks cinnamon
1 tbl. dried orange peel
2 tsp. whole cloves
1 whole nutmeg, broken
1 tsp. whole allspice berries
1/4 tsp. cardamom pod, crushed

Break up cinnamon sticks and pound other ingredients with a meat cleaver. Place in a covered jar. When ready to use, put 1 heaping tbl. of the mixture into a muslin bag or tea ball and place in 1 quart of cider or red wine. Add 1 orange, cut in rounds. Simmer mixture until hot, but do not boil. Taste before serving; add a small amount of sugar if too tart.

Rosemary Walnuts
makes 2 cups

2 tbl. butter
2 c. walnut halves
1 1/2 tsp. dried rosemary
1 1/2-2 tsp. salt
1/8 tsp. cayenne

Preheat oven to 350°. Heat butter in baking dish or cookie sheet. Add walnuts and toast 10 minutes. Add remaining ingredients and toss well. Return to oven for 10 minutes or until toasted. Stir frequently. Remove and cool on paper towels. Season according to taste. When cool, store in an airtight container.

Sources

The following is a list of our favorite places to visit, to shop, and to order plants, herbs, or specialty food items.

Gardens

Boerner Botanical Gardens
of Whitnall Park
5879 S. 92nd Street
Hales Corners, WI 53130
414/425-1130
Very large public arboretum including rose, herb, shade, and perennial gardens.

Olbrich Botanical Gardens
3330 Atwood Avenue
Madison, WI 53704
608/246-4551
Beautiful public gardens, including a 3/4-acre herb garden.

Rotary Gardens
1455 Palmer Drive
P.O. Box 8023
Janesville, WI 53537
608/752-3885
Small but beautiful garden for visiting. Includes herb garden, a sunken garden, a large Japanese garden, and more. Call for special events and hours.

Dried Herbs

Frontier Cooperative Herbs
P.O. Box 299
Norway, IA 52318
515/961-6283
Mail-order source for dried herbs. Large catalog.

Herbs, Spices and More
7352 Highway 14
Arena, WI 53503
608/753-2245
Mail-order source for dried herbs, spices, rices, grains, vinegars, and more. Call for price list and shop hours.

Penzey's Ltd.
P.O. Box 1448
Waukesha, WI 53187
414/574-0277
First-class quality dried herbs and spices with one of the most complete herb-spice catalogs. Retail store in Brookfield, WI. Call for catalog and hours.

Spice House
1031 N. Old World Third St.
Milwaukee, WI 53203
414/272-0977
First-class quality dried herbs and spices with one of the most complete herb-spice catalogs. Call for catalog & hours.

283

Periodical

Herb Companion
201 East Fourth St.
Loveland, CO 80537-9977
970/669-7672
Wonderful bi-monthly herb magazine covering all aspects of herbs: cooking, crafts, historical, medicinal, and gardening. Yearly subscription: $24

Book Dealer

Wood Violet Books
3814 Sunhill Drive
Madison, WI 53704
608/837-7207

Specializing in herb and gardening books, past and present. Wonderful catalog with good descriptions of books. ($2)

Vineyards

Botham Vineyard and Winery
8180 Langberry Drive
Barneveld, WI 53507
608/924-1412
Mail-order price list of fine Wisconsin-produced wines.

Wollersheim Winery
7876 Highway 188
Prairie du Sac, WI 53578
608/643-6515
Mail-order price list of fine Wisconsin-produced wines.

Shops

Moze's Gourmet Specialties
2701 Monroe Street
Madison, WI 53703
608/238-0300
Gourmet and specialty foods from Wisconsin, including wild rice, dried cranberries and cherries, smoked fish, and much more. Call for brochure and shop hours.

Thyme from Rosemary
N6535 State Road 120
Elkhorn, WI 53121
414/642-4042
Herb shop, plants, gifts, workshops, and luncheons. Call for hours and information.

Trailside Herb Farm
P.O. Box 246
Galena, IL 61036
800/343-6562
Seminars and workshops on herbs. Shop sells plants and related items. Call for brochure, seminar dates, and shop hours.

Plants & Seeds

The Cook's Garden
P.O. Box 535
Londonderry, VT 05148
802/824-3400
Great catalog of heirloom, exotic, and European vegetables, flowers, herb seeds, and some plants.

The Flower Factory
4062 Highway A
Stoughton, Wi 53589
608/873-8329
No mail order. Very comprehensive perennial booklet. Call for greenhouse hours.

Gryphon Gardens
P.O. Box 259299
Madison, WI 53705
608/277-8320
Very complete herb plant list. Will ship.

Hauser's Superior View Farm
Route 1, Box 199
Bayfield, WI 53714
715/779-5404
Listing of top-quality field-grown perennials for the North. Some herbs. Must buy in quantity, but worth it.

Johannsen Greenhouses
2600 W. Beltline Highway
Madison, WI 53713
608/271-6211
Complete garden center. Comprehensive list of perennial plants and roses. Shop has some herbs. Call for herbs. Call for hours.

Jung Quality Seeds
335 S. High Street.
Randolph, WI 53956
800/247-5864
Color catalog of seeds, plants, garden gifts, and bulbs. Call for catalog and shop hours in Madison, Sun Prairie, Stevens Point, and Randolph, WI.

Milaeger's
4838 Douglas Avenue
Racine, WI 53402
414/552-7118
Color catalog of perennials, some herbs. Mail order. Very large garden shop with gifts and some herbs. Call for hours and catalog.

Monches Farm
5890 Monches Road
Colgate, WI 53017
414/966-2787
Gift shop and catalog. Extraordinary gardening supplies, herb plants, and related gifts. Call for hours and catalog. $1

Nichols Garden Catalog
1190 Pacific West
Albany, OR 97321
503/928-9280
Folksy catalog—informative guide to vegetables, herbs, perennials, annuals, seeds, and plants. Call for catalog.

The Rosemary House
120 South Market Street
Mechanicsburg, PA 17055
717/697-5111
Great catalog with folksy illustrations of herbs and herbal products, seeds, and plants. Very complete catalog. $3

Sand City Gardens
7046 Reiman Road
Arena, WI 53503
608/753-2332
Specializes in topiary herb plants. No mail order. Must call for an appointment.

Sandy Mush Herb Nursery
316 Surrett Cove Road
Leicester, NC 28748
704/683-2014
A comprehensive herb plant handbook and a complete herb and seed listing. Catalog $4.

Seeds Blum
Idaho City Stage
Boise, ID 83706
208/336-8263 or 342-0858
Great folksy catalog of heirloom and speciality seeds and plants. $3

Shepherds Garden Seeds
6116 Highway 9
Felton, CA 95018
408/642-4042
Wonderful catalog of heirloom seeds, exotics, European vegetables, flowers, and herbs. $1

Speciality Foods

Bass Lake Cheese Factory
598 Valley View Trail
Somerset, WI 54025
800/368-2437 (only in MN and WI)
715/247-5586
Sheep's milk and goat's milk cheese. Many varieties. Call for mail order listing.

Cherokee Bison Farms, Ltd.
H4225 Elm Road
Colby, WI 54421
715/223-3644
Bison farm open for tours. Call for mail order listing and farm hours.

Fantome Farms
Route 1
Ridgeway, WI 53582
608/924-1266
Award-winning goat cheeses. Visiting hours by appointment. Call for brochure with price list.

Field and Forest Products
N3296 Kozuzek Road
Peshtigo, WI 54157
715/582-4997
Specialty mushrooms, dried and fresh, plus mushroom growing kits. Call for mail order list and prices.

Hollow Road Farm
W13184 Sjuggerud Road
Whitehall, WI 53773
715/983-2285
Fresh cheeses made from sheep's milk. Call for mail order list.

Indian Farm Mushrooms
N4496 Highway 78
Merrimac, WI 53561
608/742-0563
Mail-order shiitake mushrooms.

Kingsfield Gardens
Blue Mounds, WI 53517
608/924-9341
Will ship onions, shallots (many varieties) and leeks. Call for prices.

Kolb Lena Bresse Bleu (formerly Bresse Bleu)
N2002 Highway 26
Watertown, WI 53098
414/261-3036
Many varieties of award-winning Montrachet goat cheese. Call for mail-order list.

Ledge View Gardens
N8977 County Road D
Brillion, WI 54110
414/989-1952
Will mail order organic vegetables. Call for listing.

MacFarlane Pheasant Farm, Inc.
2821 S. US Highway 51
Janesville, WI 53546
800/345-8348
608/757-7881
Pheasant, fresh and smoked. Other wild game including buffalo, venison, alligator, kangaroo, ostrich, wild boar, plus assorted condiments. Call for brochure and retail shop hours.

Rushing Waters Trout Farm
P.O. Box H
Palmyra, WI 53156
800/378-7088
414/495-2998
Mail-order smoked trout and smoked salmon. Call for listing.

Renaissance Farm
P.O.Box 268
Spring Green, WI 53588
608/588-2230
Mail-order pestos and herb plants. Call for farm visiting hours and mail-order listing.

Seibel's Shiitakes
Route 3, Box 138
Bloomer, WI 54724
715/568-3886
Dried or fresh shiitakes. Mail order. Call for listing.

Sleepy Meadows
2126 Highway 147 W
Mishicot, WI 54228
414/755-2491
Mail-order lamb, sheep skins, and wool for spinning; chickens, and eggs. Call for price list.

Sohn's Forest Mushroom
617 South Main Street
Westfield, WI 53964
608/296-2456
Shiitake and oyster mushrooms. Sells mushroom growing kits. Catalog. Call for information and prices.

Trout Palace
E14214 County Road D
La Farge, WI 54639
608/625-2084
Mail order for fresh or smoked trout and trout pate. Call for prices.

Wisconsin Honey Producers Association
E3006 County Highway B
Ogdensburg, WI 54962
414/244-7620
Call for listing of honey retail outlets.

Wisconsin Maple Producers Association
33186 County Road W
Holcombe, WI 54745
715/447-5758
Call for listing of maple product outlet stores.

Wisconsin Red Cherry Growers Association
Sheila Robertson, Secretary
6025 Lake Lane
Sturgeon Bay, WI 54235-8305
Write for list of outlets for dried, fresh, or frozen tart cherries. Send self-addressed, stamped envelope.

The Authors

Suzanne Breckenridge and Marjorie Snyder began their careers together in the 1970s. Their young daughters were at the beach taking swimming lessons and, as waiting mothers are inclined to do, they began talking. One thing led to another and they soon discovered their mutual interest in cooking, gardening, and herbs.

The two began cooking professionally with "Herb Cooking" classes conducted in Marge's kitchen. As their reputation as teachers grew, they moved to conducting herb classes in several Madison gourmet cookware shops. They soon began to cater parties and to produce herbal mustards and vinegars.

Marjorie and Suzanne wrote a food column for *Wisconsin Trails* magazine, for more than ten years, and for *Isthmus*, a popular Madison weekly newspaper. They have sponsored public forums on herbs, helped to design Madison's public herb gardens, have demonstrated herb cooking techniques on TV, contributed to numerous cookbooks, and, in 1988, saw their own cookbook, *The Wisconsin Country Gourmet*, published by *Wisconsin Trails*.

Marjorie and Suzanne are self-taught cooks whose educational backgrounds have influenced their approaches to cooking. Suzanne is a food stylist with a Master of Fine Arts degree from the University of Wisconsin-Madison, and has worked as a graphic designer. Marge graduated from Bradley University with a degree in English and Business, and is a former English teacher. She is currently president of the Madison Herb Society.

Both cooks feel that good food, prepared with imagination and sensitivity, should not be just for company. Their secrets include the use of the freshest seasonal foods, the subtle incorporation of herbs and spices into recipes, and imaginative visual presentation.

The authors live in Madison, Wisconsin. Suzanne lives with her husband Bruce and their children, son Ethan and daughter Sarah. Marjorie lives with her husband Charles and their daughters Ryan and Dana.